HOW THE WEST WAS JUAN

HOW THE WEST WAS JUAN

REIMAGINING THE U.S.–MEXICO BORDER

STEVEN W. BENDER

SAN DIEGO STATE UNIVERSITY PRESS

How the West Was Juan: Reimagining the U.S.-Mexico Border
by Steven W. Bender is published by San Diego State University Press.

Unless otherwise noted, the photographs used in this collection
are by Karson Brown. Front and back cover photography
is by Carlos Solorio. Corrections, omissions, or rights queries
should be sent to SDSU Press for rectification in future editions:

Permissions @ SDSU Press
Arts & Letters 283
5500 Campanile Drive
San Diego State University
San Diego, CA 92182-6020

Electronic communications: bnericci@mail.sdsu.edu

Book Design by Guillermo Nericcio García
memogr@phics designcasa | http://bit.ly/memografix

http://sdsupress.sdsu.edu
http://facebook.com/sdsu.press
http://bit.ly/sdsu_press

ISBN-10:1-938537-93-9

ISBN-13:978-1-938537-93-6

FIRST EDITION

PRINTED IN THE UNITED STATES OF AMERICA

To Karson, with adventures and border crossings ahead.

CONTENTS

GON MANDAN

OREGON

GON

Mt Timpanogos

S. Andres

Selgemana

R. Salado

Raguapui Is.

S. Bernardo

Jutas Tabeguachis Ind.

R. de los Dolores

S. Maria

St Serafina

St Rosalina

St Rosa

Long's Peak

N. Br. or Platte R.

Platte R.

Castle Rock

James Peak

Solomon

Arkansa R.

Spanish Peaks

Saline R.

Taos

Enbudo

N. F. of Ca

or Senora la Luz

S. Rustico

V. S. Jose

Guacaros Ind.

Mt Guacaros

Timbabachi In.

St Gertrude

El Rastrillo

R. Jaquesila

R. Nabajea

Mt of Chequi

L. Trinidad

R. del Norte

Chama

S. Juan

Abicui

Cia

S. Domingo

SANTA FE

Longs Fork

Canadian R.

Red R.

puiobas Ind.

B. of the Sulphur Pyram.

Cosninas Ind.

Moqui Ind.

Gualpi

Campa

Zuni

Acoma

S. Dies

Albuquerque

Sabinez

Fonclara

Alamillo

S. del Sacramento

Chemegualba In.

Yubipias Ind.

Coquimas

Sierra de los Mimbres

S. Pasqual

Penuelas

Horse Mts.

Saline L.

Colorado

Jalchedum In.

Rio Gila

Tejua Ind.

Nijoras Ind.

Copper M.

Burras

S. Diego

Apaches

Dead Ml.

R. Jacoque

Cucapa Ind.

F. de Tubson

Apaches Gilenos In.

Jacome

Paso

Cumanches Ind.

Apaches Tontos

Mt S. Clara

F. S. Cruz

F. Tubar

Tumacacori

Apaches Chiricaquis

Las Patos

F. de Carizal

Mt de la Cola

R. Puerco

Oquitoa

Ati

Sarie

Terrenate

F. de Fronteras

Velarde

Las Boquillas

F. del Norte

Apaches Mescaleros

F. del Alter

R. Ascencion

Caborca

S. Ignatio

Arispe

SONORA

N. Andalusia

Sonora

Tarahumara

Concepcion

Agua nueva

Bisania

Tiburon

Mt del Picu

El Populo

El Aquaje

Batuco

F. of S. Buenaventura

Buchimba

Al Sauze

Dolores

Monclova

F. S. Juan

Rio Grande

Aguaverde

Nada

CHIHUAHUA

S. Diego

S. Pablo

BOLSON DE MAPIMI

Mt Gigante

S. Franc. Xav.

Matape

R. Yaqui

Cocom orachie

S. Juan

CHIHUAHUA

S. Cruz

S. Rita

S. Pedro

S. Bartolme

L. Cayman

Buenavista

Uruachi

Batopitas

R. Conchos

Villa del Fuerte

Naroqane

Zapote

S. Jose del Parral

Gertrude

R. Mayo

Tamoa

Toipahua

S. Juan

Colinte In.

Loreto

de Pulpito

R. del Fuerte

Ocroni

S. Maria

F. Cerro Gordo

F. del Gallo

S. Antonio

Parras

La Concep.

Bay of tica Viscaina

S. Jose

S. Ignatio

Sinaloa

Surutato

S. Roque

Sianori

Canelas

Al Alamo

DURANGO

COAHUILA

ACKNOWLEDGMENTS AND BACKGROUND ON A REIMAGINED BORDER

I am grateful for the comments of my Seattle law colleagues, who thoughtfully engaged my ideas during a summer scholarship series.

My librarian at Seattle University, Kerry Fitz-Gerald, provided her usual capable assistance in identifying relevant research materials, and my law students Letizia Hernández, Andrés Muñoz, and Arthur Sepulveda supplied helpful research. Colleagues and friends offered insightful comments and suggestions, particularly William Arrocha, Raymond Caballero, Ernesto Hernandez, Beto Juárez, and Lupe Salinas.

Foremost, this book benefitted from a 7,000-plus mile road trip in the summer of 2013 (which I repeated in 2015 on a slightly different route), tracing the early 1800s boundary between the United States and Mexico (freed from Spanish control in 1821) the best I could traveling paved roads and interstate highways in a rented Chevrolet Cruze nicknamed Penelope. Commencing in the southern Oregon town of Ashland about 15 miles north of the California state line, and crossing borders into Nevada twice in the coming days, my route went as far north as Twin Falls, Idaho (45 miles from the Nevada state line), then dipped into Utah and east to Wyoming through oil and natural gas country, before dropping south into Colorado ski country. Colorado roads closely follow the Arkansas River, once separating Mexico and the United States,[1] from its origins near the Continental Divide as it runs in the summertime from wet to dry riverbed once inside Kansas. Slicing through the Oklahoma panhandle, the "border" terrain became flat and agricultural. Traversing the northern agricultural region of Texas, I reached the twin cities of Texarkana, Texas, and Texarkana, Arkansas. Heading southward, my route tracing the former border concluded at the Gulf of Mexico near Port Arthur, Texas, birthplace of singer Janis Joplin, where the hotel desk clerk warned of unfriendly alligators trolling adjoining Sabine Lake that empties into the Gulf and separates Louisiana from Texas, and once Mexico from the United States. From that endpoint of the early 1800s

---

[1] As when the border was situated between Alto Mexico and the United 44 States following the Arkansas, Red, and Sabine Rivers, the U.S.-Mexico border now follows the Rio Grande. Evidencing the international commonality of transboundary waters, water shortages have prompted significant United Nations attention to equitable management of transboundary aquifers. See United Nations Department of Economic and Social Affairs, "International Decade for Action: 'Water for Life' 2005-2015, http://www.un.org/waterfor lifedecade/transboundary_waters.shtml (last visited June 22, 2014).

U.S.-Mexico border, I cut across the heart of Texas to the most significant cross-border cultural partnership on the current U.S.-Mexico
border—the companion cities of El Paso, Texas, and Ciudad Juárez, in
the Mexican state of Chihuahua. After walking across a U.S.-Mexico
border bridge connecting the two countries, and enjoying warm
chilaquiles for breakfast in Juárez, which was drying out after a spectac-
ular summer night's thunderstorm, I followed the existing border along
the U.S. side, reaching Imperial Beach, a California bordertown on the
Pacific Ocean next to Chula Vista, just south of San Diego. Driving north
through California, I traveled along the picaresque coastline on a sunny
early Saturday morning where roadside lines of parked cars of tanned
young Anglo surfers abruptly gave way to dozens of older parked cars of
young Mexican farm workers harvesting lettuce near Oxnard without
the luxury of weekend play. Eventually, I crossed the westward starting
point of the early 1800s international border, now the California-Oregon
state line on the forty-second parallel between the coastal towns of
Brookings, Oregon, and Crescent City, California (of course, in the early
1800s the United States had not yet resolved with Great Britain its claims
to ownership of the Pacific Northwest).

Throughout the journey along the current U.S.-Mexico border I encountered the realities of militarization along the border and within the
borderlands. Border Patrol checkpoints on U.S. roads near the border in
New Mexico, Arizona, and Southern California (part of the network of
more than seventy checkpoints operating in the Southwest) ensured I
looked, talked, and dressed enough like a U.S. citizen should look in order to avoid detention and search, and also that Penelope Cruze passed
a dog's sniff test for narcotics. In contrast to these reminders of the imperatives (and vulnerabilities) of national borders, I can't recall a
checkpoint between U.S. states for passenger vehicles (although some
states did inspect towed boats for invasive species), as most of the time I
had to keep a watchful eye and even backtrack to find welcome signs
signaling a crossing of U.S. state borders. Many state boundaries are not
precisely demarcated on the ground, as welcoming signs tend to be situated where convenient for tourists to pull over and take photos. The
U.S.-Mexico border, in contrast, does not invite casual photography.

While walking into Juárez, Mexico, from El Paso, Texas, using the
Paso del Norte bridge spanning the Rio Grande (known in Mexico as the
Río Bravo del Norte), I passed a Mexican border guard on the south side
who cheerily welcomed me to Mexico for my breakfast jaunt. He demanded no showing of papers, or even a slowing of my steady gait. On
my return walk to the United States, I encountered a line-up of Mexican
day workers, and dutifully showed my passport several times to the electronic readers and, finally, underwent a face-to-face interview with a U.S.
border guard about my purpose in visiting Mexico. Despite having navigated the U.S. border entry line in just 15 minutes that blustery morning,
I wondered about how different the experience might be for a Mexican
tourist or migrant when the same line can wind several hours long on

many days, and how relieved Mexican daily commuters must be to walk home to Mexico after a long day of manual labor in U.S. homes and businesses, with no lines or hassles. The dichotomy of the Mexican welcome and the U.S. border militarization was even starker at the U.S.-Mexico border separating Tijuana from Imperial Beach, California. The oceanfront Border Field State Park follows the sandy California coastline until it reaches the intrusive metal rods extending into the Pacific surf, erected by the United States to signal and secure the international border. I walked along the waterline of the state park until I reached a point about 50 feet from that wall, which I soon learned was just beyond an invisible federal property line in the sand. On the other side were a large group of Mexican children on the beach, supervised by Mexican teachers or camp counselors on a cloudy July morning. I halted when I heard a siren and barking loudspeaker coming from the hill to the east of the shoreline, as a Border Patrol vehicle rapidly approached me. Pointing to a supposed sign up the hill a few hundred yards away, the U.S. agent informed me I was trespassing on federal property, and was incredulous I had neither seen the sign, which wasn't visible from the surf line, nor heard his instructions, inaudible with the crash of the surf, until he sped down the hill to confront me near the border wall. Not sure what to do with me, he ultimately shrugged after again questioning my honesty, and told me to leave immediately. When I turned back after jogging several yards up the beach to take a picture of the border wall, it struck me how ironic that within 24 hours, I had been vigorously questioned returning from Mexico in El Paso, and prevented from even approaching the Mexico border at Tijuana, both by U.S. border officials. In contrast, had I taken advantage of a low tide to elude the U.S. border guards and slip through the gaps in the steel rods protruding through the Southern California beach sand that delineate the border wall, crossing into Mexico, I expect I would have been greeted the same as when I entered Juárez for breakfast. The unwelcoming border walls and fences that line the U.S.-Mexico border in urban locations and, gradually and potentially, throughout the reach of its entire 2,000-mile route, were erected by the United States, not Mexico.

In its current location, the U.S.-Mexico border, marked by a mounting infrastructure of security, symbolizes the exclusion of desperate migrants seeking economic opportunity and, in many instances, survival for themselves and their families. As we go forward as a nation and make policy choices toward further securitizing and militarizing the border, I hope we consider the different message of the welcoming Mexican border guard in Juárez. No doubt he appreciated I would contribute to the Mexican economy as a tourist. Yet Mexican migrants contribute much more fundamentally to our wellbeing in the United States through their labor in critical industries such as agriculture and construction. We just don't recognize or honor their contribution. This book is a small step towards celebrating the influence of Mexican culture and the contribution of Mexican labor to our wellbeing.

AN ALBUM OF BORDERED/ BORDERING SNAPSHOTS FROM MY FRONTERA SOJOURN

Unless otherwise noted all photos are by Karson Brown

The Arkansas River once divided the United States from Mexico along its route from its headlands in Colorado to southwestern Kansas.

Representative of the wide open spaces demarcating the Oregon/Nevada borderlands.

*The tiny Oregon/Nevada bordertown of Denio, Nevada exemplifies
the sparsely populated Alto Mexico borderlands in its northern reaches.*

The Arkansas River can run dry in the summertime into Kansas.

*The aptly named Red River demarcates the Oklahoma and Texas border
and once separated the United States from Mexican terrain.*

*A water tower in Texarkana, Texas, touts the connectedness
with its sister city Texarkana, Arkansas, built on land that once
demarcated the U.S.-Mexico borderlands.*

Liquor flows freely on the wet Arkansas side of the Texarkana sister cities, finally joined by Texas when Texarkana, TX voters approved beer and wine sales in 2014.

*State Line Avenue divides Texas and Arkansas through
the sister cities of Texarkana.*

*Homes in Sabine Pass, at the southeastern corner of Texas, where the
Sabine Lake and Sabine River meet the Gulf of Mexico across from
Louisiana (and once the U.S. border), are elevated to protect
against hurricane inflows.*

*Now a neighborhood in Port Arthur, Sabine Pass was
once the site of major Civil War battles.*

*Mexican daily commuters crossing the international
border headed toward work in El Paso.*

Mexican workers in Colorado's Aspen area, on the once-Mexican side of the borderlands, often commute from less affluent communities, residing in trailer parks.

Mexican residents can readily find Mexican goods such as piñatas in Jackpot, Nevada on the Nevada/Idaho border.

The Border Wall at San Ysidro
photo: Serge Dedina

The California/Oregon border at the coastline, once demarcating the northern reach of Mexican territory, offers no impediments to crossings.

INTRODUCTION

> Just as none of us is outside or beyond geography, none of us
> is completely free from the struggle over geography. That
> struggle is complex and interesting because it is not only
> about soldiers and cannons but also about ideas, about form,
> about images and imaginings.
>
> —Edward W. Said[2]

I magine a United States without California and Texas—its two most populous states and its economic leaders. And a United States without seven of its ten most populous cities (Los Angeles, Houston, Phoenix, San Antonio, San Diego, Dallas, and San Jose), as well as the eleventh largest city, Austin. New York and Chicago, the first and third largest cities, would remain U.S.-cities, but the Western region of the remaining U.S. states might be sparsely populated and home to just the now twenty-second (Seattle), twenty-third (Denver), twenty-eighth (Portland), and twenty-ninth (Oklahoma City) largest U.S. cities. The U.S. West (exclusive of Alaska) would be less than half its current size. It would lack the sunny beaches of Southern California, the Grand Canyon, the Great Salt Lake, and the international adult playground of Las Vegas.

This book imagines a different U.S.-Mexico border than the present 2,000 mile border along the southern boundaries of four U.S. states — California, Arizona, New Mexico, and Texas. Rather, it returns to the early 1800s U.S.-Mexico border, and before that the same border when Spain controlled the region as part of the Viceroyalty of New Spain (known in Spanish as el Virreinato de Nueva España),[3] that encompassed much of the present-day Western United States. Once within the boundaries of Mexico was the terrain of the entire U.S. states of California, Nevada, Utah, Arizona, New Mexico, and Texas, as well as western and southeastern Colorado, a southern portion of Wyoming, a southwestern piece of Kansas, and a slice of the western panhandle of Oklahoma. Rather than today's border endpoint cities of San Diego/Tijuana on the Pacific Ocean and Brownsville/Matamoros near the Gulf of Mexico, imagine a national border moving from west to east, and south, beginning between California's coastal Crescent City and Ore-

---

[2] Edward W. Said, *Culture and Imperialism* (New York: Knopf, 1993), 7
[3] As explained below, Spain once owned Florida, Louisiana, and held claims to the Pacific Northwest, that were resolved peaceably by treaty with the United States.

gon's Brookings, with a border endpoint near the eastern Texas city of Port Arthur on Sabine Lake that drains into the Gulf of Mexico.

As confirmed and described in the Adams-Onís Treaty of 1819 between the United States and Spain, the border demarcating Spanish, and soon thereafter Mexican, territory was specified as follows:

> ARTICLE 3
> The Boundary Line between the two Countries, West of the Mississippi, shall begin on the Gulf of Mexico, at the mouth of the River Sabine in the Sea, continuing North, along the Western Bank of that River, to the 32d degree of Latitude; thence by a Line due North to the degree of Latitude, where it strikes the Rio Roxo of Nachitoches, or Red-River, then following the course of the Rio-Roxo Westward to the degree of Longitude, 100 West from London and 23 from Washington, then crossing the said Red-River, and running thence by a Line due North to the River Arkansas, thence, following the Course of the Southern bank of the Arkansas to its source in Latitude, 42. North and thence by that parallel of Latitude to the South-Sea [the Pacific Ocean] . . . But if the Source of the Arkansas River shall be found to fall North or South of Latitude 42, then the Line shall run from the said Source due South or North, as the case may be, till it meets the said Parallel of Latitude 42, and thence along the said Parallel to the South Sea: all the Islands in the Sabine and the Said Red and Arkansas Rivers, throughout the Course thus described, to belong to the United States; but the use of the Waters and the navigation of the Sabine to the Sea, and of the said Rivers, Roxo and Arkansas, throughout the extent of the said Boundary, on their respective Banks, shall be common to the respective inhabitants of both Nations. The Two High Contracting Parties agree to cede and renounce all their rights, claims and pretensions to the Territories described by the said Line: that is to say.—The United States hereby cede to His Catholic Majesty, and renounce forever, all their rights, claims, and pretensions to the Territories lying West and South of the above described Line; and, in like manner, His Catholic Majesty cedes to the said United States, all his rights, claims, and pretensions to any Territories, East and North of the said Line, and, for himself, his heirs and successors, renounces all claim to the said Territories forever.[4]

In its entirety, I refer to the current U.S.-controlled land once owned by Spain and Mexico as **Alto** (Spanish for upper) **Mexico**, and use that terminology interchangeably with the U.S. Southwest.

---

[4] http://www.tamu.edu/faculty/ccbn/dewitt/adamonis.htm (last visited August 24, 2015). In 2014, a University of Arizona professor marked the coordinates of this border with steel monuments, a project documented at http://delimitationsblog.tumblr.com (last visited August 26, 2015).

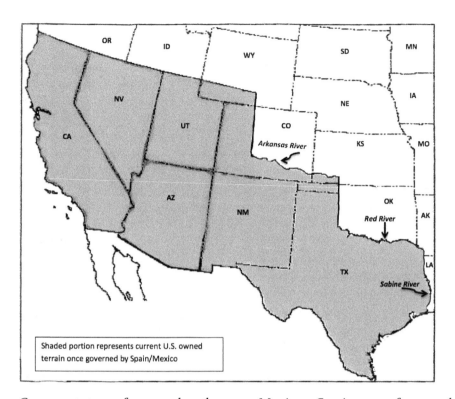

Shaded portion represents current U.S. owned terrain once governed by Spain/Mexico

Commentators often employ the term Mexican Cession to reference the smaller territory lost to the United States under the 1848 Treaty of Guadalupe Hidalgo, but I prefer the term Alto Mexico for its sense of the loss of the entire northern half of Mexico that includes Texas, the independence of which Mexico had never accepted until that treaty. Mexico, and before that Spain, once referred to a large portion of this Alto Mexico terrain, including the present-day U.S. state of California, as the territory of Alta California, but my reference to Alto Mexico, in addition to including the former boundaries of Alta California, also encompasses the massive state of Texas, once part of the Mexican state of Coahuila y Tejas and other Mexican states.[5] Having separated out Alto Mexico from the United States, I refer to the remainder of the United States as the **United 44 States**, making the assumption that the portions of the present-day states of Colorado, Kansas, Oklahoma, and Wyoming not included within Alto Mexico's Spanish/Mexican ownership would nonetheless have been carved into four separate U.S. states. The six missing states from the union given a Mexico-governed Alto Mexico, would be the entire states of California, Nevada, Utah, Arizona, New Mexico, and Texas, resulting in the configuration of the United 44 States.

Long part of Spain's empire, the terrain of Alto Mexico was held only briefly by an independent Mexico—from Mexico's independence from

---

[5] The Laredo, Texas region was part of the Mexico state of Tamaulipas and El Paso part of the state of Chihuahua. Under Mexico's 1824 Constitution, today's U.S. state of Arizona was once part of the Mexican state of Sonora y Sinaloa and the Alta California territory.

Spain in 1821 until the independence of the Republic of Texas in 1836, followed by the loss of the remainder of Alto Mexico with the signing of the Treaty of Guadalupe Hidalgo in 1848 ending the U.S.-Mexican War and completed by the U.S. purchase from Mexico of southern Arizona and southern New Mexico a few years later. During its Spanish/Mexican control, only part of Alto Mexico was settled by Spaniards/Mexicans. Spaniards established missions primarily in today's California (the site of twenty-one missions), New Mexico, and Texas (building twenty-nine missions there). Most Spaniards/Mexicans in Alto Mexico settled in New Mexico around the missions, and there were no settlements in Nevada, Utah, Wyoming, Kansas, or Oklahoma. Rather, these areas remained under control of indigenous peoples who vastly outnumbered both Mexicans and Anglos in Alto Mexico, as a whole, before the U.S.-Mexican War.[6]

Imagining a relocated border separating Alto Mexico from the United 44 States is worthwhile not for purposes of advocating a forcible or even political reconquest of the Southwest, which this book in no way invites, but rather as a novel lens to examine contentious border issues that divide many U.S. residents. In discourse today about Mexico and Mexicans, most discussed are concerns over the undocumented entry of Mexicans, and relatedly the supposed failure of even documented Mexican immigrants to assimilate into the Anglo culture. Moreover, our conceptions of Mexico and Mexicans are marked by fears of illicit drugs crossing the border and the possibility of the drug cartel violence that erupted in Mexico seeping into U.S. territory. Relocating the border for purposes of discussing U.S. immigration policy serves the dual purposes of disconnecting the heated debate from the current physical border, while allowing exploration of the physical and cultural space of the entirety of Alto Mexico, where most U.S. Mexicans reside today,[7] as a means of identifying and emphasizing the cultural and historical connections and synergies between the United States and Mexico. Ultimately, this book posits Alto Mexico as a cultural convergence zone between the United 44 States—which especially in the last few decades is increasingly populated by Mexicans—and Mexico, in which Anglo re-

---

[6] See David J. Weber, *The Mexican Frontier, 1821-1846: The American Southwest Under Mexico* (Albuquerque: University of New Mexico Press, 1982), xv. Arguably, under the Mexican Constitution these tribal members were considered as Mexican, and thus it is awkward to say that Mexicans occupied only part of the Alto Mexican terrain. Perhaps it is more accurate to say the Mexican government only controlled and governed part of Alto Mexico, as the sovereign tribes controlled (and populated) much of the rest.

[7] By U.S. Mexicans I mean to refer to the full range of U.S. residents with Mexican heritage, encompassing those Mexican residents who trace their roots to Spanish/Mexican residents in the Southwest before the Treaty of Guadalupe Hidalgo and undocumented immigrants from Mexico, as well as everyone falling in between from U.S. citizens to documented immigrants, regardless of whether any of these residents retain Mexico citizenship.

tirees and part-time residents from the United States have begun to arrive in significant numbers, again mostly in the last few decades. Given its large Mexican population and presence dating back centuries, Alto Mexico invites study as a timely reminder of the shared legacy of the Americas,[8] and the place from which compassionate immigration reform may spring, in contrast to the imperatives of recent decades and especially since the election of Donald Trump to fortify and militarize a physical border between the United States and Mexico, to the symbolic exclusion of the Mexican people and culture.

With Los Angeles, founded by a group of Spanish settlers in 1781, as its cultural capital and the locus of national/international cultural influence through motion pictures and the television industry, Alto Mexico is an opportune space for the development of respect and appreciation for a bilingual/bicultural society in which physical borders matter little, or at least less than under our border-centric emphasis of late. Indeed, the question is fairly posed whether U.S. or Mexico ownership fundamentally matters in the everyday lives of most Alto Mexico residents, a question confronted below. The rise in Mexican population within Alto Mexico makes locating the physical border less critical. Rather, the ascendancy of Mexican population may ultimately bring with it the political influence and cultural evolution that make ownership of the Southwest matter less for the everyday lives of its residents. Ultimately, the realization may come that people and their wellbeing and dignity matter more than our physical borders.

A fresh perspective on immigration and culture wars is needed to break the stalemate of hostile, dismissive attitudes by (mostly Anglo) xenophobes in the United States imploring that Latin-appearing residents "go back to Mexico," often countered by immigrant rights groups who respond, "we didn't cross the border, the border crossed us," in effect situating themselves within Mexico, at least when challenged within the terrain of Alto Mexico. The reality is more complex, as the diaspora of Mexican immigration has reached the entirety of the United States. Moreover, demands for self-deportation are wholly ineffective and even abusive as an immigration policy, despite Mitt Romney's hapless embrace of the notion in his 2012 presidential campaign that U.S. states might justifiably make life so miserable for undocumented entrants that they might elect to flee. The four U.S. border states, ground zero for today's fortified border along their southern boundaries, are centered in the discussion below given the residence in the early 1800s there of virtually all the Mexican residents in what is now the United States, and, together with Colorado, as the residence of 90 percent of the U.S. Mexican-origin population in 1930,[9] and the location still today of most of the

---

[8] By the Americas I mean to reference both North and South America.
[9] Rogelio Saenz, "The Changing Demography of Latinos in the Midwest," in *Latinos in the Midwest*, ed. Rubén O. Martinez (East Lansing, MI: Michigan State University Press, 2011), 33.

U.S. Mexican-origin population, (albeit a smaller percentage than prior decades given the inroads of Mexican residents to the United 44 States). Although the U.S. immigration policy conundrum is broader than just Mexicans, encompassing other migrants from Asia, Africa, and Latin America, among other locations, the emphasis below on residents and immigrants of Mexican origin allows exploration of our symbiotic relationship with the largest immigrant group living and working in the United States today,[10] by comparing how and when the West was Juan.

* * *

Chapter 1 reviews the history of Spanish and Mexican ownership of Alto Mexico, and its fall to the United States, from the revolution in Mexico's Tejas state and the subsequent annexation of the Republic of Texas by the United States, to the Treaty of Guadalupe Hidalgo ending the U.S.-Mexican War in 1848. Pointing to the origins of the loss of Alto Mexico, and especially Tejas, in the preservation of the Southern institution of slavery by Anglo slaveowners within the Mexican state of Coahuila y Tejas, the chapter addresses the reality of a potentially different border if the internal U.S. struggles over the immorality of slavery were resolved sooner. Although not essential to the book's ultimate conclusion calling for the cultural embrace of Spanish and recognition of the shared legacy of Mexicans and Anglos in the Southwest, the real potential in history for a different physical border helps demonstrate the folly of reinforcing the existing border to exclude Mexican migrants and their culture from a region they once governed.

Chapter 2 addresses the roots of the Spanish/Mexican presence in the current states of California and New Mexico, the latter the venue of the largest Spanish-speaking population within Alto Mexico at the time of the U.S.-Mexican War and the former now home to the largest Mexican-origin population in the United States. The decades-long delay in statehood for New Mexico, in comparison to the near immediate statehood for California, reflected tensions over culture and demographics that still animate immigration policy and other laws and attitudes affecting Alto Mexico and its Mexican residents. In contrast to California, that was flooded with Anglo settlers at the onset of the Gold Rush in the late 1840s and early 1850s, New Mexico's population remained majority Spanish-speaking for decades, dooming statehood until the 1910 Census

---

[10] Chiamaka Nwosu, Jeanne Batalova, and Gregory Auclair, "Frequently Requested Statistics on Immigrants and Immigration in the United States," http://www.migrationpolicy.org/article/frequently-requested-statistics-immigrants-and-immigration-united-states (posted April 28, 2014; last visited June 25, 2014) (in 2012, Mexico-born immigrants accounted for 28 percent of foreign-born U.S. residents, by far the largest group, with the next largest group, from India, accounting for only about 5 percent). More than half of these Mexican immigrants reside in California (37 percent) and Texas (22 percent), with Illinois third at 6 percent.

signaled a sufficient ascendancy of Anglo settlers speaking English. As revisited in Chapter 8, Spanish has long been seen as an illegitimate language despite its deep roots in the United States. Our inevitable cultural recognition and embrace of the value of Spanish must (and will) surmount this history of suppression.

Chapter 3 considers the potential economy of a Mexico-governed Alto Mexico, mindful that most immigration to the region historically has been job-related and thus the economy is essential to predicting and analyzing the demographics of the region. Tracing the evolution of the Alto Mexico economy from subsistence farming on Mexican ranchos before the U.S.-Mexican War, through the exploitation of mineral resources and industrialization, to today's diverse economy where Mexican workers tend to occupy lower-paid service positions, Chapter 3 details more than a century of the Mexican contribution to the Alto Mexico economy. Regardless of who controls the Southwest, if the United States ever acknowledged the value of this labor contribution, perhaps immigration policies would soften toward our neighbor Mexico, that has supplied labor for decades when needed, and usher in the good neighbor policies the book's conclusion urges.

Chapters 4-6 map the potential racial/ethnic composition of the United States and Mexico, both historically and under the model of a Mexico-governed Alto Mexico and its northern and eastern neighbor, the smaller United 44 States. As Chapter 4 details, although Mexicans did not make substantial inroads to the U.S. South (aside from Texas) until recently, in the last few decades they came in considerable numbers to the South, as well as to the Midwest and Pacific Northwest, accompanied by surging anti-immigrant animus in Southern states such as Alabama and Georgia. Expecting these same anti-immigrant sentiments to accompany reimagined national borders, this chapter discusses how the tensions in the four current U.S.-Mexico border states might simply migrate to the eight Alto Mexico/United 44 States border states (Oregon, Idaho, Wyoming, Colorado, Kansas, Oklahoma, Arkansas, and Louisiana), and speculates as to which of the United 44 States might assume the mantle from Arizona as the hub of anti-immigrant attitudes and law.

Chapters 5 and 6 emphasize the demographics of Alto Mexico, with Chapter 5 documenting the migration of Anglos to the region, from the immigration of Anglo slaveowners to the Mexican state of Coahuila y Tejas before the U.S.-Mexican War, to the influx of Anglo retirees and younger job-seekers to the Sun Belt states since the 1950s. Chapter 5 also addresses the recent influx of Anglo retirees to Mexico, as one of the factors suggesting that Anglos would have a substantial presence in a Mexico-governed Alto Mexico.

No doubt Mexicans too would enjoy a substantial numerical presence in a Mexico-governed Alto Mexico, as they do in the Southwest today despite restrictive U.S. immigration controls that have governed Mexican immigration since 1965, requiring most Mexican immigrants to enter the United States without papers. Chapter 6 details this history of Mexican migration to Alto Mexico that resulted in at least 22 million current U.S. residents of Mexican background in the region, by far the most of any U.S. region—a population, combined with other Latina/o groups, that has surpassed Anglo residents in the states of California and New Mexico, and will soon surpass Anglos in Texas. Completing the demographic survey of Alto Mexico is a review of certain groups (indigenous peoples, Chinese, blacks, and Latina/o immigrants from Central American countries such as Guatemala, Honduras, and El Salvador who migrate through Mexico) in the U.S. Southwest who share a significant history in Mexico that signals the potential presence of these groups in a Mexico-governed Alto Mexico, and more important how they might be treated different, if at all, from their past and present marginalization in the United States.

Chapter 7 looks at the current U.S.-Mexico borderlands to predict the economy and landscape of the Alto Mexico/United 44 States borderlands, including the extent to which the maquiladora factory model would be replicated in a reimagined border location. Augmenting the discussion of immigration policy in other chapters, Chapter 7 details the fortification of the border and its impact on undocumented immigration; it also examines the equally controversial border issue of illicit drug trafficking, questioning in either case whether a relocated border will have any impact on the entry of undocumented labor and illicit drugs bound for U.S. employers and users.

Chapter 8 details the history of a contentious issue that surrounds the immigration debate—the extent to which the Mexican culture, particularly the centrality of the Spanish language, survives and has a proper place in today's U.S.-governed Alto Mexico given the history of language suppression in that region.

Given the absence of any threat of a Reconquista of the Southwest by force, and of any political retaking of that terrain, Chapter 9 considers fears of a cultural/demographic retaking of Alto Mexico through the ascendancy of Mexican population in the Southwest. Rather than succumbing to nativist fears of a cultural Reconquista that pits one culture against another, Chapter 9 sketches a vision of Alto Mexico as a cultural convergence zone for bilingual/bicultural expression. Given its nearing equality in numbers, although not power, of Anglo and Mexican residents, Alto Mexico can serve as an intermediary for the United 44 States, with its own increasing Mexican population, and Mexico, with its increased Anglo presence of retirees and entrepreneurs. Rather than being a candidate for some future secession from the United States, Alto Mexico is an opportunity for a zone of cultural synergy, fueled by ongoing immigration, that unites the Americas. With this cultural breakthrough, the book's Conclusion argues for compassionate immigration policies welcoming Mexican laborers and their families to the United States rather than the anti-immigrant policies that have dominated the borderlands and beyond.

Regardless of who owns and governs the U.S. Southwest, we are in-extricably bound with Mexico in history, culture, and economy. This text imagines a different border than the current configuration, but at bottom, our connected destiny suggests that we should worry less about locating, marking, and securing our national border with Mexico, and more about recognizing, celebrating, and strengthening our shared connections with Mexico and Mexicans.

1. REMEMBERING THE ALAMO: THE ORIGINS OF TEXAS AND THE U.S. SOUTHWEST

> Let the great measure of annexation be accomplished, and with
> it the questions of boundary and claims. For who can arrest the
> torrent that will pour onward to the West? The road to Cali-
> fornia will be open to us. Who will stay the march of our
> western people?
>
> —President James Polk (1845)

The U.S.-Mexico border has remained virtually unchanged in location for more than 150 years. Before that, Mexico lost more than half its land to the United States in the span of twenty years through events that encompassed the secession of Texas from Mexico and its subsequent U.S. annexation, the U.S. acquisition of most of the current Southwest by a wartime treaty and, once the Southwest had been lost to the United States, an 1854 purchase from Mexico of an additional 30,000 square mile expanse, primarily in southern Arizona, to complete the border's current alignment.[11] The premise of this book, which assumes the early 1800s U.S.-Mexico border remained intact, relies on epiphanies of humanity and immorality that arrived too late, and in fundamental ways still lag.[12]

No doubt an array of factors set in motion and ensured Mexico's loss of more than half its territory in those monumental twenty years of the mid-nineteenth century. Constituting the largest U.S. state in size other than Alaska, Texas is central to that loss. As discussed below, among the crucial dynamics that led to its secession from Mexico, and its annexation into the United States a decade later as the 28th state, were the interest among Anglo immigrants to the region to preserve their rights to own black slaves, and their disfavor at being governed by Mexicans, whom they regarded, along with blacks and Natives, as subhuman. Of course, none of this reality aligns with the myths of heroism and freedom-fighting that surround the Alamo, particularly as constructed in the mythology of Hollywood, unless the freedom Anglo immigrants sought is acknowledged rightly as the freedom to own and torture black slaves. Realities of a slave-owing culture, and one that consigned Mexicans to a lesser humanity, better explain the current

---

[11] Although most sources specify the land acquired as encompassing about 29,640 or 29,670 square miles, some sources list the acquisition as comprising 45,000 square miles.

[12] Steven W. Bender, *Mea Culpa: Lessons on Law and Regret from U.S. History* (New York: New York University Press, 2015), ch. 9.

geography of the borderlands, and suggest that an epiphany of humanity, earlier realized, may have preserved intact the early 1800s U.S.-Mexico border, with consequences for both countries examined in later chapters.

Critics of a historical emphasis on the roles of slavery and perceptions of Mexican subhumanity instead attribute Mexico's loss of the Southwest to less startling and even laudatory motives. In the case of Texas, they would point to a broader cultural disconnect between Anglo immigrants and Mexicans, encompassing religious freedom from the predominant Catholicism of the Mexican people, and the locally unpopular move in 1835 initiated by Mexican President Antonio López de Santa Anna to centralize Mexico's government and draw power away from the Mexican states that coincided with the battle for independence of Texas (then part of the Mexican state of Coahuila y Tejas as well as other Mexican states and regions).[13] In this vein, today's visitors to the Alamo are informed by signage that this centralization of authority sparked the struggle for independence and local autonomy.[14] Relatedly, Mexico's decision in 1830 to prohibit further Anglo migration from the United States to Mexico's Tejas state alienated Anglo immigrants. Further aggravating Anglo immigrants, the Mexican government rescinded an exemption from property taxes favoring Anglo immigrants, and increased tariffs on goods shipped to them from the United States.[15] The

---

[13] At the time, the El Paso region was part of the Mexican state of Chihuahua; part of the present-day Texas panhandle and Laredo—the latter being part of the Mexican state of Tamaulipas, were also outside the Mexican state of Coahuila y Tejas. For convenience, the text refers to Coahuila y Tejas as encompassing the entirety of present day Texas, as that Tejas region was the venue for most Anglo migration preceding the Texas Revolution. In 1835, Mexico abandoned the 1824 Constitution and abolished its states and state legislators, replacing the states with departments headed by governors and councils selected by the Mexican President. Technically, then, the Texas region was comprised of departments rather than states at the time of the revolutionary unrest. Although most sources point to 1835 for the imposition of centralist government, one source specifies 1834. D.W. Meinig, *The Shaping of America: A Geographical Perspective on 500 Years of History, Volume 2, Continental America 1800-1867* (New Haven, CT: Yale University Press, 1993), 139. This discrepancy might be reconciled by acknowledging that the centralization of government was set in motion by President Santa Anna in 1834 when he formed a centralist Catholic government that acted to abolish the states in 1835 and replace them with centralized departments under federal control.
[14] Similarly, Texas guidelines for the teaching of U.S. history are meant to cast the Civil War as a battle for states' rights, rather than the desire to maintain slavery in the South. Emma Brown, "Texas Officials: Schools Should Teach that Slavery Was 'Side Issue' to Civil War," *Washington Post*, https://www.washingtonpost.com/local/education/150-years-later-schools-are-still-a-battlefield-for-interpreting-civil-war/2015/07/05/e8fbd57e-2001-11e5-bf41-c23f5d3face1_story.html (posted July 5, 2015; last visited September 5, 2016).
[15] "Texas Revolution," http://en.wikipedia.org/wiki/Texas_Revolution (last visited January 19, 2014) (specifying the property tax exemption as lasting ten years).

salad days of luring Anglos to populate Tejas as loyal Mexican citizens were no doubt short-lived.

Explaining Mexico's broader loss of the rest of the Southwest on racially neutral terms, the U.S. acquisition of California (once part of what was called Alta California by Mexico) and the current states of Nevada, Utah, and other Southwestern terrain might be attributed by historians to the U.S. desire for access to natural ports (particularly San Diego and San Francisco) to anchor a trade pipeline to Asian markets, enabling competition with Europe. Nevertheless, concurrent with the start of the U.S.-Mexican War in 1846, the United States had obtained sole rights from Great Britain to similarly protected ports within the Strait of Juan de Fuca, now home to Seattle and Tacoma, Washington.

Critics of ignoble motives for the Texas Revolution and the resultant U.S.-Mexican War might also suggest that the territorial desires of the United States and its evident economic prosperity (albeit on the backs of slave labor) filling the national treasury would have accomplished the same territorial acquisition from Mexico through voluntary purchase without the secession of Texas and the hostilities of the U.S.-Mexican War.[16] Still, Mexico consistently rejected cash offers from the United States for its terrain, forcing the United States to resort to military intervention and force. Moreover, by means of the 1854 Gadsden Purchase, Mexico sold 30,000 square miles now encompassing southern Arizona and New Mexico only after its northern territory was taken by a bloody war and Mexico was reminded about the consequences of denying the United States its desired land.

Even more factors potentially weighed into the loss of much of Mexico's territory to the United States. Among them are factors that contributed not to the roots of the U.S. desire for Mexican terrain, but to Mexico's inability to defend it, such as the distractions posed by ongoing tribal raids on Mexican cattle and residents in the borderlands that one historian blames for Mexico's ill-preparedness for war with the United States.[17] Financial and political instability in Mexico, that saw eight different men serving as president in the ten years leading to the U.S.-Mexican War,[18] also contributed to Mexico's military demise and even

---

Compare Timothy J. Henderson, *A Glorious Defeat: Mexico and its War with the United States* (New York: Hill and Wang, 2007), 38 (stating settlers were exempt from all taxation for their first six years in Mexico).
[16] Amy S. Greenberg, *A Wicked War: Polk, Clay, Lincoln, and the 1846 U.S. Invasion of Mexico* (New York: Alfred A. Knopf, 2012), 97.
[17] Brian DeLay, "Independent Indians and the U.S.-Mexican War," *American Historical Review* 112 (February 2007).
[18] "List of Heads of State of Mexico," http://en.wikipedia.org/wiki/List_of_heads_of_state_of_Mexico (last visited January 20, 2014). See also Juan Carlos Moreno-Brid and Jaime Ros, *Development and Growth in the Mexican Economy: A Historical Perspective* (New York: Oxford University Press, 2009), 31 (observing that from 1821 to 1867 Mexico experienced 56 different administrations).

presented the option to U.S. leaders, which they eventually rejected, of taking control of the entirety of Mexico instead of just the Southwest.[19]

Although no doubt several factors played some role in the vast territorial loss of Mexican terrain to the United States in the mid-nineteenth century, I focus here on protection of the slave economy and culture, and on disdain for Mexican ownership and control of the area's natural resources, as best explaining our territorial acquisitions from Mexico by force. In brief, slavery figured in the three main events that transferred control of the Tejas/Texas region to the United States—the Anglo slave-owning immigrants' decision to forcibly secede from Mexico and form the independent Republic of Texas, the agreement of the United States to annex the Republic as the 28th state, and the U.S. imperative to fix the Texas border at the Rio Grande by military force. As explained below, Mexico's moves to invalidate the institution of slavery and, later, the desires of Southerners for the political power of another U.S. slave-state, dictated these outcomes, none of them consistent with the favorable lore of Texas history that still surrounds the state. Augmenting this drive to protect slave labor in the lucrative Texas cotton fields, and explored first below, was the view of Mexicans as inferior to the arriving Anglo immigrants and thus unworthy to govern them and imperil their livelihoods and chance at prosperity through slave labor. This poor regard for the humanity of Mexicans still underlies our restrictive immigration policies and holds back our potential to recognize and celebrate the vital contribution of Mexicans to our economy and culture. Thus, the roots of our present anti-Mexican policies and practices extend to the early encounters and perceived incompatibilities of Anglos and Mexicans in Tejas.

Conceptions of the inferior Mexican prevailed both among Anglo immigrants in Mexico's Tejas region and, outside that terrain, in the U.S. public generally. Historian Arnoldo De León documents how Anglo immigrants in Tejas constructed Mexicans as a subhuman and mongrel breed. With this framing, he characterizes the Texas Revolution for independence as one of "racial adjustment" and supremacy of the white settlers over the "barren wastes and Mexicanos" in Tejas: "For Anglo-Texans to have accepted anything other than 'white supremacy and civilization' was to submit to Mexican domination and to admit that Americans were willing to become like Mexicans. The prospect of being dominated [and governed] by such untamed, uncivil, and disorderly creatures made a contest for racial hegemony almost inevitable."[20] These same views propelled the Manifest Destiny of U.S. territorial and eco-

[19] A successor to this volume will examine the possibility of the United States having acquired control of the entirety of Mexico as a result of the U.S.-Mexican War, examining contentious border issues such as undocumented immigration, culture, and the war on drugs through the lens of that relocated border.
[20] Arnoldo De León *They Called Them Greasers: Anglo Attitudes toward Mexicans in Texas, 1821-1900* (Austin, TX: University of Texas Press, 1983), 13.

nomic expansion from coast to coast across Native American lands seen as wilderness possessed by mere tribal savages,[21] while appropriating Mexican territory seen as ripe for the taking from undeserving hands, all to the benefit of Anglos using slave labor of blacks they viewed as "beasts" to harness the abundant natural resources. Not what you would expect to read in a U.S. high school history textbook!

Known as the Father of Texas, and one of the organizers of the Texas Revolution, Stephen F. Austin, well captured the derogatory sentiment directed at Mexicans in describing his aspirations for more worthy Anglo settlement of the Tejas region: "My object, the sole and only desire of my ambitions since I first saw Texas, was to redeem it from the wilderness—to settle it with an intelligent[,] honorable and interprising [sic] people."[22] As Sam Houston, another Texas founder, put it even more bluntly, "Mexicans are no better than Indians."[23] These sentiments permeated the U.S. military forces during the territorial war with Mexico. As one writer described, "Like most Americans, [President] Polk felt a deep disdain for the racially mixed population of Mexico."[24] The U.S. soldiers battling Mexico, in turn, "felt deep enmity for the people of Mexico, and conflated them with Indians and African American slaves."[25] Popular press embraced the juxtaposition of the subhuman savage Mexican and the honorable Anglo cause for liberating the Southwest, as in this pre-War editorial in the *New York Morning News* in late 1845: "We are contiguous to a vast portion of the globe, untrodden save by the savage and the beast, and we are conscious of our power to render it tributary to [the white] man."[26] Addressing California's terrain, the *St. Louis Daily Missourian* remarked that under Mexican control, the land was "doomed to desolation and a barren waste, instead of the garden of the world" and that unless "settled by our countrymen" the region was a mere "theatre for robbery and plunder, instead of being devoted to the uses [for] which nature and nature's God designed it."[27] As shown in later chapters, these attitudes of Anglo superiority survived the war.

---

[21] The Supreme Court employed the derogatory conception of Native Americans as mere "savages" to justify the U.S. acquisition of title to native lands by the force of conquest. *Johnson v. M'Intosh*, 21 U.S. 543 (1823).
[22] De León, *They Called Them Greasers*, 3.
[23] Greenberg, *Wicked War*, 57.
[24] Ibid., 76.
[25] Ibid., 131-132. Of course, given that many Tejanos (Mexicans in Tejas) had black roots given the reliance on black slaves when Spain controlled Mexico, this conflation of Mexicans and African Americans was not entirely inappropriate, despite the stain of dehumanization embedded in these conceptions.
[26] Natsu Taylor Saito, *Meeting the Enemy: American Exceptionalism and International Law* (New York: New York University Press, 2010), 131.
[27] Norman A. Graebner, *Empire of the Pacific: A Study in American Constitutional Expansion* (New York: Ronald Press Company, 1955), 100.

* * *

The brutal origins of slavery in the United States and its once celebrated place within the Southern culture and economy are well documented and still the frequent grist for Hollywood films and U.S. writers. Less known is the use of African slaves by Spaniards in colonial Mexico. Prompted by the labor shortage in the 16th century after the Spanish annihilated Mexico's indigenous population through murder, mistreatment, and the widespread introduction of disease to natives without natural immunities, Spanish conquistadores came to rely on African slave labor to work silver mines, sugar cane fields, and other labor-intensive enterprises of the evolving Mexican economy.[28] An estimated 200,000 African slaves were brought to Mexico during the allowance of the slave trade under Spanish rule.[29] In relation to the percentage of slaves in the U.S. South, however, where millions of slaves resided by 1860, the Mexican numbers were indeed small.[30] As soon as Mexico was freed from Spanish rule in 1821, slavery as an economic and cultural institution was in jeopardy.[31] Yet concurrent with Mexico's newfound autonomy, Anglo immigrants began arriving in Mexico's Tejas region, predominantly coming from the U.S. South, many bringing their black slaves with them. Although Mexico never physically prevented the entry of slaves into or demanded their freedom once inside the Tejas region, the showdown over Mexico's concurrent enactment of anti-slavery laws, clashing with the culture and fortunes of newly arrived Anglo slaveowners, ensured confrontation.

Coinciding with frequent changes in Mexican leadership after securing freedom from Spanish control were Mexican laws challenging slavery's legitimacy. Effective in early 1823, Mexico's Imperial Colonization Law was a compromise between Mexican abolitionists and property rights advocates, prohibiting the "purchase or sale of slaves that may be introduced into the empire."[32] As applied to the Tejas region, presumably U.S. immigrants could bring slaves with them into Mexican territory,

---

[28] Colin A. Palmer, *Slaves of the White God: Blacks in Mexico, 1570-1650* (Cambridge, MA: Harvard University Press, 1976).

[29] Ibid., 3.

[30] See William D. Signet, *Introduction to the Mexican Real Estate System* (Durham, NC: Carolina Academic Press, 2010), 9 (noting that African slaves carried immunities from most European diseases that annihilated indigenous populations, and also that by 1810, the number of full or mixed-race blacks in Mexico through generations of births was 634,461).

[31] By then, slavery had declined in economic necessity in the region, as it was cheaper to rely on indigenous labor for seasonal agricultural work. Earlier, in 1810, one of the leaders of the Mexican independence movement, Miguel Hidalgo de Costilla, decried the institution of slavery in 1810, setting the tone for one of the outcomes of independence.

[32] Randolph B. Campbell, *An Empire for Slavery: The Peculiar Institution in Texas, 1821-1865* (Baton Rogue, LA: Louisiana State University Press, 1989), 16.

but not trade them. Further, the 1823 Mexican law provided that "[t]he children of such slaves, who are born within the empire, shall be free at fourteen years of age." The law was annulled in short order with the overthrow of Mexican Emperor Agustín de Iturbide in 1823. The next year, a new Mexican constitutional congress adopted an opaque anti-slavery provision that read: "Commerce and traffic in slaves proceeding from any country under any flag whatsoever, is forever prohibited in the territory of the United Mexican States,"[33] which included the Mexican state of Coahuila y Tejas. Unclear under this law was whether slave-owning Anglo immigrants could bring their slaves with them into Mexi-can terrain because the law, by referring to "commerce and traffic," arguably outlawed only the entry of slaves for the purpose of their even-tual sale. A few years later, in 1827, the Mexican state of Coahuila y Tejas enacted its own compromise constitutional provision that purported to ban entries of additional slaves after a grace period, but failed to abolish the practice of slavery: "[N]o one shall be born a slave in the state, and after six months the introduction of slaves under any pretext shall not be permitted."[34] Anglos migrating to the region, however, quickly seized upon a potential loophole to the state constitutional denial of entry of new slaves. Taking advantage of the Mexican allowance of debt peonage, and foreshadowing evasions of eventual anti-slavery laws in the U.S. South in later decades after the Civil War, Anglo slaveowners merely converted their slaves to the status of an indentured servant owing a money debt to their former slave master. With this subterfuge, Anglo slaveholders migrating to Tejas simply drew a contract before a U.S. magistrate with their slaves, who agreed to pay their master their worth as a slave plus their travel costs to Tejas, less room and board. With wages set as low as possible, presumably the former slave, although technically free in Tejas, would be bound to work for a lifetime to repay the debt.[35] The Coahuila y Tejas state congress even formally approved this circumvention, decreeing that "All contracts, not in opposition to the laws of the state, that have been entered into in foreign countries [the United States], between emigrants who came to settle in this state, or between inhabitants thereof, and the servants and day laborers or workingmen whom they introduce, are hereby guaranteed to be valid in said state."[36]

Notwithstanding the ready circumvention by indenture contracts, Mexican law kept circling dangerously closer to the Anglo slaveholder's financial interests. In 1829, Mexico's president decreed the emancipation of slaves in Mexico, which has stood since and predated the U.S. Civil War by decades. Still, a few months later he exempted Tejas from the

---

[33] Ibid., 16-17.
[34] Ibid., 21.
[35] Ibid., 23.
[36] Ibid.

decree.[37] In 1832, however, the Mexican state of Coahuila y Tejas confronted the ongoing evasion of anti-slavery laws through use of indentured servant contracts, imposing the following time-restriction: "Servants and day laborers, hereafter introduced by foreign colonists, cannot be obligated by any contract to continue in the service of the latter longer than ten years."[38] As one historian noted, although the prospect for actual enforcement of these various Mexican federal and state laws against slavery was uncertain, in their aggregate, "slavery's foothold in Texas was far from secure as the [U.S. immigrant] revolution against Mexico developed in 1835."[39] Moreover, the move in 1835 to centralize Mexico's government and take power away from its states must have worried Anglo slaveowners given the anti-slavery imperatives of the Mexican government. No doubt Anglo slaveholders could see the looming threats to their lucrative slave culture while remaining under Mexican control, yet within easy reach of the U.S. South, from which many had come, where slavery was celebrated.

As Mexico was moving toward abolishing slavery in all its reaches, the Tejas region became a popular destination for Anglo migrants from the United States. Once these immigrants, comprised significantly of Southerners, many of them with slaves, overtook Mexicans in population, the writing of rebellion in Tejas was on the wall. At the time the first Anglos began to arrive in the region, few Spaniards/Mexicans lived in the vast territory that became the Republic of Texas, and now the U.S. state of Texas—a 1785 Spanish census counted only 2,919 residents.[40] Most of the region's non-indigenous residents during Spain's control of Mexico were military soldiers and officers aiming to prevent foreign encroachment and to reign in the native tribes that populated the region.[41] Forty-three of these residents counted in 1785 were slaves,[42] but it is not possible to tell whether they were brought by the very few early Anglo immigrants or if they were slaves of Spanish residents during the time of Spanish rule of Mexico. The Anglo immigrant who almost single-handedly altered the composition of the Tejas region toward rebellion, soliciting hordes of Anglo immigrants and their slaves, was Stephen F. Austin, the namesake of Austin, Texas. Austin's father, a slaveowner, had obtained permission (and land) from the Spanish government to settle a colony of Anglo immigrants on the Brazos River east of Houston, a settlement zone extending from the Gulf of Mexico to near Dallas,

---

[37] Ibid., 26.
[38] Ibid., 29.
[39] Ibid., 34.
[40] Ibid., 11. The census taker no doubt failed to count tribal residents. Unclear too is whether the census encompassed the Spanish region of Nuevo Santander in today's southern Texas.
[41] Samuel Harman Lowrie, *Culture Conflict in Texas 1821-1835* (New York, AMS Press, 1967), 30.
[42] Campbell, *Empire for Slavery*, 11.

with its center point the present day town of San Felipe, founded in 1824 as the colony's main settlement, San Felipe de Austin. At the time, the eastern reaches of Tejas between the Trinity and Sabine rivers were off limits to Anglo settlement as a sort of buffer zone between Mexico and the United States, instead reserved as territory for native tribes considered hostile to the United States.[43] Attracting Anglo migrants to inland Tejas seemed potentially in the interest of the Spanish and then Mexican government, as immigrants loyal to Mexico might embrace Mexican citizenship and presumably help hold native tribes at bay, as well as ward off any threat of U.S. expansion.[44] Mexicans were justifiably uneasy about their neighbor's intentions, and of the downside of permitting Anglo migration, following the experience of Spain in Florida. Once Spanish territory, Florida fell to the United States in the early 1800s, preceded by the entry of Anglo immigrants into east Florida.[45] Settled by treaty (the Adams-Onís Treaty) in 1819 without war given Spain's distractions elsewhere in the hemisphere, the land dispute ended when Spain ceded Florida to the United States, in exchange for setting the western border of the Louisiana Purchase (and thus the boundary between Spain/Mexico and the United States) at the Sabine River separating the current U.S. states of Louisiana (which Spain controlled between 1762 and 1800) and Texas, rather than at the Rio Grande.[46]

After his father died in 1821, Stephen F. Austin, then twenty-eight years old, took over the role of soliciting Anglo immigrants into the Brazos River region beginning later that year. Now governed by Mexican law, Austin served as a land agent, known as an *empresario*, to distribute lands to Anglo immigrants of his selection in order to populate the vast region, even learning Spanish to better negotiate with the Mexican government for immigrant land grants. Austin had a financial stake in attracting Anglo immigrants, slave-owners or not, as he received vast acreage of fertile Tejas land totaling almost a quarter million acres and conveyed it in parcels to the Anglo newcomers for next to nothing, ad-

---

[43] W.T. Block, *Cotton Bales, Keelboats and Sternwheelers: A History of the Sabine River and Trinity River Cotton Trades, 1837-1900* (Woodville, TX: Dogwood Press, 1995), 2.

[44] See S. C. Gwynne, *Empire of the Summer Moon: Quanah Parker and the Rise and Fall of the Comanches, the Most Powerful Indian Tribe in American History* (New York: Scribner, 2010), 25 (noting the irony that one of the reasons Mexico had encouraged Anglo settlement in Tejas was to serve as a buffer against the Comanches, yet it was the Anglos who ultimately took control of the region).

[45] See Saito, *Meeting the Enemy*, 125 (explaining that although at the time Spaniards were not cast as uncivilized to justify the takeover, their failure to control the "savage" tribes inhabiting the region was seen as a sufficient justification for the U.S. powerplay).

[46] Henderson, *Glorious Defeat*, 34 (noting Spain also relinquished and ceded any claim it had of discovery to the Pacific Northwest, leaving Britain and the United States to resolve title later, which they did in 1846, and in turn received $5 million of forgiveness of claims owned by Spain to U.S. citizens).

vertising widely for immigrants in U.S. journals.[47] For his part, Austin collected a commission fee per acre transferred to the immigrants, paid on easy terms over three years.[48] In one example, Austin granted land to a slaveowner coming from Georgia whose 90 slaves established a Tejas cotton plantation, with a large home for their master and cabins for themselves, on the thousands of acres the slave master received from Austin.[49] Most Anglo migrants to the region came from the U.S. South (particularly from Mississippi, Louisiana, and Arkansas), and many brought their slaves, either overtly as slaves or under the guise of indentured servants. By 1825, black slaves accounted for almost 25 percent of the population of Austin's colony.[50] As a slaveholder himself,[51] Austin appreciated the realities of slave ownership in Texas and their necessity for deriving the most profit in the cotton plantation culture emerging in the region. To preserve that culture, in 1825 Austin wrote to the governor of the Mexican state of Coahuila y Tejas urging protection of slavery to ensure Tejas would attract Anglo immigrants of means rather than mere shepherds and the poor.[52] Later, in 1833, Austin wrote that "Texas must be a slave country. Circumstances and unavoidable necessity compel[] it. It is the wish of the people there, and it is my duty to do all I can, prudently, in favor of it. I will do so."[53] Earlier, in 1824, Austin drafted a slave code for his Anglo colony, criminalizing harboring any runaway slave and inflicting cruel punishments on misbehaving slaves.[54]

Having tolerated the entry of Anglo immigrants with their slaves for almost a decade, the Mexican government altered its pro-immigrant position in 1830, when Mexican President Anastasio Bustamante decreed that no further immigrants from the United States, whether Anglo slaveowners or their black slaves, were allowed. Presumably slavery was

---

[47] Joel H. Silbey, *Storm Over Texas: The Annexation Controversy and the Road to Civil War* (New York: Oxford University Press, 2005), 6.

[48] Gregg Cantrell, *Stephen F. Austin: Empresario of Texas* (New Haven, CT: Yale University Press, 1999), 152-153. Explaining the intense interest of immigrants in Texas was the shift in U.S. policy from financing the sale of public land to demanding full payment up front, in contrast to the terms of sale that Austin offered in Texas. Ibid., 109. For background on Austin, see also Eugene C. Barker, *The Life of Stephen F. Austin: Founder of Texas 1793-1836, A Chapter in the Westward Movement of the Anglo-American People* (Austin: University of Texas Press, 1926, 1990 ed.) (suggesting that without Austin's empresario contract with Mexico, there would have been no Anglo settlement of Texas, no revolution, no U.S. annexation, and no U.S.-Mexican War, leaving the boundary of the United States at the Louisiana Purchase).

[49] Campbell, *Empire for Slavery*, 14.

[50] Ibid., 19.

[51] Ibid., 32.

[52] Ibid., 18.

[53] Ibid., 3. See also Barker, *Life of Stephen F. Austin*, 201-202 (suggesting how Austin's views on slavery underwent changes over the years).

[54] Ibid., 18-19 (including lashes for slaves away from home without a pass from their master).

at the forefront of that decree, as Anglo immigrants to Tejas at the time
were blatantly evading restrictions on slavery by their subterfuge of la-
beling their slaves as indentured servants. But additional reasons explain
the immigration bar—presumably Anglo disdain for Mexican leadership
was evident and given the numerical predominance in Tejas of Anglo
immigrants over Mexican residents, the Mexican government must have
realized the possibility for disloyalty that erupted only a few years later.
To address the mounting disproportion of Anglo immigrants to Mexican
residents, Mexico's 1830 immigration law also encouraged Mexicans to
migrate to Tejas: "Mexican families that voluntarily want to colonize will
be helped with the trip; maintained for a year, given lands and other
tools for work."[55] Rather than holding treason at bay, the 1830 immigration law was ignored by Anglos and likely helped spur rebellion. Despite
the ban, Anglos kept coming to Tejas, essentially as undocumented immigrants akin to today's Mexican migrants without papers seeking
economic opportunity in the United States. Anglo immigrants held con-
ventions in 1832 and 1833 seeking repeal of the Mexican anti-
immigration law, and establishment of their own state government for
the Tejas region,[56] which was then conjoined with the current Mexican
state of Coahuila—most of the Mexican state's population at the time
was in the Coahuila region which therefore dominated state government.[57] Although Mexican President Antonio López de Santa Anna
rejected the Anglo immigrant request for a separate state government,
he did agree to repeal the ban on U.S. immigration to Tejas, effective in
1834.[58] Notwithstanding that concession, the Texas Revolution, including the famous Battle of the Alamo in late February-early March 1836,
soon followed as Anglos rebelled against Mexican rule. By that time,
Anglo immigrants far surpassed Tejas residents of Mexican heritage
(Tejanos) in number—an 1834 census taker reported a Mexican population of about 4,000, with Anglos comprising 17,000 residents owning
2,000 slaves. Two years later, after the independence of Texas, a U.S. official counted 3,500 Mexicans, 30,000 Anglos, and almost 5,000 black
slaves.[59] The various counts shared the conclusion that Anglos dramatically outnumbered residents of Mexican heritage in the Tejas region at
the time of the hostilities.

In the military battles that ensued, it was evident the Mexican government viewed the eradication of slavery as a pivotal goal in defeating

[55] José Angel Hernández, *Mexican American Colonization During the Nineteenth Century: A History of the U.S.-Mexico Borderlands* (New York: Cambridge University Press, 2012), 59.
[56] Campbell, *Empire for Slavery*, 29.
[57] *Foreigners in Their Native Land: Historical Roots of the Mexican Americans*, ed. David J. Weber (Albuquerque: University of New Mexico Press, 1973, 2003), 89.
[58] Campbell, *Empire for Slavery*, 30.
[59] Lowrie, *Culture Conflict in Texas*, 31. By 1847, the first official census of Texas counted 38,753 black slaves and 102,961 whites. Rosalie Schwartz, *Across the Rio to Freedom: U.S. Negroes in Mexico* (El Paso: Texas Western Press, 1975), 32.

the Anglo insurgency. Before the Battle of the Alamo, for example, Mexican President Santa Anna wrote his minister of war, articulating a compelling moral justification for defending the Tejas region that romanticized versions of the struggle ignore: "There is a considerable number of slaves in Texas . . . who have been introduced by their [Anglo] masters under cover of certain questionable [indentured servitude] contracts, but who according to our laws should be free. Shall we permit those wretches to moan in chains any longer in a country [Mexico] whose kind laws protect the liberty of man without distinction of cast[e] or color?"[60] Santa Anna applauded Mexico's unwillingness to profit from "the sweat, blood and tears of the African race," and, after the Texas Revolution, predicted that Mexico's anticipated reclaiming of Tejas would be "blessed by all those who esteem sincerely the inalienable rights of the human species."[61] Clearly, any narrative of the Texas Revolution as somehow seeking religious freedom or freedom from control by a remote government (notwithstanding the Texas Republic's later joinder with the United States), must explain the reality of the overriding economic justification to preserve slavery in the Tejas region. It must also explain why so many of those who fought the Mexican soldiers for Texas independence were not settled immigrants to Tejas enduring suppression of their freedoms, but rather were Anglos who came to Tejas after the battle for independence began.[62] Any student of history knows the rest of the story—despite morality on his side, Santa Anna was defeated, the Republic of Texas established, and eventually (in 1845) the United States annexed the region as the 28th state of Texas. But protection of slavery continued to animate the events that led to the U.S.-Mexican War a decade after the Republic of Texas was formed.

Weeks before defeating the Mexican forces, the Anglo insurgents desiring independence adopted a new constitution for the soon-to-be Republic of Texas, ensuring slavery's protection under law and denying emancipation to thousands of slaves while prohibiting the residency of any free blacks:

> All persons of color who were slaves for life previous to their emigration to Texas, and who are now held in bondage, shall

---

[60] Campbell, *Empire for Slavery*, 42.

[61] Schwartz, *Across the Rio*, 26.

[62] Henderson, *Glorious Defeat*, 100. Nevertheless, some Mexican residents of Tejas joined with Anglos in seeking independence from Mexico. Ray Suarez, *Latino Americans: The 500-Year Legacy That Shaped a Nation* (New York: Penguin Group, 2013), 27-34 (describing a prominent Mexican who sided with the Anglo immigrants). Among the reasons for Mexican unrest were the dictates of Santa Anna who declared all Mexican states as mere administrative districts to the federal government. See generally Meinig, *Shaping of America*, 139. In the same vein, some Mexican residents of the adjoining Mexican states of Coahuila (after the loss of Tejas), Nuevo León, and Tamaulipas unsuccessfully tried to establish an independent Republic of the Rio Grande in 1840, for which they sought but failed to obtain support from the Republic of Texas.

remain in the like state of servitude: Provided, the said slave shall be the bona fide property of the person so holding the said slave as aforesaid. [The Texas] [c]ongress shall pass no laws to prohibit emigrants from bringing their slaves into the republic [of Texas] with them, and holding them by the same tenure by which such slaves were held in the United States; nor shall [the Texas] congress have power to emancipate slaves; nor shall any slave holder be allowed to emancipate his or her slave or slaves without the consent of congress, unless he or she shall send his or her slave or slaves without the limits of the republic. No free person of African descent, either in whole or in part, shall be permitted to reside permanently in the republic, without the consent of congress; and the importation or admission of Africans or negroes into this republic, excepting from the United States of America, is forever prohibited, and declared to be piracy.[63]

As the Supreme Court of Texas recognized later in 1851, this constitutional provision of the Texas Republic was meant to replace the disappearing rights of slaveholders under Mexican law with a law establishing a master's dominion over his slaves. Its "true object and meaning," thus, was to "fix and establish the title of the master, whatever may have been the legal effect of Mexican legislation to impair that right and to nullify all Mexican legislation on the subject."[64] Clearly, as a Republic, and later as a U.S. slave state until the Civil War's outcome, Texas was an empire for slavery. Evidencing the reliance on slave labor in its cotton fields and the explosion in migration of slaveowners and their slaves once Texas was liberated from Mexico's anti-slavery regime, by the start of the Civil War in 1861, almost 200,000 slaves resided in Texas,[65] which by then had seceded from the United States and joined the Confederacy in yet another move by Anglo slaveowners to ensure their abominable institution survived.

Mexico never assented to the loss of Tejas. Although Mexican President Santa Anna signed a treaty (the Treaty of Velasco) acknowledging the region's independence from Mexico, he did so while captured by Anglos, and the Mexican government repudiated his authority and never ratified the treaty. Mexico's objection to the usurpation of the Tejas terrain, in fact, likely kept the United States from annexing the region for several years, knowing it would prompt war, which eventually proved true.[66] But an equally powerful impediment to annexation, which prevailed for a decade, was U.S. opposition among Whig Party politicians to the entry of another slave state or even multiple slave states, as the Republic of Texas (ostensibly encompassing parts of the modern day

---

[63] Campbell, *Empire for Slavery*, 46-47 (as modified slightly to reflect wording in *Guess v. Lubbock*, 5 Tex. 535 (1851)).
[64] *Guess v. Lubbock*, 5 Tex. 535 (1851).
[65] Campbell, *Empire for Slavery*, 231.
[66] Greenberg, *Wicked War*, 10.

states of New Mexico, Colorado, Wyoming, Kansas, and Oklahoma)[67] was perhaps five states large in size and would alter the balance of federal power. In 1837, and in 1844, these anti-slavery U.S. politicians were able to block admission of Texas as a state[68] in which slavery would be permitted given its location mostly below the line of the Missouri Compromise of 1820.[69] Although 97 percent of voters in the Republic of Texas supported U.S. annexation in a 1837 referendum, the realities of its admission as a slave state(s) squelched that possibility. At the time, the U.S. Senate was equally split between free and slave states, and admitting Texas as a slave state would upset that balance.[70] Ensuring the delicate balance of slave/free state power had meant that as part of the 1820 Missouri Compromise, Missouri was admitted as a slave state and Maine as a free state to even out U.S. Senate representation.[71] Moreover, in addition to tilting the U.S. Senate, admitting Texas would increase the political power of slaveowners in the U.S. House, where they would get credit for three-fifths of each slave in accordance with the U.S. Constitution.

Because the Republic of Texas was an independent nation, its joinder to the United States presumably required a diplomatic treaty, ratified by a two-thirds majority of the U.S. Senate. With the narrow presidential victory of James Polk in 1844, however, a new opportunity emerged to admit Texas as a slave state. Polk, a Democrat, had run for president under a party platform proclaiming that "the re-occupation of Oregon and the re-annexation of Texas at the earliest practicable period, are great American measures."[72] Although framed in the supposed

---

[67] Of course, the limits of the Republic of Texas were hard to define. Although it was in the interest of the secessionists to claim as expansive a territory as possible, their efforts to assert authority over regions such as today's Santa Fe, New Mexico and Laredo, Texas, were met with resistance.

[68] Laura E. Gómez, *Manifest Destinies: The Making of the Mexican American Race* (New York: New York University Press, 2007), 131.

[69] While most of the initial Republic of Texas terrain was below the Missouri Compromise line, that terrain encompassed parts of northeastern New Mexico, southwestern Kansas, Colorado, and Wyoming, that lay above it. For a map of the Republic of Texas, see David Montejano, *Anglos and Mexicans in the Making of Texas, 1836-1986* (Austin: University of Texas Press, 1987), 17.

[70] Steven E. Woodworth, *Manifest Destinies: America's Westward Expansion and the Road to the Civil War* (New York: Alfred A. Knopf, 2010), 111.

[71] Richard Bruce Winders, *Crisis in the Southwest: The United States, Mexico, and the Struggle over Texas* (Wilmington, DE: Scholarly Resources, 2002), 78.

[72] Robert McNutt Mc Elroy, *The Winning of the Far West: A History of the Regaining of Texas, of the Mexican War, and the Oregon Question; and of the Successive Additions to the Territory of the United States, within the Continent of America: 1829-1867* (New York: G.P. Putnam's Sons, 1914), 86. Polk's fanciful use of "re-annexation" was meant to attack the 1819 Adams-Onís Treaty by which the United States acquired Florida from Spain and agreed to set the western boundary of the Louisiana Purchase at the Sabine River separating the current

greatness of Manifest Destiny, at bottom the U.S. move the next year to annex Texas was solely to protect the institution of Southern slavery. U.S. officials acknowledged as much. U.S. Secretary of State John C. Calhoun claimed annexation was needed to strengthen slavery, which he called an institution "essential to the peace, safety, and prosperity" of the U.S. South.[73] His predecessor, Abel Upshur, agreed that admitting Texas was "indispensable" to the security of southerners, and urged political parties to unite on this "Southern question" of protecting the institution of slavery.[74] Adding to the imperative for admitting Texas to the union, despite the potential for conflict with Mexico, was the fear of Great Britain's apparent interest in the Republic of Texas. Southerners were afraid that in the hands of British abolitionists, Texas would become a refuge for runaway slaves[75] or that Britain would ignite a slave rebellion that would spread throughout the U.S. South.[76]

Although a move to annex Texas by treaty failed in 1844 when the U.S. Senate voted 16 in favor and 35 in opposition,[77] nowhere near the two-thirds majority needed, the election of Polk, and the looming British threat to slavery, overcame the fear of war with Mexico and brought Texas into the union the next year. Still, the potential for opposition to adding another slave state(s) required some political maneuvering that scholars still question[78]—rather than admit the Republic of Texas by a Senate-confirmed treaty, Texas became part of the United States by means of a joint resolution needing the simple majorities of the U.S. Senate (where it passed 27 to 25) and House (where it passed 135 to 76) with the aid of Democratic party support from some of the northern states.[79] The Republic of Texas approved the measure and newly elected President Polk signed it on December 29, 1845, admitting Texas as the

---

states of Texas and Louisiana, thus giving up any claim to having acquired the Texas region through the Louisiana Purchase. See Greenberg, *Wicked War*, 33.

[73] Silbey, *Storm Over Texas*, xi.

[74] Ibid.

[75] Woodworth, *Manifest Destinies*, 112 (revealing that Republic of Texas president Sam Houston had invited diplomatic negotiations with the British not meaning to conclude them with British joinder, but to spark U.S. fear and jealousy to prompt U.S. annexation).

[76] Silbey, *Storm Over Texas*, 41.

[77] Woodworth, *Manifest Destinies*, 124.

[78] E.g., Juan F. Perea, "A Brief History of Race and the U.S.-Mexican Border: Tracing the Trajectories of Conquest," *UCLA Law Review* 51 (2003): 283; Mark A. Graber, "Settling the West: The Annexation of Texas, the Louisiana Purchase, and *Bush v. Gore*," in *The Louisiana Purchase and American Expansion, 1803-1898*, ed. Sanford Levinson and Bartholomew H. Sparrow (Lanham, MD: Rowman & Littlefield, 2005), 83. But see *DeLima v. Bidwell*, 182 U.S. 1 (1901) (ruling annexation by joint resolution as lawful in case involving Puerto Rico).

[79] Winders, *Crisis in the Southwest*, 87.

28th state.[80] In order to balance the admission of Texas as a slave state, Polk placated abolitionist politicians in 1846 by settling the dispute with Britain over the Oregon territory (encompassing the current states of Oregon, Washington, and Idaho), which lay above the Missouri Compromise line.[81] Previously, under the Adams-Onís Treaty of 1819 with Spain,[82] the United States had acquired Spain's claim to the Pacific Northwest—territory north of the forty-second parallel west of the Rockies that demarcates the border between Oregon and Idaho to the north, and the retained Spanish/Mexican territory of today's California, Nevada, and Utah to the south. With the U.S. Senate's approval of the boundary treaty with Britain at the forty-ninth north parallel coinciding with the start of the U.S.-Mexican War in 1846, and obviating the need for hostilities in the Pacific Northwest, the *New York Herald* suggested cavalierly that "We can now thrash Mexico into decency at our leisure."[83]

Reflecting its designs to protect the institution of slavery and the abhorrent notion of slaves as property, the initial U.S. state constitution of Texas, adopted in 1845, directed in a provision titled "Slaves" that:

> The legislature shall have no power to pass laws for the emancipation of slaves, without the consent of their owners; nor without paying their owners, previous to such emancipation, a full equivalent in money for the slaves so emancipated. They shall have no power to prevent emigrants to this State from bringing with them such persons as are deemed slaves by the laws of any of the United States, so long as any person of the same age or description shall be continued in slavery by the laws of this State: Provided, That such slave shall be the bona fide property of such emigrants. . . .[84]

---

[80] Ibid., 88. Although portions of the Texas region extended above the Missouri Compromise line, particularly as it extended into the present-day states of Oklahoma, Kansas, and Colorado, the bill admitting Texas stipulated that slavery would not exist above the Missouri Compromise line, in which all of the current state of Texas falls beneath. Woodworth, *Manifest Destinies*, 140. Rather, with the consent of Texas, up to four additional states could be formed out of the region, with slavery prohibited in those north of the Missouri line.

[81] Silbey, *Storm Over Texas*, xii.

[82] Mexico, which obtained its independence from Spain shortly after Spain and the United States ratified the treaty, ultimately ratified the treaty itself in 1831 as part of the so-called Treaty of Limits.

[83] Michael Golay, *The Tide of Empire: America's March to the Pacific* (Hoboken, NJ: John Wiley & Sons, 2003), 305.

[84] Perea, "Brief History of Race," 291 (excerpting Article VIII of Texas Constitution of 1845).

Mexico had communicated it would consider U.S. annexation of Tejas as an act of war,[85] but apparently protecting slavery mattered more to U.S. interests. The U.S.-Mexican War began just a few months after the annexation, in 1846. Although Mexico never formally ceded Tejas to the Republic of Texas or to the United States, these hostilities began over an ongoing dispute about the location of the southern border of Tejas/Texas that survived annexation. The United States claimed it owned Texas down to the Rio Grande, its current border, but Mexico claimed the confines of Tejas (once it was separated from Coahuila in the 1835 centralization of Mexican government) ended more than 100 miles north at the Nueces River, which flows into the Gulf of Mexico at Corpus Christi.[86] The land between the two rivers was arid and sparsely inhabited (aside from settlements along the Rio Grande), but aims of Manifest Destiny deployed the disputed boundary as a pawn for a bigger prize. Just a few weeks after the Texas annexation, Polk provoked war by sending troops south to the Rio Grande where U.S. troops blockaded the river at the Mexican city of Matamoros, and war erupted along the Rio Grande.[87] As Polk spun the confrontation to Congress seeking approval and funding for battle, "Mexico has passed the boundary of the United States, has invaded our territory and shed American blood upon the American soil."[88] Opposition to the war was scant at this juncture, limited to those seeking the abolition of slavery[89] and who understood that combat was aimed primarily to protect the slave culture and economy of Texas.

The U.S.-Mexican War dragged on for almost two years, and only after more than 10,000 soldiers died on both sides from combat or disease, and the U.S. forces captured Mexico City, did Mexico relent and accede in 1848 to the Treaty of Guadalupe Hidalgo, named for the shrine where it was signed a few miles from Mexico City. Although Mexico sought to

---

[85] James Ford Rhodes, "The Conspiracy Thesis," in *The Mexican War: Was It Manifest Destiny?*, ed. Ramón Eduardo Ruiz (New York: Holt, Rinehart and Winston, 1963), 9, 15.

[86] Earlier, the 1824 Mexico Constitution combined the Spanish provinces of Coahuila and Tejas into the Mexican state of Coahuila y Tejas. When the 1835 repeal of that Constitution centralized government and replaced Mexican states with centralized "departments" managed by presidential appointees, Coahuila y Tejas was split into the two departments of Coahuila and Tejas. Presumably that department boundary fell along the Nueces River, giving rise to the Mexican government's claim that, while not assenting to the loss of control of Tejas, the southern boundary of what was taken by the Republic of Texas and then the United States ended at the Nueces River.

[87] Greenberg, *Wicked War*, 101.

[88] Ibid., 104.

[89] Woodworth, *Manifest Destinies*, 167. Those opposed to the war included Abraham Lincoln, then an Illinois Senator. See http://global.oup.com/us/companion.websites/9780195375701/pdf/SPD4_Opposition_Mex_Am_War.pdf (last visited September 21, 2014).

keep today's Southern California (unaware that gold had been discovered just a few days earlier in Northern California), New Mexico (where the most Mexicans resided in Alto Mexico) and, more than anything, to set the Texas/U.S.-Mexico boundary at the Nueces River rather than farther south at the Rio Grande, the United States, holding the cards at that point, refused to relent and Mexico gave away much of its territory, as well as assented to the prior U.S. annexation of Texas. In all, counting Texas to which Mexico had never relinquished its claim until the Treaty of Guadalupe Hidalgo, the lands subject to that treaty encompassed a staggering 915,000 square miles of former Mexican territory.[90] Mexico did obtain compensation of $15 million for its relinquished territory (albeit as a credit against money Mexico already owed the United States), and the United States agreed to assume a few more million in Mexico's debts owed to U.S. citizens. Although some historians have viewed those payments as fair and just, the riches in timber, gold, silver, oil, natural harbors, and raw land acquired from the California coast to Texas make that claim laughable. Moreover, Mexico had routinely refused to sell its territory when pursued by the United States for a voluntary transfer, even for much more money than paid under the treaty, so no doubt the monies agreed to in the treaty reflected the involuntary end to a war that had been lost to a more powerful empire.

Given its stranglehold on Mexico by occupying Mexico City, many urged that the United States simply seize control of the whole of Mexico—for example the *New York Herald* championed annexing all of Mexico as a "glorious prospect."[91] Yet, ironically, some of the same sentiments that led Anglo Texans to revolt for independence and the United States to battle against Mexican control of valuable Southwestern resources this time prompted restraint, as many recoiled at the idea of inviting Mexicans en masse into the union. One of them, Senator John C. Calhoun of South Carolina, remarked:

> We have never dreamt of incorporating into our Union any but the Caucasian race—the free white race. To incorporate Mexico would be . . . incorporating an Indian race; for more than half of the Mexicans are Indians, and the other is composed chiefly of mixed tribes. I protest against such a union as that! Ours . . . is the Government of a white race. The greatest misfortunes of Spanish America are to be traced to the fatal error of placing these colored races on an equality with the white race. That error destroyed the social arrangement which formed the basis of society.[92]

---

[90] "Mexican Cession," http://en.wikipedia.org/wiki/Mexican_Cession (last visited January 20, 2014).

[91] U.S. Mexican War 1846-1848 (PBS Video, 1998).

[92] Jean Stefancic, "*Terrance v. Thompson* and the Legacy of Manifest Destiny," *Nevada Law Journal* 12 (2012): 532, 536.

Instead, the United States was happy to cherry-pick, taking the northern territory of Mexico most scarcely populated by Mexicans, and drawing boundary lines in the Treaty of Guadalupe Hidalgo that best appropriated the known resources of the region—for example, establishing the southernmost boundary of what soon became the state of California below the natural Pacific harbor of San Diego. The United States did suffer a lack of foresight—failing to draw the borderline southward enough through Arizona and New Mexico. What seemed like barren desert populated by Native tribes soon had great value for routing a transcontinental railway from the Southeastern United States through El Paso and to the U.S. West Coast, potentially transporting California's riches to eastward markets, but avoiding impassable mountainous terrain to the north. With the experience of conquest freshly in Mexico's mind, the United States was able to negotiate purchase of about 30,000 square miles of that terrain, by the Gadsden Purchase ratified in 1854, encompassing Tucson, Arizona, which had been founded by Spaniards as the presidio of San Augustin de Tucsón in 1776.[93] Although the United States also desired additional terrain in northern Mexico, including the entirety of Baja California, its negotiator, James Gadsden, was unable to persuade Mexico to part with that much territory. Mexico likely only acceded to the sale of what was needed for railway construction because of the threat of forceful acquisition. Gadsden, who negotiated with an iron fist, had warned: "The projected railroad from New York to California must be built by way of the Mesilla Valley, because there is no other feasible route. . . . The valley must belong to the United States by [payment] . . . or we will take it [by force]."[94]

Slavery factored into the Treaty of Guadalupe Hidalgo, if only in the absence of its mention. During treaty negotiations, Mexico sought a provision prohibiting slavery in the surrendered territories,[95] but, given the location of part of California and some of the territory acquired (which ultimately became the states of Arizona and New Mexico) below the Missouri Compromise line, the United States refused to contract away that Southern institution. As well, the issue of slavery came up in the congressional ratification of the Hidalgo Treaty, but abolitionists failed to similarly restrict the territory acquired from Mexico.[96] Earlier, the U.S. Congress had rejected a provision, known as the Wilmot Proviso, that a Pennsylvania congressman had attempted to attach to an 1846 appropriations bill funding the U.S.-Mexican War. The Wilmot provision would have banned slavery in any territory acquired in the war:

---

[93] See generally David Devine, *Slavery, Scandal, and Steel Rails: The 1854 Gadsden Purchase and the Building of the Second Transcontinental Railroad Across Arizona and New Mexico Twenty-Five Years Later* (New York: iUniverse, 2004).
[94] Leonard L. Richards, *The California Gold Rush and the Coming of the Civil War* (New York: Alfred A. Knopf, 2007), 151.
[95] Rhodes, "Conspiracy Thesis," 17.
[96] See Gómez, *Manifest Destinies*, 132.

"[A]s an express and fundamental condition of the acquisition of any territory from the Republic of Mexico . . . neither slavery nor involuntary servitude shall ever exist in any part of said territory."[97] In contrast, a provision the United States may have wished it included in the Treaty of Guadalupe Hidalgo was one to address the problem of fugitive slaves escaping Texas to Mexican free soil, effectively constituting a southbound "Underground Railroad," with the aid of Mexicans living in Texas.[98] By the 1850s, more than 4,000 black slaves were thought to have fled to Mexico,[99] prompting Texans to urge the United States to negotiate an extradition treaty with Mexico to return the slaves to their U.S. owners. When those urgings failed, and the Mexican government refused to cooperate with Texas, Texans turned to bounty hunters to chase their former slaves inside Mexico. The Texas state government even enacted a law (the "Act to Encourage the Reclamation of Slaves, Escaping Beyond the Limits of the Slave Territories of the United States") rewarding successful bounty hunters out of the Texas treasury.[100] The same year, 1857, that Mexico's Constitution, with unanimous approval, formally protected fugitive slaves who reached Mexico, the U.S. Supreme Court issued its *Dred Scott* decision denying freedom to a slave brought into free U.S. territory.[101] Subsequently, black slaves from the United States continued to escape to freedom in Mexico, until the end of the Civil War.

Despite the defeat of the Wilmot Proviso, the battle over admission of U.S. states as slave or free persisted until the conclusion of the Civil War a few decades later. For all the struggle of Anglo Texans to gain independence from Mexico to preserve their institution of slavery and then to join the United States to protect that institution, it was ironic to see them secede from the United States a few years later and align with the Confederate States of America, sparking the Civil War.[102] As with the

---

[97] Henderson, *Glorious Defeat*, 180.

[98] E.g., Carey McWilliams, *North From Mexico: The Spanish-Speaking People of the United States* (New York: Praeger, 1948, 1990), 103 (discussing Anglo suspicions of Texas Mexicans helping fugitive slaves).

[99] Karl Jacoby, "Between North and South: The Alternative Borderlands of William H. Ellis and the African American Colony of 1895," in *Continental Crossroads: Remapping U.S.-Mexican Borderlands History*, ed. Samuel Truett and Elliott Young (Durham, NC: Duke University Press, 2004), 217.

[100] Bruce Zagaris and Julia Padierna Peralta, "Mexico-United States Extradition and Alternatives: From Fugitive Slaves to Drug Traffickers—150 Years and Beyond the Rio Grande's Winding Courses," *American University Journal of International Law and Policy* 112 (1997): 519, 524.

[101] Schwartz, *Across the Rio*, 51.

[102] One of the ironies of the loss of Tejas and the U.S.-Mexican War was that the slave state-status of Texas helped precipitate an additional war, the Civil War. See José E. Limón, *American Encounters: Greater Mexico, the United States, and the Erotics of Culture* (Boston: Beacon Press, 1998), 13-14 (noting some Mexican residents fought on the Confederacy side).

secession from Mexican control, protecting slave ownership in the region trumped any national allegiance.

For the at least 75,000 Mexican citizens residing in the Mexican lands acquired by the United States, most of them living in today's New Mexico rather than in today's Texas, the Treaty of Guadalupe Hidalgo supplied a choice—they could remain Mexican citizens (continuing to live in the United States or returning to Mexico) or choose U.S. citizenship, with those not specifying their preference within a year deemed U.S. citizens.[103] Still, as explained in Chapters 2 and 8, these Mexican residents failed to attain the full rights of U.S. citizens. The majority of them, living in New Mexico, were denied full political participation in the United States when statehood languished for decades, awaiting the assurance of an English-speaking, Anglo majority in the region. Moreover, their status as Mexicans, or even as Mexican Americans, still meant their second class citizenship in Texas and elsewhere in the Southwest, as they were subjected to longstanding and still-evident segregation and discrimination in schools, the workplace, and fundamentally every aspect of their everyday lives, as Chapter 8 details. In the United States, as Senator Calhoun had reminded, there was to be no equality between so-called mixed tribes and whites.

---

[103] Saito, *Meeting the Enemy*, 130.

2. ALL THAT GLITTERS
THE ORIGINS OF CALIFORNIA
AND NEW MEXICO

> [T]he march of emigration is to the West, and naught
> will arrest its advance but the mighty ocean.
> —Alfred Robinson[104]

In addition to squelching Mexico's claims to the U.S.-annexed state of Texas, the U.S.-Mexican War stripped Mexico of the current U.S. states of California, Nevada, Utah, Arizona, and New Mexico (with the present configuration of the latter two states completed through the subsequent Gadsden Purchase), as well as parts of Colorado, Wyoming, Kansas, and Oklahoma. The discussion below focuses on California, probably the most important state economically and culturally to the United States of the group (and the third largest U.S. state in physical size), as well as New Mexico, encompassing the region most heavily populated by Mexicans at the time of the U.S.-Mexican War and the slowest state to experience the Anglo inroads of population and culture that soon enveloped the others. The materials in this chapter are important background to understanding the deep roots and ongoing suppression of Mexican culture in the United States, as developed in later chapters. The difference in timing of U.S. statehood between California and New Mexico reveals the poor regard for Mexicans and the Mexican culture that still constrains our willingness to accept and embrace our connected destiny with Mexico and Mexicans despite that Latina/os (most of them Mexican) in California and New Mexico exceed Anglos in number.

Isolated by geography, California (when part of the Spanish and later the Mexican territory known as Alta California that encompassed the current states of California, Nevada, Arizona, Utah, and parts of Colorado and Wyoming), received few U.S. immigrants while under Spanish and then Mexican control. Spanish immigration policies were restrictive, but immigration of Anglos ran low in California (and New Mexico) even under more welcoming Mexican rule. In contrast to the Mexican partnership with Anglo empresarios such as Stephen F. Austin who distributed land in the Mexican state of Coahuila y Tejas to Anglo immigrants, there were no such colonization grants available in New Mexico or California.[105] In 1830, only some 120 "foreigners" (namely, Anglos)

---

[104] Alfred Robinson, *Life in California: During a Residence of Several Years in that Territory* (New York: Da Capo Press, 1969) 226 (originally published in 1846).
[105] Weber, *Mexican Frontier*, 180-182.

lived in California, mostly trappers and traders, matched by a similar scant number of outsiders, thirty-four, counted in an 1839 census of New Mexico.[106]

Among other factors constraining early Anglo interest in these regions, missions already occupied the most desirable lands, although the secularization of missions and the increased market for products of California ranches prompted some Anglos to successfully petition for rancho land grants in California from the Mexican government in the 1830s and 1840s.[107] Still, after the uprising in Tejas, Mexican officials in Alta California appreciated the threat Anglo newcomers posed in their sparsely populated region. Indeed, the United States had early designs on acquiring California, with President Andrew Jackson offering Mexico $500,000 in 1835 for San Francisco Bay and its natural port, and the northern portion of Alta California.[108] The Pacific Coast offered access to the Asian markets, which desired the pelts of resident sea otters and other products from the region. [109] At the time, the United States was still embroiled in a dispute with Great Britain over the territory of today's states of Oregon, Washington, and Idaho, elevating the importance of acquiring a foothold in California to the Pacific trade routes. In 1845, the United States upped its ante, with President James Polk, riding an expansionist mandate, sending an envoy to Mexico who offered to purchase Northern California (and New Mexico) for substantially more money, described by commentators variously as $20 million and $25 million, than the prior purchase offer.[110] But the concurrent U.S. efforts to annex the Republic of Texas scuttled any such friendly dealmaking with Mexico, leaving Polk to pursue his target through war. At the start of those hostilities in 1846, California was thinly populated, primarily by indigenous residents, and most of its Spanish/Mexican settlements were along the coast. Even El Pueblo de Nuestra Señora la Reina de los Ánge-

---

[106] Ibid., 179-180. Of course, from an indigenous perspective, the Spanish/Mexican settlers were outsiders too.

[107] Ibid., 196-197.

[108] Rodolfo Acuña, *Occupied America: A History of Chicanos* (New York: HarperCollins, 3d ed. 1988), 109. Compare John S.D. Eisenhower, *So Far From God: The U.S. War With Mexico 1846-1848* (New York: Random House, 1989), 199 (specifying the amount offered as $5 million for territory north of Monterey).

[109] Greenberg, *Wicked War*, 57.

[110] Compare David J. Weber, "Editor's Introduction" in *Foreigners in Their Native Land*, 88, 95 (stating Polk sent an envoy with instructions to purchase Upper California and New Mexico for up to $25 million) with Lisa García Bedolla, *Latino Politics* (Cambridge, UK: Polity Press, 2009), 38 (Polk empowered an offer of up to $20 million for New Mexico and California, apparently all of the latter). See also Meinig, *Shaping of America*, 145 (Polk's envoy was empowered to offer up to $20 million for land west of New Mexico that included the San Francisco Bay, as well as $5 million more for land encompassing Monterey, California and another $5 million for New Mexico).

les de Porciúncula (known today as simply Los Angeles or even just "L.A."), had only fifteen hundred residents, and California's current port cities, such as San Francisco, San Pedro, and San Diego, were mere trading posts,[111] established typically in the location of the Spanish missions that carried their namesakes.

Following a similar path of revolt as in Texas, Anglo immigrants in Northern California, described as a band of horse thieves and runaway sailors,[112] led an uprising against Mexico in 1846, planting a flag with a red grizzly bear in the plaza of Sonoma (an Indian word meaning Valley of the Moon) in present-day wine country, and declaring an independent republic. The U.S.-Mexican War had already begun along the Rio Grande, but word hadn't reached California. When U.S. naval forces arrived in Monterey, California by sea, joined by U.S. troops arriving from the east by land, the struggle for independence based in Sonoma simply merged into the greater fight for U.S. acquisition of California and the rest of Alto Mexico, and the U.S. flag soon flew in Sonoma. Polk explained in his diary: "Although we had not gone to war for conquest, yet it was clear that in making peace we would if practicable obtain California and such other portion of the Mexican territory as would be sufficient to indemnify our claimants on Mexico, and to defray the expenses of war."[113]

At the time of the signing of the Treaty of Guadalupe Hidalgo, Mexico City was unaware of the discovery of gold a few days earlier in Northern California's Sutter's Mill, and Mexican officials relinquished the Alta California region to the United States. The resultant Gold Rush flood of Anglo immigrants overnight changed the demographics of California to a decidedly Anglo population that maintained its dominance for the next 150 years until recently, and set the stage for speedy approval of U.S. statehood that eluded the Mexican-dominated region of New Mexico for decades. By the time of its first state constitution, which took effect in 1850, California's population had swelled to 380,000, most of them Anglos, with Mexicans constituting only 15 percent of that total, and a scant 4 percent by 1870.[114]

In contrast to the predominance of Mexicans that delayed New Mexico's aspiration for statehood, it was slavery that almost derailed California's statehood. Southerners demanded the Missouri Compromise line extend to the Pacific Ocean, which would ensure the entry of all of Southern California as a slave state separate from Northern California. But Californians held a constitutional convention in 1849, adjusting the eventual state line westward to exclude the current states

---

[111] Eisenhower, *So Far From God*, 200.
[112] U.S. Mexican War 1846-1848 (PBS Video, 1998).
[113] Peter Laufer, *Wetback Nation: The Case for Opening the Mexican-American Border* (Chicago: Ivan R. Dee, 2004), 63.
[114] David J. Weber, "Editor's Introduction," in *Foreigners in Their Native Land*, 140, 148.

of Nevada and Arizona, and proposing a free state for its entire reach north. That vote for free status stemmed less from a sense of the immorality of slavery and more from prejudice. Anglo voters, who approved the California constitution, were generally non-slaveholders who nonetheless did not want to live near blacks, whether slaves or free.[115] Presumably, if California were established as a slave state, blacks would reside in greater numbers and upset that expectation. When California's slave-free constitution arrived in Washington D.C., Southern politicians were outraged—they framed the prohibition as preventing them from entering and residing in California. In Congressional statehood negotiations that included New Mexico's territory, one Georgia congressman fumed: "[I]f by your legislation you seek to drive us from the territories of California and New Mexico, purchased by the common blood and treasure of the whole people, and to abolish slavery in this district, thereby attempting to fix a national degradation upon half the States . . . I am for disunion."[116] Equally offensive to Southerners was the political reality that admitting California as the 31st state would upset the then balance (Iowa and Wisconsin were added as free states in 1846 and 1848 respectively following the admissions of Florida and Texas in 1845) of fifteen slave and fifteen free states,[117] with the prospect of additional free states should other states be carved from its expansive reach. A possible solution called for splitting California into two states, extending the Missouri Compromise to the Pacific Ocean, with a free north and a slave south.

In what followed as the Compromise of 1850, California was admitted in its entirety as a free state,[118] and the Utah Territory was established, as was the New Mexico Territory, the latter with its slave status (despite existing mostly south of the Missouri Compromise) and statehood aspirations, as discussed below, unaddressed and unresolved. Slave owning interests were dealt a further blow when, as part of that 1850 Compromise, the slave state of Texas dropped its territorial claim to most of what is now eastern New Mexico (along with the once-Alto Mexico lands in Kansas and Oklahoma, and some of the once-Alto Mexico terrain in Colorado and Wyoming) in exchange for debt relief by the United States.[119] As a bone thrown to the slaveholding states, however,

---

[115] Woodworth, *Manifest Destinies*, 332.

[116] Ibid., 335.

[117] Ibid., 332.

[118] As the Mexican Minister to the United States observed in 1889, of all the territory seized in the U.S.-Mexican War, the only region to become a slave state was Texas. M. Romero, "The Annexation of Mexico," *North American Review* CCCXC (May 1889): 525, 529 (posing the question: "Could the (U.S.] leaders of the Mexican War have foreseen this result, it is not likely that they would have been so much in earnest for the acquisition of that territory.").

[119] Gómez, *Manifest Destinies*, 132.

as part of the 1850 Compromise, Congress adopted the Fugitive Slave Act of 1850 to require state officials to capture runaway slaves.[120]

* * *

New Mexico's prolonged bid for statehood reflected the dual factors that led previously to its seizure from Mexico—protection of slavery and conceptions of Mexicans as unfit to govern their territory. Petitioning for U.S. statehood in 1848 and 1850, New Mexico hurt its cause among Southern politicians by rejecting slavery.[121] The Compromise of 1850, which established the Territory of New Mexico, gave its inhabitants the right to decide the slavery question for themselves, which New Mexicans exercised against the Southern institution.[122] At the time, some of the territory extended above the Missouri Compromise line, although most lay below. Even though the upheaval of the Civil War in the 1860s finally settled the U.S. slavery question, New Mexico's bid for statehood lagged several decades longer, now attributable to negative attitudes toward its majority Mexican population. In contrast to the rest of the lands the United States acquired through the Treaty of Guadalupe Hidalgo and its earlier annexation of Texas, the New Mexico region was home to a substantial number of Mexicans who far outnumbered Anglo immigrants. Some Anglo immigrants did arrive in the New Mexico region before the U.S.-Mexican War, entering through the Santa Fe Trail, but in New Mexico, home to more than two-thirds of the Mexicans living in the vast Alto Mexico terrain ceded to the United States,[123] they failed to dominate the region's population and politics. Presumably anticipating a delay in statehood for this decidedly Mexican region, in approving the Treaty of Guadalupe Hidalgo, the U.S. Senate altered its negotiated language contemplating statehood, and statehood's attendant political advantages, "as soon as possible," to read "at the proper time." While awaiting statehood, New Mexico's territory was carved by Congress into other territories and eventually into states, with New Mexico in 1912 and, a month later, Arizona becoming the last admitted U.S. states in the past 100 years, apart from Alaska and Hawaii. Originally included, in part, within the reach of the New Mexico Territory, Colorado, Nevada, and Wyoming all became states before New Mexico. When carved out of the Territory of New Mexico as its own territory in 1863, Arizona too had a predominance of Mexicans over Anglo settlers, which lasted through the 1870s,[124] which helps explain its own delay in statehood.

---

[120] Ibid.

[121] David V. Holtby, *Forty-Seventh Star* (Norman, OK: University of Oklahoma Press, 2012), 3.

[122] Robert W. Larson, *New Mexico's Quest for Statehood 1846-1912* (Albuquerque, NM: University of New Mexico Press, 1968), 55.

[123] Gómez, *Manifest Destinies*, 7.

[124] David J. Weber, "Editor's Introduction," in *Foreigners in Their Native Land*, 144.

Accusations of the unfitness of Mexican residents for the privileges of statehood plagued New Mexicans from the outset. In the first statehood bid, in 1848, Massachusetts Senator Daniel Webster balked at the prospect of Mexicans in governance: "Have they any notion of popular government? Not the slightest. . . . It is farcical to talk of such people making a constitution for themselves."[125] Webster proceeded to quote from a racist narrative that claimed Mexicans in New Mexico were "as deficient in energy of character and physical courage as they are in all the moral and intellectual qualities. In their social state [they are] but one degree removed from the veriest savages."[126] These prejudicial attitudes dominated subsequent discussions of statehood decades later in the early 1900s, with Senator C.K. Davis, of the Senate Committee on Territories, suggesting, "[t]he large Mexican population of that territory is a mighty undesirable element out of which to form a state."[127] By then, the 1900 Census revealed that of the New Mexico territory's 195,310 residents, 69 percent (135,000) were Mexicans, and another 13,200 of the residents were Indians. Equally damming to conceptions of sufficient Americanization needed for statehood was the Census finding that more than half (51 percent) of the territory's native-born residents did not speak or understand English.[128] Perceptions of a territory overrun with monolingual Spanish-speakers led U.S. Senator Albert Beveridge to call for the Americanization of these residents, along with the residents of other U.S. territories such as the Philippines: "American soldiers, American teachers, American administrators are all instruments of the Nation in discharging the Nation's high duty to the ancient and yet infant people which circumstance has placed in our keeping."[129] Evidencing the assumption that Americanization eventually would come through more Anglos settling in New Mexico, Beveridge wrote:

> On the whole, the [Senate] committee [on Territories] feel[s] that in the course of time, when education . . . shall have accomplished its work; when the masses of the people or even a majority of them shall in the usages and employment of their daily life have become identical in language and customs with . . . the American people; when the immigration of English-speaking people who have been citizens of other States does its modifying work with the "Mexican element"—when all these things have come to pass, the committee hopes and believes that this mass of people unlike us in race, language, and social customs, will finally come to form a creditable portion of American citizenship.[130]

---

[125] Holtby, *Forty-Seventh Star*, 4.
[126] Ibid.
[127] Ibid., 34.
[128] Ibid., 53.
[129] Ibid., 44-45.
[130] Perea, "Brief History of Race," 300.

Local Spanish language dominance factored into the Senate statehood debates, with Senator Knute Nelson of Minnesota calling New Mexico "more of a Spanish country than an American country," and, relying on the 1900 Census data, charging "In respect to language, in respect to education, in respect to intelligence, and all that goes to make-up the leading and prominent characteristics of a self-governing American citizen, the people of that Territory were to a large extent deficient," as well as lacking "homogeneousness in language and in fitness for self-government."[131] Even residents of the Arizona Territory, since carved from New Mexico, sought to disassociate themselves from what they saw as the lesser Mexican people of the region. When voters in both regions went to the polls in 1906 to decide on a proposal for joint statehood of the Arizona and New Mexico Territories, voters in New Mexico favored the proposal but Arizonans, by then with an Anglo majority in place, overwhelmingly balked and killed the measure.[132] As one legislator put the issue, "Can Arizona as a single state control it better by itself, or shall we join the [New] Mexican greasers to Arizona and let them control it?"[133]

A single demographic factor explains the eventual success of the statehood campaign for New Mexico in 1912—the results of the 1910 Census. In the decade after the 1900 Census that showed a considerable Mexican majority in New Mexico, an Anglo settler influx soon closed the gap. Growing 68 percent in the decade, to an overall population of 327,301, New Mexico saw its Mexican population increase only 15 percent while Anglos jumped 382 percent, to fall just a few thousand residents short of the region's Mexican population.[134] With this trend of dominant Anglo migration, statehood, finally, was earned as the 47th state, along with Arizona as the 48th (in contrast, Anglo-dominated Utah received statehood in 1896, Colorado in 1876, and Nevada in 1864).

The United States today is no more receptive to the Spanish language, nor to Mexican residents. Yet the hybridity of New Mexico just before statehood, with a substantial Spanish-speaking population and a near equal number of Anglo residents speaking English, mirrors today's Alto Mexico terrain where Latina/o and Spanish-speaking residents are catching Anglos in population. Rather than the prize of U.S. statehood connecting New Mexico to the United States in laws and governance, as later chapters explain the more fundamental consequence of the current demographic shift may be to connect Alto Mexico to the Americas as a cultural convergence zone where bilingualism is respected rather than discouraged.

---

[131] Holtby, *Forty-Seventh Star*, 60.
[132] Ibid., 117.
[133] David J. Weber, "Editor's Introduction," in *Foreigners in Their Native Land*, 145.
[134] Holtby, *Forty-Seventh Star*, 159.

3: IMAGINING ALTO MEXICO'S ECONOMY

There she is, folks—the land a milk an' honey—California!

—Grapes of Wrath screenplay[135]

This chapter charts the economic development of the Southwest from Mexican control to the region's current economic strength, as supplemented by Chapter 6's discussion of how Mexicans went from landowners of vast rancho properties to supplying the majority of today's labor on U.S. farms. Examining the economy of the Southwest today and historically (both as U.S. and Mexican owned) is critically important for the undertaking in later chapters to construct and imagine the demographic composition of the Southwest under Mexican control and for engaging the contentious issues that dominate today's U.S.-Mexico relations at the border and beyond. No single factor is more important than the economy in drawing immigrants to the United States. Both for Mexicans and most other immigrants, the primary lure of the United States as a migrant receiving country has been the prospect of jobs, rather than family reunification, social services, or even escape from oppression elsewhere.

Relying on Mexican immigrant labor for more than 100 years, as well as drawing Anglos within the United States toward Sun Belt jobs, the Southwest economy has helped create the two most populous U.S. states of California and Texas which, together with the rest of what was once Alto Mexico, account for about one-fourth of the U.S. population (approximately 80 million of 314 million U.S. residents). From another perspective, the current population of Alto Mexico equals about two-thirds of Mexico's entire population. The states of California and Texas play a critical role in constituting the United States as the international leader in gross domestic product (with Mexico ranked fourteenth). Aligning with their standing as the most populated U.S. states, California and Texas similarly rank first and second in gross state product,[136] although coming in only thirteenth and seventh respectively in per capita production (internationally, the United States ranks sixth in per

---

[135] Nunnally Johnson, "The Grapes of Wrath Screenplay," http://www.aellea.com/scripts/grapes_of_wrath_the.html (last visited June 3, 2014).
[136] "List of U.S. States by GDP," http://en.wikipedia.org/wiki/ List_of_U.S._states_by_GDP (last visited May 14, 2014) (2009 figures).

capita gross national product and Mexico only sixty-sixth).[137] With a
Mexico-controlled Alto Mexico, the United 44 States would still claim
New York City, the nation's financial capital, helping New York state ac-
count for the third ranked state in gross product, but California and
Texas together triple the economic output of New York state and Cali-
fornia's economy alone well surpasses the Mexican economy.

No doubt some feel that our current economic strength stems from
longstanding Anglo control of the Southwest (and the rest of the United
States), and presumably that if under Mexican control, the Southwest
economy would have withered rather than flourished. The cavalier sentiment driving Manifest Destiny to usurp wilderness from the control of
"savages" ill-equipped to maximize its resources still surfaces today in
comparisons of the U.S. and Mexican economies. For example, actor Ben
Stein and Phil DeMuth maligned Mexico in their 2008 book, *How to Ruin the United States of America*, opining that "if we hadn't taken over the
sparsely populated territory [of northern Mexico], the economy of the
American Southwest would today resemble that of . . . well, Mexico, to
the detriment of the entire world."[138] Evidencing a contrary view of the
fortunes of Mexico that hinged on its loss of valuable resources, historian Rodolfo Acuña suggests the U.S.-Mexican War left Mexico with
"shrunken resources," while the United States gained key ports to facili-
tate trade, along with "rich farmlands and natural resources such as gold,
silver, zinc, copper, oil, and uranium, which would make possible its
unprecedented industrial boom."[139] Moreover, the author of an acclaimed history of cotton suggests that without the U.S. acquisition of
Alto Mexico, Mexico "might have been the world's premier cotton producer by the early twentieth century."[140]

Focusing on the power of geography, historian Oscar Martínez contended that had Mexico retained its territory, its economic future would
have been "significantly more prosperous."[141] Instead, with its acquisition
of strategic Mexican land conferring the blessings of a broad coast-to-
coast geography, the United States became a "land of opportunity."[142]

Although at the time of the War most Mexican citizens resided in
the fertile tropical highlands at its center, and the northern Mexican territory lost to the United States was sparsely populated by Mexicans, that
Alto Mexico terrain was nonetheless resource-rich with minerals and

---

[137] "List of Countries by GDP (PPP) Per Capita,"
http://en.wikipedia.org/wiki/List_of_countries_by_GDP_(PPP)_per_capita (last
visited May 14, 2014) (2013 International Monetary Fund figures).
[138] Ben Stein and Phil DeMuth, *How to Ruin the United States of America* (Carlsbad, CA: New Beginnings Press, 2008), 125.
[139] Acuña, *Occupied America*, 20.
[140] Sven Beckert, *Empire of Cotton: A Global History* (New York: Alfred A. Knopf,
2014), 353.
[141] Oscar J. Martínez, *Mexico's Uneven Development: The Geographical and Historical Context of Inequality* (New York: Routledge, 2016), 68.
[142] Ibid., 72.

deposits, such as gold and oil, or other resources (such as ski slopes) that became vital to the regional economy after the War. Because the economy of the Southwest is driven significantly by natural resources, such as through the tapping of oil or natural gas reserves, or through rich soils, favorable climate, and the availability of water for agriculture, these natural advantages would have inured to the benefit of Mexico's economy if the U.S. Southwest had remained in Mexican control, rather than somehow being untapped in Mexican hands. Although some factors in economic development are dependent on local law (such as the allowance of appropriating water for off-site use, [143] the private/government ownership of oil reserves, and the extent of worker protections under law), much of the revenue stream, particularly from resource-based economies, stems from the fortuity of geography rather than the race/ethnicity of those owning the land and other tools of production, or those controlling the government.[144] As Oscar Martínez has argued, in sum, Mexico's loss of nonfuel minerals, "coupled with the additional loss of fuel minerals, vast fertile lands, fecund forests, and exceptional harbors on the Pacific and Gulf Coasts, represent an incalculable economic setback."[145]

At the time of the U.S.-Mexican War, Alto Mexico was thinly populated by Mexicans, with its indigenous inhabitants well outnumbering the Mexican residents who migrated to the region and resided mostly in today's New Mexico. Most Mexican (and Anglo settler) residents lived in rural settings, and towns were very small. For example, El Pueblo de Nuestra Señora la Reina de los Ángeles de Porciúncula (today's Los Angeles) boasted only about 1,500 wartime residents, soon swelling to 5,000 by 1854 when Anglos began arriving in larger numbers after the War.[146] Mexican residents of the Southwest tended to live on large ran-

---

[143] Lawrence J. Jelinek, *Harvest Empire: A History of California Agriculture* (San Francisco: Boyd & Fraser, 1979), 55-56 (describing early development of California water law). For discussion of water rights under Spanish and Mexican law in Alto Mexico, see Andrea Bottorffa, "The Legal History of a Changing Population: Integrating Mexican and U.S. Legal Customs in the American Southwest," *University of Pittsburgh Law Review* 73 (2012): 699.

[144] But see Daron Acemoglu and James A. Robinson, *Why Nations Fail: The Origins of Power, Prosperity, and Poverty* (New York: Crown Publishers, 2012) (positing that open and inclusive, pro-growth political systems are responsible for economic wealth of nations, in contrast to the political systems of poor nations).

[145] Martínez, *Mexico's Uneven Development*, 196-97 (noting that the ceded Mexican territory accounted for 42 percent of the total U.S. nonfuel mineral production value in 2008). See also ibid., 87 (stating that Mexico's coastlines are deficient in natural harbors vital for coastal and overseas trade).

[146] Leonard Pitt, *The Decline of the Californios: A Social History of the Spanish-Speaking Californians, 1846-1890* (Berkeley, CA: University of California Press, 1966), 122 (1,500 to 2,000 of the 5,000 postwar residents were Anglo settlers from the United States, in contrast to just 75 wartime Anglo settlers in the city).

chos, making a subsistence living by cattle ranching on the vast estates, while growing other crops for familial consumption and trading in cattle hides and tallow. As described in Chapter 1, Anglo immigrants in the Mexican state of Coahuila y Tejas (and later the Republic of Texas and the U.S. state of Texas) established labor-intensive cotton plantations serviced by black slave labor. But elsewhere in Mexico-governed Alto Mexico, subsistence farming was the norm. Now the leading U.S. agricultural producing state, California, when part of Mexico-owned Alto Mexico, had little opportunity to market products to the distant eastern and southern United States before the advent of railways and refrigerated railcars later in the nineteenth century. Moreover, as the territory of Alta California under Mexican control, its Mexican population was thinly distributed, constraining the development of local markets. Of course, the population explosion that accompanied the 1848 discovery of extensive deposits of gold in Northern California altered the incentives and economics of agriculture, and set California on a path toward becoming an agricultural giant in its quantity and variety of production.

With the onset of the Gold Rush, and the loss of ranchos through the onus of land title confirmation and other treachery described in Chapter 6, agriculture in California shifted to serve the enormous influx of hungry miners. For example, the Northern California wine industry, vital in today's economy of specialized agriculture, originated in the 1850s in response to the demand among nearby miners for wine and brandy (produced from wine), while taking advantage of the favorable growing climate.[147] The predominance of livestock agriculture, now helping to feed miners,[148] eventually gave way in California to wheat production by 1872,[149] shipped to England, among other places, which in turn was replaced by the early 1900s with today's agricultural emphasis in California on fruits and vegetables. By 1900, 25 percent of canned fruits and vegetables in the United States originated in California.[150] These agricultural advancements in no way derived solely from Anglo settler inspiration. Coming from an arid climate in Europe, Spaniards had introduced many of these crops within California long before the U.S.-Mexican War, including figs, oranges, grapes (for eating and wine), apricots, pears, olives, and lemons, as well as wheat seeds suited for the region's climate.[151] Today, almost half of U.S. produced fruits, nuts, and

---

[147] Jelinek, *Harvest Empire*, 35.

[148] Donald J. Pisani, *From the Family Farm to Agribusiness: The Irrigation Crusade in California and the West, 1850-1931* (Berkeley, CA: University of California Press, 1984), 3 (discussing how miner demand for cattle led to cattle drives from Mexico, Texas, and the Midwest to increase the supply and quality of meat from the Spanish cattle valued for hides but not as a source of meat or milk).

[149] Jelinek, *Harvest Empire*, 70.

[150] Pisani, *Family Farm*, 284.

[151] McWilliams, *North From Mexico*, 40-41.

vegetables are grown in California, with its state agriculture generating a $45 billion annual revenue stream.

Technology eventually developed machinery to harvest cotton and tomatoes, among other crops, but generally the California fruit, nut, and vegetable crops have been and remain dependent on human labor.[152] Initially, before the U.S.-Mexican War, Mexican rancho owners in California relied mostly on Mexican and Indian labor on their ranchos, but the labor-intensive agriculture of more specialized crops that displaced the subsistence rancho model required a significant pool of cheap labor. Chinese immigrants first served this role, having built the western railroads along with Mexican laborers and then moving to the fields where they were willing to accept lower wages than other workers.[153] By the 1880s, Chinese workers comprised more than half of California's farm laborers.[154] But anti-Chinese prejudice prompted the federal Chinese Exclusion Act of 1882, excluding their entry into the United States, and led to their replacement in the agricultural workforce by Japanese immigrants, who similarly received lower wages than white workers. Backlash too against Japanese workers and farm owners culminated in federal immigration laws and policies barring their entry and state Alien Land laws in the early twentieth century in California (and other states) prohibiting their ownership of agricultural land.[155] Replacing the Japanese workers, so-called Okies came to labor in California during the Dust Bowl drought of the 1930s, and Filipino immigrants arrived in significant numbers to work the California fields—for example, 60 percent of the 30,000 Filipino entrants to California in the 1920s became farm laborers.[156]

But with a boost from the Bracero guest labor program, an accord between the United States and Mexico initially intended to meet U.S. domestic labor needs in agriculture during World War II, over time Mexican immigrants replaced workers from other groups as the dominant source of U.S. farm labor as they had previously done in maintaining the Western U.S. railroads.[157] California's agricultural workforce, less than half of which was Latina/o in 1965, became over 97 percent Latina/o, the vast majority of Mexican background, by the mid-

---

[152] Jelinek, *Harvest Empire*, 4.
[153] Ellen Liebman, *California Farmland: A History of Large Agricultural Land-holdings* (Totowa, NJ: Rowman & Allanheld, 1983), 63-64.
[154] *A Guidebook to California Agriculture*, ed. Ann Foley Scheuring (Berkeley, CA: University of California Press, 1982), 15.
[155] See generally Keith Aoki, "No Right to Own? The Early Twentieth-Century 'Alien Land Laws' as a Prelude to Internment," *Boston College Third World Law Journal* 19 (1998): 37.
[156] Jelinek, *Harvest Empire*, 70.
[157] McWilliams, *North From Mexico*, 156 (describing how by 1880 Mexican laborers comprised 70 percent of the section crews and 90 percent of the extra work gangs on the main Southwestern rail lines).

1990s.[158] When the Bracero Program terminated and Congress placed restrictive limits on legal Mexican immigration in the mid-1960s, the agricultural workforce in California and elsewhere in the Southwest and the United States remained reliant on a Mexican workforce, yet now comprised of undocumented Mexican immigrants who surmounted the stingy lawful entry limits in their search for opportunity in scorching U.S. fields. As they did in California's fields, Mexican workers eventually replaced black labor in the Texas cotton fields in advance of mechanization—Texas today leads the United States in cotton production. By 1940, two-thirds of the migratory cotton pickers in the region were Mexican, and tens of thousands of migratory Mexican workers followed the development of cotton production into Arizona and California.[159] Overall, no matter the crop nor the advent of mechanization, and throughout the food production chain from slaughterhouses to processing and packaging plants, Mexican workers are now the dominant food labor force in the U.S. Southwest and beyond, supplying affordable food to the nation.

Within an Alto Mexico under Mexico control, the same dynamic of a decidedly Mexican farm labor force would surely have taken hold, although sooner and without the risk and consequences of undocumented entry—with the exception of migrants from Guatemala and Central America who today cross Mexico as undocumented migrants in search of U.S. opportunities, as Chapter 6 addresses. Given the expense and peril of undocumented crossings for Mexican and other migrants who enter the United States with the aid of compensated coyotes, family members often are left behind, as they were in the official Bracero Program where families were unwelcome and Mexican workers were expected to leave after completing their harvests. As with the Bracero Program, migrant Mexican farm workers today tend to arrive solo and work as long daily and live as cheaply as they can, while sending remittances to family members who remain south of the border, effectively supporting two lonely households. In a Mexico-governed Alto Mexico, presumably with a similarly significant agricultural economy, Mexican laborers within that geography could more easily travel and live with their families. Even for those jobs too transitory for family joinder without disrupting school and stable residency, today's undocumented Mexican laborers in U.S. fields, having paid so much for an unauthorized crossing in this era of militarized borders, cannot afford to return to Mexico and their family in off-seasons or for holidays or family celebrations, and then surreptitiously recross the border. In a Mexico-governed Alto Mexico, though, such travel would be as commonplace as it used to be between the U.S. fields and Mexican residences for decades until the U.S.-Mexico border was fortified to deny easy entry to migrant workers.

---

[158] Daniel Rothenberg, *With These Hands: The Hidden World of Migrant Farmworkers Today* (Berkeley: University of California Press, 1998), 44.
[159] McWilliams, *North From Mexico*, 157-162.

Although farmers within a Mexico-governed Alto Mexico would have even more ready access to Mexican laborers, cynics of Mexican agriculture might point to struggles of Mexican farms to remain competitive with U.S. agri-business. In the Mexico-governed Alto Mexico, and still today in Mexico, farming often involved small-scale cooperative efforts known as ejidos protected under Mexican law from sale or use as collateral for loans that might prompt an involuntary foreclosure sale and loss of the livelihood of land. By the 1970s, however, Mexico was importing significant quantities of its food staples, and critics there blamed the imbalance on the lack of access to credit markets and inefficiencies of the traditional ejido system of farm ownership. Spurred by NAFTA (the North American Free Trade Agreement), in the early 1990s Mexico's Constitution underwent reform to "modernize" the ownership rights of ejidos by authorizing voluntary privatization. Lifting some of the restrictions on transfer and foreign ownership, the constitutional amendments authorized transfer of individual land title to other ejido members or to outsiders, the creation of joint ownership ventures with multinational agriculture corporations, and offering the loan collateral of ejido ownership to obtain agricultural loans.[160] The expectation was that these longstanding smaller-scale community-based agriculture operations would be replaced by multinational efforts with ready access to capital and familiarity with the dictates of capital markets.

The fruits of the recent agricultural reform, however, were sour for many of the ejidatarios (ejido owners). Reminiscent of the loss of rancho lands by Mexicans in the U.S. Southwest after the U.S.-Mexican War discussed in Chapter 6, many Mexican ejidatarios lost their land at bargain prices, not with the aim of maximizing productivity, but because of financial emergency through sale or loans that led to foreclosure.[161] The post-NAFTA upheaval of Mexico's agricultural economy launched millions of rural Mexicans north across the border, leaving behind lands they own or used to own. Inabilities to compete with U.S. farmers of staple crops, such as corn, stemmed less from inefficiencies of the Mexican ejido structure and more from government subsidies and largess conferred on U.S. agribusiness that Mexican farmers did not similarly

---

[160] James J. Kelly, Jr., "Article 27 and Mexican Land Reform: The Legacy of Zapata's Dream," *Columbia Human Rights Law Review* 25 (1994): 541, 562; Wayne A. Cornelius and David Myhre, ed. *The Transformation of Rural Mexico: Reforming the Ejido Sector* (San Diego: Center for U.S.-Mexican Studies, University of California, 1998). Foreign private investors that enter into production associations or joint ventures with the ejido owners are subject to a limit of 49 percent of the equity capital in the venture.

[161] Wenonah Hauter, "The Limits of International Human Rights Law and the Role of Food Sovereignty in Protecting People from Further Trade Liberalization Under the Doha Round Negotiations," *Vanderbilt Journal of Transnational Law* 40 (2007): 1071, 1075; Joseph M. Whitmeyer and Rosemary L. Hopcroft, "Community, Capitalism, and Rebellion in Chiapas," *Sociological Perspectives* 39 (Spring 1996): 517, 524.

enjoy. These advantages resulted in unfair competition and the irony of Mexican farmers displaced from their land and relegated to migrant labor, often as undocumented workers traveling to the United States for subsistence work in the fields of U.S. agri-business. As one writer described this ongoing transformation from Mexican land owner to migrant laborer:

> [C]ampesinos [farm workers] are becoming minimum wage workers on what were once their own lands. . . . Campesinos are now free to move north to the burgeoning industrial farms of Baja and Sonora, the bustling, if wholly degrading, Maquila districts [in Mexico borderlands], and of course [media] have no trouble turning up indentured Zapotec peasants living in converted chicken sheds on flower farms in San Diego and Riverside, and their even less fortunate compatriots living without shelter in the ravines below Southern California's sprawling, faux-Spanish suburbs.[162]

Given the U.S. "Corn Belt" centered in the states of Iowa, Illinois, Nebraska, and Minnesota, all outside the boundaries of Alto Mexico, presumably the same dynamics may have occurred within the United States to disrupt the agricultural economy of a Mexico-governed Alto Mexico. As occurred in the United States, the economy in Mexico eventually shifted away from subsistence agriculture as residents moved from rural regions to cities—Mexico's rural population fell from 26 to 15 percent between 1980 and 2005.[163]

Some of Mexico's current agricultural challenges stem from climate and inadequate access to water, particularly in its arid northern region, which enjoys a scant three percent of Mexico's total river flow.[164] Similarly, California farmers once faced similar obstacles of a long dry season. They overcame climate, at least temporarily, by building an irrigation system (initially as collaborations between farmers and eventually as massive government irrigation districts) that appropriates water from California's northern mountainous regions to service a majority of the

---

[162] Don M. Mitchell, "The Geography of Injustice: Borders and the Continuing Immiseration of California Agricultural Labor in Era of 'Free Trade,'" *Richmond Journal of Global Law and Business* 2 (2001): 145, 163.

[163] Robert A. Pastor, *The North American Idea: A Vision of a Continental Future* (New York: Oxford University Press, 2011), 94-95.

[164] David Barton Bray, "Of Land Tenure, Forests, and Water: The Impact of the Reforms to Article 27 on the Mexican Environment," in *Reforming Mexico's Agrarian Reform*, ed. Laura Randall (Armonk, NY: M.E. Sharpe, 1996), 215, 217; see also Martínez, *Mexico's Uneven Development*, 117, 150 (lamenting the small fraction of Mexico's navigable waterways, amounting to only 1,800 miles, in comparison to the United States, and debunking the myth of Mexico's unlimited agricultural potential with the reality of difficult terrain, the scarcity of cultivable soil, and the shortage of rainfall).

state's cropland.[165] Population growth and agricultural development generally followed the irrigation channels. Some of the water diverted for irrigation in the Southwest would have otherwise found its way to Mexican users south of the border, as seen most starkly in the dry Colorado riverbed in Mexico, drained by the All-American Canal along the U.S.-Mexico border that delivers water to California's Imperial Valley,[166] with Mexico allocated only ten percent of the Colorado's flow.[167] Not only the Colorado is running dry—the Arkansas River that once demarcated the U.S.-Mexico border in modern day Colorado and Kansas now is drained off for irrigation early in its path and usually dries up in summertime by the time it reaches the Kansas interior on its long journey to the Mississippi.[168] Similarly, the Rio Grande along the Texas-Mexico border, at least before Mexican rivers replenish it in South Texas, is "almost nonexistent most of the year. You can drive across it."[169] Following years of negotiation between the United States and Mexico toward increased water flow, the Colorado River briefly reached the Gulf of California for the first time in decades in spring 2014, a reminder of its mighty past. Yet, as discussed at the chapter's end, climate change and prevailing drought in much of Alto Mexico may diminish the region's natural advantage over northern Mexico for agricultural production, imperiling the agricultural economy of both regions and even the prospects for sustainable population growth.

* * *

Although preceding its acquisition by the United States the Southwest economy was primarily dependent on agriculture, an extraction-based economy of minerals and deposits developed almost immediately after

---

[165] Jelinek, *Harvest Empire*, 3.
[166] Jonathan Waterman, *A Journey from Source to Sea Down the Colorado River* (Washington D.C.: National Geographic, 2010) (discussing how the canal follows an ancient river and travels some of its route on Mexican soil in exchange for some of the water, and also discussing water treaties between the United States and Mexico).
[167] Jonathan Waterman, "Where the Colorado Runs Dry," http://www.nytimes.com/2012/02/15/opinion/where-the-colorado-river-runs-dry.html?_r=0 (posted February 14, 2012; last visited January 8, 2014). Mexico owes reciprocal treaty obligations to deliver water to the United States, through the Río Conches that flows from the Mexican state of Chihuahua to the Rio Grande.
[168] Oliver W. Holmes, *The Arkansas: Lifeline of Empire* (Washington D.C.: Potomac Corral of the Westerners, 1969), 22-23 (describing early twentieth century litigation between Colorado and Kansas that reached the Supreme Court twice, and ultimately prompted the Arkansas River Compact to divide waters).
[169] Peter Eichstaedt, *The Dangerous Divide: Peril and Promise on the US-Mexico Border* (Chicago: Lawrence Hill Books, 2014), 85 (remarks of chief agent for U.S. Border Patrol's Big Bend Sector).

the U.S.-Mexican War, soon rivaling and even eclipsing agriculture's contribution to the region's economy. Just nine days before the signing of the Treaty of Guadalupe Hidalgo ending the War in early 1848, an Anglo migrant, native to New Jersey, discovered gold in Northern California in what proved to be a motherlode of riches. Spaniards/Mexicans were no strangers to the allure and pursuit of gold, but fortunate timing, and the then-prevailing lack of speedy communication, favored Manifest Destiny as word never reached the Mexican government in time—news of El Dorado riches arrived some three months after the treaty signing.[170] Indeed, some Protestant preachers credited the handiwork of God with shielding the discovery from Mexican Catholics until the usurpation of Anglo ownership of the region.[171] The resultant crush of gold-hungry prospectors—known as forty-niners (1849), swiftly transformed the region from Catholic to Protestant, and from a cattle ranching economy to one driven by gold. Gold riches dominated the economy almost overnight. By just 1852, gold production in California reached the then staggering total of $81 million.[172] Initially, at a time when agricultural workers earned no more than $1 a day, prospectors panning for gold could readily make $20 daily and even more at the outset of the frenzy before the easiest pickings disappeared and mining became industrialized.[173] Agriculture in the region initially could not keep up with the prospector demand, requiring reliance on food imports shipped from around the world—European cheese, Chilean flour, and Mexican oranges,[174] but eventually spurring the growth of local agriculture. Having attracted just 2,700 overland Anglo migrants from 1841 to 1848,[175] California became the destination of choice following the discovery of gold and, concurrently, the U.S. acquisition of control over the region. Anglos arrived in droves overland from the east, and by ship to San Francisco, constituting the largest transcontinental migration to date. Settlers from the U.S. South came by land through Texas and the Southwest, while Easterners tended to arrive by ship, which involved a pre-Panama Canal trek through the Nicaraguan or Panamanian jungle. Many of the prospectors expected to remain west only temporarily and to return home

---

[170] See generally Pitt, *Decline of the Californios*, 49 (speculating on impact of Spaniards/Mexicans having discovered gold in California before Anglos, with possibilities ranging from California being the most heavily defended terrain in the Spanish empire to an even more crushing defeat in the U.S. Mexican War).
[171] J.S. Holliday, *The World Rushed In: The California Gold Rush Experience* (New York: Simon and Schuster, 1981), 25.
[172] Ibid., 303.
[173] Malcolm J. Rohrbough, *Aspen: The History of a Silver Mining Town, 1879-1893* (New York: Oxford University Press, 1986), 9 (describing how pioneer farmers labored with limited economic expectations—the end result of their lifetime of work would be only modest land to pass on to their children to repeat the cycle; sadly, however, today's farm worker immigrants acquire even less).
[174] Holliday, *World Rushed In*, 354.
[175] Ibid., 30.

wealthy. From 1848 to 1852, California's population increased an amazing 2,500 percent, and by 1870 reached 560,000 residents,[176] on its way to becoming today's most populous and most diverse state (at least in the mainland United States),[177] nicknamed the Golden State in homage to its economic history.

Not just Anglo migrants pursued gold riches, as newspaper reports of the gold strike drew Mexicans north to California, now crossing international borders in an era before border control, along with South Americans and other immigrants from around the world such as Chinese. Prejudice against the Mexicans and other "foreign" arrivals, such as the Chinese and Chileans (although conveniently not encompassing Anglo newcomers) soon surfaced, however, with Anglo California legislators passing a foreigner miner's tax in 1850 requiring a monthly payment of $20 for the "privilege of taking from our country the vast treasure to which they have no right."[178] Succeeding in driving Mexican immigrants from the mines, the discriminatory tax was the first salvo in a legacy that followed of racially-motivated laws and policies in California targeting newcomers of color, encompassing Alien Land laws directed at Asian farmers and culminating in the 1990s anti-immigrant initiative, Proposition 187, directed at Mexican immigrants. Lynchings of dozens of Mexican miners and other acts of violence against them also enforced the new subordinate racial order throughout Alto Mexico that has remained entrenched for generations. Memorialized in the film, *Salt of the Earth*, the early 1950s struggles of Mexican American zinc miners in New Mexico for pay equality with white workers and against other injustices revealed the continuing reality for many Mexican American miners of so-called Mexican wages in contrast to higher wages paid to Anglo workers. Whether in agriculture, mining, or other U.S. industries, it seems many Mexican laborers today still effectively pay a "foreigner's" tax for their vulnerable immigration status that ensures them paltry wages and treacherous working conditions.

Mineral wealth in the middle and late nineteenth century was by no means confined to Northern California, as most of the Alto Mexico region joined the mining frenzy as other reserves were discovered. Now an international destination for wealthy skiers, Aspen, Colorado, began as a booming silver mining town producing one-sixth of U.S.-mined silver, with 12,000 residents at its mining peak in the late 1880s and early 1890s, just a decade after the initiation of silver mining there, and just before the collapse of silver markets with the repeal in 1893 of the Sherman Silver Purchase Act of 1890 and the accompanying economic depression of

---

[176] Ibid., 455.

[177] http://www.mainstreet.com/slideshow/lifestyle/most-diverse-states-america (last visited March 20, 2014) (pegging California as the second most diverse state after Hawaii).

[178] J.S. Holliday, *Rush for Riches: Gold Fever and the Making of California* (Berkeley, CA: University of California Press, 1999), 135.

1893. By 1910, Aspen counted just 1,834 residents, as mining survived but continued on a much smaller scale.[179] Similarly, Colorado's Leadville, forty miles east of Aspen, experienced its own silver boom in the late 1870s, spurting from 200 to 15,000 residents by 1880 to become Colorado's second largest city over Aspen,[180] but eventually withering to a population today of just 2,500. The mining boom of the late 1800s established the state's largest city of Denver, located outside the Alto Mexico terrain, as the gateway to the Rockies. In Nevada, nicknamed the Silver State, silver miners flooded the Washoe region (near Reno) beginning in 1859, with nearby Virginia City swelling to 9,000 residents by 1865, buoyed by the silver and gold mines in that region which produced $300,000,000 in riches between 1860 and 1880.[181] Arizona was at the heart of the copper mining boom, with the mining epicenter of Cochise County near the current U.S.-Mexico border more than tripling in population from 1900 to 1910.[182]

Liquid gold in the form of oil (and natural gas) reserves soon generated a more sustained fortune from the U.S.-governed Alto Mexico region, surviving to this day as an important sector of the economy. California's first oil well, drilled in 1861 in Humboldt County,[183] preceded drilling throughout California by the early twentieth century. Oil eventually dominated the economy in other parts of the region, notably in oil-rich Texas which produces one-fifth of U.S. oil and one-third of its natural gas,[184] and Wyoming, a leading producer of coal, oil, and natural gas, with mining comprising a larger portion of that state's economy than in any other U.S. state.[185] Elko, Nevada, still thrives as the mining capital of Nevada's Gold Belt, at least when prices are high. Texas oil operations continue to boom, now using the controversial fracking process of pumping pressurized water into the ground to dislodge oil and gas, in a region beset by longtime drought and consequent water scarcity. Consuming billions of gallons of water through fracking, most newly drilled oil and gas wells are located in areas of water scarcity in the Alto Mexico states of California, Texas, New Mexico, Utah, and Wyoming.[186]

[179] See generally Rohrbough, *Aspen*; Sally Barlow-Perez, *A History of Aspen* (Aspen, CO: Who Press, 1991); John O'Rear and Frankie O'Rear, *The Aspen Story: Including Skiing the Aspen Way* (New York: A.S. Barnes, 1966).
[180] Rohrbough, *Aspen*, 13-14.
[181] Ibid., 13.
[182] Rachel St. John, *Line in the Sand: A History of the Western U.S.-Mexico Border* (Princeton, NJ: Princeton University Press, 2011), 71.
[183] Liebman, *California Farmland*, 71.
[184] http://www.netstate.com/economy/tx_economy.htm (last visited January 9, 2013).
[185] http://www.netstate.com/economy/wy_economy.htm (last visited January 9, 2013).
[186] William Rivers Pitt, "Diary of a Dying Country," http://www.truthout.org/opinion/item/21691-william-rivers-pitt-diary-of-a-dying-country (posted February 6, 2014; last visited May 13, 2014).

As in its former Alto Mexico terrain, Mexico has enjoyed considerable oil reserves, although those reserves deteriorated in recent decades.[187] A substantial difference between the two countries, however, is that unlike the United States, oil reserves and production are nationalized in Mexico, with all oil reserves belonging to the government following a 1938 presidential decree by Lázaro Cárdenas that established the government-run Petróleos Mexicanos (Pemex) to extract and refine oil.[188] Monies from the nationalized Mexican oil industry eventually accounted for about one-third of the federal budget. In 2013, however, responding to the fear of declining reserves, Mexico moved toward privatizing its petroleum reserves by allowing Pemex to strike agreements with domestic and foreign private companies to explore and develop Mexico's oil fields.[189] Later, in 2014, Mexico moved further toward privatization by opening investment in its oil fields to foreign and private companies, except for those fields set aside by Pemex.[190]

After its initial reliance on natural resources, the economic base for the Alto Mexico region, in U.S. hands, evolved and broadened away from resource-extractive industries to an industrial manufacturing economy, and then to today's U.S. diverse economy in which services (encompassing health care, lawyers, financial services, retail, and other sectors) are dominant. Within the Alto Mexico region, unique economies prompted by climate, state laws, or other factors emerged, at least some of them (e.g., the Disneyland amusement park and Hollywood, which with few exceptions produces only English-language films and television shows) not likely to have been duplicated in a Mexico-governed Alto Mexico. These unique economies include tourist attractions such as the Grand Canyon; ski resorts such as those near Park City, Utah, and Colorado's Aspen, once a mining town as addressed above which reinvented itself as a ski destination in the late 1940s (and contributed to 29.5 million tourists visiting Colorado in 2012, generating $11.2 billion in annual tourist revenue); the hotel/gambling /entertainment industry in Las Vegas, which county-wide generated

---

[187] Duncan Wood, "Energy Challenges for the Peña Nieto Administration," in *The End of Nostalgia: Mexico Confronts the Challenges of Global Competition*, ed. Diana Villiers Negroponte (Washington D.C., Brookings Institution Press, 2013), 57, 61.

[188] "Mexican Oil Expropriation," http://en.wikipedia.org/wiki/Mexican_oil_expropriation (last visited January 9, 2013).

[189] "Mexico Reverses History and Allows Private Capital Into Lucrative Oil Industry," http://www.forbes.com/sites/doliaestevez/2013/12/11/mexico-reverses-history-and-allows-private-capital-into-lucrative-oil-industry/ (posted December 11, 2013; last visited June 22, 2014).

[190] Mark Stevenson, "Mexico's President Enrique Pena Nieto Signs Landmark Energy Reform Into Law," http://www.huffingtonpost.com/2014/08/12/mexico-energy-reform_n_5672055.html (posted August 12, 2014; last visited September 21, 2014).

$9.4 billion in gambling revenues in 2012 alone and drew almost 40 million visitors that year, supplying tourism jobs to a whopping 47 percent of the local workforce;[191] professional sports teams in baseball, football, basketball, soccer, and other sports situated throughout the region; and the high-tech sector in the San Francisco Bay Area—known as Silicon Valley. Although integral in these economies, U.S. born Mexican Americans and Mexican immigrants, documented or not, tend to occupy lesser-paying positions behind the scenes rather than being visible at the forefront of these Southwestern U.S. sectors. For example, Mexicans are more likely to labor in landscaping, maintaining, and cleaning the houses of Hollywood film and televisions stars than in front of the cameras. Within Alto Mexico, the dichotomy of rich (and not-so-rich) Anglo tourists serviced by low-wage immigrant Mexicans is perhaps most stark in monuments to income inequality such as the resort town of Aspen:

> The visual images that gloss Aspen magazine covers feature stretch Range Rover limousines, black-tie fund-raisers, world-class ski slopes, and film celebrities who live part of the year in multimillion dollar, single-family homes. At the same time, Aspen is also a place where foreign-born workers drive thirty to one hundred miles round-trip daily to work in low-status jobs for low wages with few benefits. Many of these workers live in deplorable housing conditions, including cars, campers, and even caves.[192]

Within the expensive Aspen resort hotels and condominiums, Mexican immigrants work to clean rooms and staff the restaurants of a town whose residents are 95 percent white, while commuting daily on treacherous roads from their residences in cheaper locations far from Aspen's accommodations priced well beyond their reach, helping to keep Mexican workers in the shadows. Despite the relative invisibility of the Mexican workers and their vital contributions, anti-immigrant sentiment gripped that mountain region, prompting the Aspen City Council in 1999 to unanimously pass a resolution asking the U.S. Congress and the executive branch to restrict the number of immigrants to the United States, both by enforcing laws against the undocumented, and by reducing lawful entries, all in the interest of preventing supposed environmental degradation attributed to immigrants. Not limited to the Aspen city limits, the anti-immigrant sentiment infected the surrounding county, Pitkin County, anchored by Aspen, which voiced its own approval for a resolution seeking "population stabilization" by reducing

---

[191] http://www.lvcva.com/stats-and-facts/ (last visited January 9, 2014). Nevada legalized gambling in 1931 as a revenue-source.
[192] Lisa Sun-Hee Park and David Naguib Pellow, *The Slums of Aspen: Immigrants vs. the Environment in America's Eden* (New York: New York University Press, 2011), 17.

immigration and concomitantly the national growth rate.[193] Ironically, wealthy tourists from Mexico and other Latin American countries flock to Aspen and Vail in the wintertime, suggesting life can be equally splendid within a U.S.-governed Alto Mexico whether you are Anglo or Mexican, so long as you are wealthy.[194]

As they do throughout Alto Mexico today, Mexican workers, particularly immigrants both documented and undocumented, occupy low-wage jobs in the Las Vegas casinos and hotels, particularly in entry-level positions such as maids.[195] Mexican hospitality workers are also evident in the Alto Mexico/United 44 States casino-driven "bordertown" of Jackpot, Nevada, where the sole supermarket stocks piñatas and Mexican treats for workers and their families. In California, the epicenter of the modern era "Gold Rush" is located in the high technology and digital information economy of Silicon Valley.[196] Home to multimillionaire entrepreneurs, the region is serviced by low-wage earning Mexican immigrants, including thousands of workers who clean office buildings but are excluded from the vast riches enjoyed by the technoelite.[197] Like the immigrants who service the Aspen resort town, Silicon Valley immigrants tend to live a considerable distance away from their unstable low-wage jobs, often residing in the barrios of San Jose (founded by Spanish settlers in 1777 as El Pueblo de San José de Guadalupe), California. Janitors, in particular, work a largely invisible job at night and reside equally invisibly by day in the barrios away from the glitter of Silicon Valley's gleaming development. Within Los Angeles, the de facto capital of the Alto Mexico region, Mexican immigrants, and those from Central American and Caribbean countries, anchor low-income service professions such as domestic work and landscaping that better the lives of the Anglo elite and upper middle-class. As in California's agriculture industry, reliance on immigrant Latina/os evolved from dependence for domestic work on Chinese "houseboys" and, later, Japanese workers.[198] Of course, Mexicans in the Southwestern U.S. have reached and labored in all em-

---

[193] Ibid., 7.

[194] "Latin Americans Bring Culture, Currency to Colorado's High Country Ski Resorts," http://www.summitdaily.com/news/obituaries/9909530-113/million-vail-latin-aspen (last visited September 21, 2014).

[195] M.L. (Tony) Miranda, "The Mexicans," in *The Peoples of Las Vegas: One City: Many Faces,* ed. Jerry L. Smith and Thomas C. Wright (Reno, NV: University of Nevada Press, 2005), 56.

[196] See generally David Naguib Pellow and Lisa Sun-Hee Park, *The Silicon Valley of Dreams: Environmental Injustice, Immigrant Workers, and the High-Tech Global Economy* (New York: New York University Press, 2002).

[197] See generally Christian Zlolniski, *Janitors, Street Vendors, and Activists: The Lives of Mexican Immigrants in Silicon Valley* (Berkeley, CA: University of California Press, 2006).

[198] Pierrette Hondagneu-Sotelo, *Doméstica: Immigrant Workers Cleaning and Caring in the Shadows of Affluence* (Berkeley: University of California Press, 2001).

ployment and class sectors, serving as doctors, lawyers, judges, scientists, educators, firefighters, police officers, business leaders, and more. Still, Mexicans in the United States, and the Southwest, as a group, whether citizens, or documented or undocumented immigrants, disproportionately work in low-wage jobs, many of which service the Anglo elite and powerful. Indeed, they often enable the profits of their employers, and contribute to the economic growth and rewards of the Southwest and the rest of the United States, in which they do not fully share.

* * *

Although it is difficult to predict the future, economically or otherwise, one critical factor in the continued prosperity of the U.S. Southwest, regardless of which country controls it, is access to water. Impacts of climate change and long term drought have raised alarm throughout the Southwest region, with diverse consequences that encompass threats to the agricultural economy that uses much of the water supply, devastating wildfires and consequent impediments to the viability of national parks, and even the ability of the Southwest to sustain the continued Sun Belt expansion of cities and resort destinations such as Phoenix, Los Angeles, Palm Springs, and Las Vegas, whose water needs far exceed the local supply. Los Angeles, the second largest U.S. city, relies on shrinking water supplies moved great distances—although 80 percent of California's population lives from Sacramento south to the Mexican border, 70 percent of the state's fresh water supply originates north of the San Francisco Bay.[199] In recent decades, Palm Springs, a desert oasis of resort pools, golf courses, and verdant gardens, became one of California's largest per-capita water users in a region beset by drought.[200] Absent widespread conservation initiatives; technological advances in fresh water generation, preservation, conservation, or agricultural production methods and mineral extraction; changes in crops grown; or climate shift in unexpected and sustained ways, notwithstanding the unusual heavy rains of the 2016-17 winter, the Southwest may lose its capacity to absorb and attract new immigrants, retirees, and other residents, and its tourists and the economy they sustain, as quality of life, and employment in construction and other industries, wane. In that environment, might the Southwest actually decline in population, as did Nevada in the 1880s and 1890s? How will agriculture survive, particularly

---

[199] Alexis C. Madrigal, "American Aqueduct: The Great California Water Saga," *Atlantic*, http://www.theatlantic.com/features/archive/2014/02/american-aqueduct-the-great-california-water-saga/284009/ (posted February 24, 2014; last visited February 24, 2014).

[200] Ian James, "Dry Times Redefining Storied Palm Springs Desert Oasis," http://www.desertsun.com/story/news/environment/2014/04/13/dry-times-redefining-storied-palm-springs-desert-oasis/7665993/ (posted April 14, 2014; last visited September 21, 2014) (discussing new water-saving initiatives in Palm Springs).

crops grown for export to Asia and other world markets? In early 2014, officials estimated that without increased precipitation, 200,000 acres of prime farmland would go unplanted in California's Fresno County alone,[201] victimized by the worst drought in recorded California history—calendar year 2013 was the driest there in 119 years of formal weather recordkeeping. In 2015, California's governor announced mandatory restrictions on residential and commercial water use while, for now, shielding the agricultural industry that uses 80 percent of the state's water. Can extraction of oil through fracking continue for long in a droughted-landscape, imperiling another revenue source within the Southwest? What regions of the United States will endure or even prosper through drought—the Pacific Northwest? Given the inroads of Mexican immigrants throughout the United States, as detailed below in Chapter 4, no doubt Mexican immigrants will continue to serve vital U.S. labor needs. But the Southwest region may have reached its capacity, at least in the grip of a U.S. culture of excess that demands manicured green lawns, golf courses, artificial lakes and water features, and backyard swimming pools. A Mexico-governed Alto Mexico may be no better positioned to navigate the challenges of drought. Rather, as some predict, drought may force a migration of Southwestern (and Mexico) residents north toward wetter U.S. regions such as the Pacific Northwest in search of a hospitable environment. At bottom, the predictions on Alto Mexico's demographics and culture suggested in subsequent chapters are tempered by the possibility of dramatic upheaval wrought by scarcity of water.

---

[201] Norimitsu Onishi and Malia Wollan, "Severe Drought Grows Worse in California," *New York Times*, January 17, 2014.

4. SOUTHERN HOSPITALITY? MEXICAN MIGRATION TO THE UNITED 44 STATES

> It's a trespassing issue. Federal law, properly enforced, would be sufficient. If we close the border and enforce the law, states wouldn't have to pass these kinds of laws. It's an issue nationally, Alabama just had the courage to deal with it.
>
> —Alabama State Senator Scott Beason, on the 2011 Beason-Hammon Alabama Taxpayer and Citizen Protection Act[202]

With Alto Mexico under Mexican control, the United 44 States would still encompass Hawaii, Alaska, the Pacific Northwest and most of the Rocky Mountain region, the Midwest and Plains states (with the exception of Southwestern Kansas), most of the South (with the exception of Texas and a sliver of Oklahoma), and the Northeast. Presumably these U.S. regions would draw Mexican immigrants seeking economic opportunity, as they did during the last century, prompting the questions addressed in this chapter of how U.S. border and immigration policy would manage or deter those migrations, and how the remaining forty-four U.S. states might join or lead the campaign to deter undocumented migration as many U.S. states are doing today. Anti-immigrant measures tend to accompany demographic changes, and no doubt the longstanding U.S. reliance on low-income labor would have drawn significant numbers of Mexican immigrants to the United 44 States and sparked xenophobic backlash, particularly when that labor reliance on Mexican immigration accelerated as in the last few decades, and particularly when an economic downturn arrives in which immigrants are the first to be scapegoated. Thus, I suggest in this chapter that regardless of who controls Alto Mexico, U.S. immigration law and policy would likely reflect the same attitudes and prejudices toward Mexican newcomers seen, as they were during the Gold Rush, as interlopers in the economy, especially in times of financial turmoil. A reimagined U.S.-Mexico border transcends none of the hostility of the present immigration debate, as prejudice is not limited to the geography and confines of Alto Mexico. Rather, prejudice is long embedded in the United 44 States as well, serving to impede compassionate immigration policy that awaits recognition of the connected destiny and goals of Anglos and Mexicans. Instead of

---

[202] Daniel Trotta and Tom Bassing, "In Alabama, Strict Immigration Law Sows Discord," http://www.reuters.com/article/2012/05/30/us-usa-immigration-alabama-idUSBRE84T16P20120530 (posted May 30, 2012; last visited June 5, 2014).

bringing us closer to this realization, the recent boost in Mexican migration to the United 44 States sparked an anti-immigrant and anti-
Mexican backlash in many of these states. Impetus for a compassionate
embrace of Mexicans and the Mexican culture, then, may have to come
from the terrain of Alto Mexico where Mexican culture and Mexican
homesteads predate Anglo arrival.

Having served U.S. labor needs for decades, Mexican immigrants are
lured to el Norte by jobs and economic opportunity. During the Great
Recession that began around late 2007, removing millions of jobs from
the U.S. economy, migration from Mexico to the United States slowed to
a crawl. Even a reverse migration occurred of Mexican migrants unable
to find work returning to Mexico. So long as the United 44 States supplies jobs at wages well exceeding those paid in Mexico, which generally
is the case in all of these states, immigration is assured when the economy prospers. Although most Mexican migrants to the United States
traditionally remained within the terrain of Alto Mexico, predominantly
settling in California and Texas, Mexican migrants, documented or not,
have reached every U.S. state, particularly those reliant on low-wage labor offered by such U.S. industries as agriculture, food processing, food
service, construction, and the hospitality industry. Evident in this Mexican migration is that the roots of present-day migrant journeys to U.S.
regions including the Southwest and those beyond Alto Mexico extend
at least a century, prompted initially by U.S. labor demand pulling and
the Mexican Revolution pushing migrants north in the 1910s, and later
by the Bracero Program (a guest labor accord between the United States
and Mexico) established to serve U.S. wartime labor needs. Especially in
the mid-1990s, another push-pull of economic crisis in Mexico and demand for low-wage labor in the increasingly industrialized U.S.
agricultural sector drew documented and undocumented migrants from
Mexico toward jobs in the U.S. South, Northwest, and Midwest, as addressed below.

Probably the most sustained migration of Mexicans outside of Alto
Mexico during the last century has been the diaspora to Chicago. Trailing only the Alto Mexico cities of Los Angeles, San Antonio, and
Houston in Mexican population, Chicago is home to some 578,000 residents of Mexican descent, constituting almost 22 percent of the city's
population.[203] Starting in 1916 with the upheaval from the Mexican Revolution, and continuing into the 1920s when Mexicans (and other
Western Hemisphere migrants) were protected from the restrictive entry limits for many disfavored European groups imposed by the
Immigration Act of 1924,[204] the first significant arrivals of Mexican im-

---

[203] Michael Innis-Jiménez, *Steel Barrio: The Great Mexican Migration to South
Chicago, 1915-1940* (New York: New York University Press, 2013), 3.
[204] Ibid., 27 (discussing how lobbying of agricultural interests in Texas, California, and the Southwest was effective in procuring and maintaining the

migrants to the Chicago area found work in agriculture and the railroad/steel industry. Chicago's garment factories employed Mexican women, while Mexican men worked in the steel, meatpacking,[205] and railroad industries,[206] joined later by Puerto Ricans. Mexican workers came directly from Mexico to Chicago, but they also arrived from nearby regions where they had worked in agriculture, such as in the sugar beet fields of Michigan, Wisconsin, and Minnesota.[207] As with the later experience of Mexican migrants brought as strikebreakers to the Southwestern agricultural fields, the 1919 U.S. Steel strike drew Mexican replacement workers to Chicago, where discriminatory mill employers favored them over African American laborers. Similarly, steel mills in nearby Gary, Indiana, hired Mexican workers. But mirroring the invitation and exile cycle of Mexican workers elsewhere in the United States throughout the 1900s tied to economic prosperity and declines, Chicago officials rounded up Mexican-appearing residents during the Great Depression and sent them south on trains to the U.S.-Mexico border, scapegoating Mexican workers and refusing to recognize unemployed Mexican workers as deserving government assistance. These Depression-era repatriations purged nearly half of Chicago's Mexican population, leaving only about 16,000 Mexicans in Chicago by 1940.[208] Overall, although only 3.6 percent of all U.S. Mexicans at the time lived in Illinois and the states of Indiana and Michigan, more than 10 percent of repatriated Mexicans during the Depression came from these states.[209] Enjoying a boost in production during World War II, the Chicago steel mills restored Mexican migration to the region, this time under the auspices of the Bracero Program that brought more than 15,000 Mexican workers to Chicago between 1943 and 1945 alone.[210] As Mexicans entered other industries and through their entrepreneurship opened new businesses from construction companies to restaurants,

---

exemption of Mexicans and other Western Hemisphere countries from the restrictive limits).

[205] Wilfredo Cruz, *Chicago Latinos at Work* (Chicago: Arcadia Publishing, 2009), 24 (recounting that Latina/os in the meatpacking industry worked mostly in the freezers and on the killing floor).

[206] http://www.encyclopedia.chicagohistory.org/pages/824.html (last visited September 22, 2013); Innis-Jiménez, *Steel Barrio*, 77 (noting Chicago's rail track work force was 74 percent Mexican by 1928).

[207] Innis-Jiménez, *Steel Barrio*, 21.

[208] http://www.encyclopedia.chicagohistory.org/pages/824.html (last visited September 22, 2013); Innis-Jiménez, *Steel Barrio*, 144 (describing the Chicago repatriations as falling into categories of forced, coerced, or voluntary; also counting a different population decline, from a peak of 19,632 Mexicans in 1930 to 13,021 in 1934, and up to 16,000 by the decade end).

[209] Innis-Jiménez, *Steel Barrio*, 148.

[210] http://www.encyclopedia.chicagohistory.org/pages/824.html (last visited September 22, 2013).

Chicago's Mexican population continued to swell during the ensuing decades to become the largest outside of Alto Mexico.

Mexican bracero workers also came to the Pacific Northwest states of Oregon, Washington, and Idaho in considerable numbers during the last century, primarily as agricultural laborers. Even before implementation of the Bracero Program, Mexican workers migrated to the Northwest, such as to the Twin Falls, Idaho countryside to pick sugar beets, contributing to a ninefold increase in Idaho's Mexican population from 1910 to 1920.[211] Additional Mexican laborers came to the Northwest in the early 1900s to maintain railroad lines. Still, during World War II, Pacific Northwest farmers initially opposed importing Mexican agricultural laborers en masse to address the labor shortage, until that labor crisis worsened.[212] By 1943, Northwest sugar beet farmers alone requested more than 21,000 bracero workers.[213] Although the Bracero Program remained in effect until late 1964, Northwest farmers ended their reliance on this labor importation program of Mexican nationals after World War II, instead hiring, among other groups, Mexican American migrant seasonal workers who were U.S. citizens.[214] Eventually, though, as they did in other U.S. regions, non-citizen Mexican immigrants came in substantial numbers to serve the current agricultural labor needs of the Pacific Northwest.

Aside from the longstanding migration of Mexicans to Chicago and the surrounding region, to Denver, Colorado, where Mexican residents now comprise one-quarter of the population, and to the Pacific Northwest, not until the last few decades did significant Mexican migration, particularly of undocumented workers, reach the rest of the United 44 States.[215] Following the termination of the Bracero Program and the adoption by Congress a few months later in 1965, for the first time, of inflexible limits on Mexico and Western Hemisphere immigration, family reunification with immediate relatives (albeit following a long wait) and limited numbers of visas for daily commuter labor near the border, and for U.S. farm labor, became the only practical means of legal entry for Mexican immigrants supplying low-wage labor. After these 1960s and subsequent changes in federal immigration law, "Mexico went from enjoying access to 450,000 annual guest worker [bracero] visas and an unlimited number of residence visas to having no guest worker visas at

---

[211] Erasmo Gamboa, *Mexican Labor and World War II: Braceros in the Pacific Northwest, 1942-1947* (Austin: University of Texas Press, 1990), 8.
[212] Ibid., 40.
[213] Ibid., 50 (noting these farmers ultimately received only 7,686 laborers).
[214] Ibid., 130.
[215] Of course, apart from Mexicans, other Latina/o groups migrated in substantial numbers during the twentieth century to the United 44 States, with substantial Cuban inroads in Florida, and Puerto Ricans, as U.S. citizens, migrating to New York City among other mainland locations.

all and just 20,000 [annual] visas for permanent residence."[216] Because U.S. employers kept calling, however, Mexican migrants kept coming, now primarily as vulnerable undocumented immigrants given the unrealistically stingy visas available for Mexican laborers. Evidencing this shift in lawful status of migrants from Mexico, by 1970 the United States was deporting almost one-half million Mexicans annually, a number that rose to almost one million annually by 1977.[217] By the early 1980s, estimates of the U.S. undocumented population, many of them Mexican, ranged from two to eight million. Although the Immigration Reform and Control Act of 1986, which ultimately legalized between 2.7 and 3.1 million undocumented workers, aimed to legalize the existing undocumented migrant population while at the same time preventing future undocumented migration through employer sanctions, ready availability of false documents and inconsistent enforcement rendered those penalties useless. Instead, U.S. employers kept hiring and migrants, documented or not, many of them from Mexico, kept coming.

By 2013, some 11 million undocumented immigrants, most of them from Mexico, were living in the United States, the backlog of an economic system that lures and relies on low-wage immigrant labor in numbers far exceeding lawful paths of worker entry. Whether as U.S. citizens, documented workers, or undocumented laborers, Mexican workers fanned out across the United States, in all cases responding to employer demand. For example, Mexicans became the fastest growing ethnic group in New York City by 2000, with a population then of 186,872[218] that ballooned further to 319,263 by 2010. Despite Mexican immigrants enjoying an exceptionally high rate of employment in New York City, their dismal wages meant nearly two-thirds of the Big Apple's Mexican residents, whether immigrants or native-born, lived in low-income households in one of the world's most expensive cities.[219] Denver, Colorado, home to about 150,000 Mexican residents in 2010, constitutes the third largest city for Mexican population outside of Alto Mexico (trailing Chicago and New York City).[220]

In recent years, Mexican migration to the United 44 States increased most in the South and Midwest. Beginning around 1990, the U.S. South experienced tremendous growth rates in Mexican (and other Latina/o) immigrants. Several factors, all connected to employment opportunities,

---

[216] Douglas S. Massey, "Only by Addressing the Realities of North American Economic Integration Can We Solve the Problem," *Boston Review* (May/June 2009).

[217] Steven W. Bender, *Run for the Border: Vice and Virtue in U.S.-Mexico Border Crossings* (New York: New York University Press, 2012), 126-127.

[218] http://www.tc.columbia.edu/news.htm?articleID=4495 (last visited September 22, 2013).

[219] Kirk Semple, "Mexican New Yorkers Are More Likely To Live in Poor Households," *New York Times*, March 21, 2013.

[220] http://factfinder2.census.gov/bkmk/table/1.0/en/DEC/10_DP/DPDP1/1600000US0820000 (2010 Census) (last visited September 22, 2013).

explain that demographic transformation in the Southern region. Supplying legalization to more than two million Mexican undocumented immigrants, the federal Immigration Reform and Control Act of 1986 offered a new cheap and mobile labor source to U.S. employers, prompting many immigrants to leave California and the Southwest for opportunities in other U.S. regions.[221] The mid-1990s peso crisis in Mexico spurred additional migration from Mexico in search of better-paying U.S. jobs. Given its low unemployment rates, the U.S. South actively recruited Mexican laborers into a variety of industries to supply low-wage, non-unionized labor. Offering a lower cost of living, particularly for housing, than California, the South drew thousands of Mexican immigrants, some of them undocumented, along with Latina/os from other backgrounds such as Puerto Ricans and immigrants from Guatemala, El Salvador, and other Central and South American countries. Once Mexican immigrants (and other Latina/os) established cultural, labor, and residential footholds in Southern communities, migration streams developed that drew additional migrants to these enclaves that promised employment.[222] Mexican immigrants to the South found work in several industries, most of them offering low wages for difficult and sometimes dangerous manual labor. Opportunities ranged from construction—particularly during Atlanta's push to prepare for the 1996 Olympic Games, the textile industry, such as in Dalton, Georgia, the "Carpet Capital of the World," and chicken-processing and meatpacking plants, to agricultural work in the tobacco fields of North Carolina, and picking other staple Southern crops such as watermelons, peaches, tomatoes, and cucumbers. Immigrants replaced Southern blacks and poor whites that previously supplied this low-wage agricultural labor. Outside of agriculture, Mexican and other Latina/o migrants also replaced blacks and poor whites in such Southern occupations as janitorial and other service industries, including landscaping and construction.[223]

Aside from Florida (and Texas), until 1990, Latina/os were relatively "absent from the demographic, economic, cultural and political landscape" of the South, constituting less than 1 percent of the mid-South population.[224] Within the 1990s decade, however, profound growth occurred, as the Southern Latina/o population increased a whopping 104 percent.[225] Florida's Latina/o population increased by 1.15 million residents in the decade. Alabama's Latina/o growth rate during the 1990s

---

[221] *Latino Immigrants and the Transformation of the U.S. South*, ed. Mary E. Odem and Elaine Lacy (Athens, GA: University of Georgia Press, 2009), xvi.
[222] Ibid.
[223] Raymond A. Mohl, "Globalization and Latin American Immigration in Alabama," in *Latino Immigrants*, 60 (discussing racial tensions that resulted).
[224] Owen J. Furuseth and Heather A. Smith, "From Winn-Dixie to Tiendas: The Remaking of the New South," in *Latinos in the New South: Transformations of Place*, ed. Heather A. Smith and Owen J. Furuseth (Burlington, VT: Ashgate, 2006), 1,2,4.
[225] Ibid., 4.

decade was 300 percent (from 24,629 to 75,830 residents), as was the increase in South Carolina. Other Southern states had even higher Latina/o growth rates, much of it stemming from Mexican immigrants and likely not counting significant numbers of undocumented Mexican immigrants—in the 1990s decade, Arkansas' Latina/o population jumped from 19,876 to 86,866, Georgia's from 108,922 to 435,227 (many of them settling in the Atlanta metropolitan area), North Carolina's from 76,726 to 378,963, and Tennessee's from 32,741 to 123,838 residents.[226] At the same time, although substantial, the overall U.S. growth rate for Latina/os in the 1990s decade was a smaller 58 percent. Growth through Mexican immigration to the South continued into the first decade of the 2000s, albeit at a slower rate, with the 2010 Census counting 629,718 Florida residents of Mexican background alone, along with 519,502 Georgia residents, 486,960 in North Carolina, 186,615 in Tennessee, 155,067 in Virginia, 138,358 in South Carolina, 138,194 in Arkansas, and 122,911 in Alabama, with smaller but still significant numbers of Mexican residents in Kentucky, Mississippi, and Louisiana (including Mexican immigrants who helped rebuild New Orleans after Hurricane Katrina but failed to receive proper credit for their contribution).[227]

In contrast to the South (aside from Texas), Mexicans had been coming to the U.S. Midwest in significant numbers for at least 100 years to supply the region's labor needs. As discussed above, migrants headed for Chicago and the region's sugar beet fields in the 1910s, 1920s, and later as bracero workers. But, like the South, the 1990s was the most pronounced decade of expansion in the Midwest Latina/o population. Although lower than in the South, the Midwest growth rate of 80 percent for Latina/os in the 1990s, comprised mostly of Mexican immigrants, surpassed the overall national Latina/o growth rate in that decade of 58 percent and easily eclipsed the overall population rise in the Midwest—a modest 8 percent in the 1990s. Some of the same labor dynamics occurred in the Midwest that drew Mexican migrants (whether documented, undocumented, or born in other U.S. regions— primarily from California and Texas) to jobs in the South. The transformation of Midwestern agriculture from family farms to labor-intensive agri-business that disdained unionization supplied low-paying, physically taxing, and sometimes dangerous jobs for immigrants,[228] who tend to occupy the worst jobs in the hierarchy of the industrial workplace. Evidencing a general shift of large-scale food processing jobs from unionized urban regions to rural locations, many meatpacking plants

---

[226] Ibid., 5.

[227] Kevin R. Johnson, "Hurricane Katrina: Lessons About Immigrants in the Modern Administrative State," *Houston Law Review* 45 (2008): 11.

[228] Sylvia R. Lazos Vargas, "'Latina/o-ization' of the Midwest: Cambio de Colores (Change of Colors) as Agromaquilas Expand into the Heartland," *Berkeley La Raza Law Journal* 13 (2002): 343, 346-348.

relocated from cities to rural Iowa, Kansas, and Nebraska.[229] Spurred by newfound employment in these rural areas, the Kansas Latina/o population doubled in the 1990s from 93,670 to 188,252, and kept growing. By 2010, the state's Mexican population alone was 247,297.[230] Missouri's Latina/o population also doubled during the 1990s, from 61,702 to 118,592, with Mexicans counted at 147,254 by 2010. Growing at even higher rates in the 1990s, Latina/o populations in Nebraska (from 36,969 to 94,425) and Iowa (32,647 to 82,473) continued their spurt in the 2000s (128,060 Nebraskan and 117,090 Iowan Mexican residents respectively by 2010). Reflecting the reality of additional thousands of uncounted undocumented Latina/o immigrants arriving in the Midwest was the notorious round-up by federal ICE (Immigration and Customs Enforcement) officials and the subsequent deportation of 398 suspected undocumented immigrants at a kosher meatpacking plant in Postville, Iowa, in 2008, although the arrested workers were mostly Mayan immigrants from Guatemala rather than Mexicans. Earlier, from 1992 to 1997, federal officials raided fifteen workplaces in Iowa and Nebraska, arresting 1,000 undocumented laborers, signaling the Midwest's newfound reliance on undocumented Latina/o labor.[231]

Straddling the Arkansas River on the north side of the Alto Mexico/United 44 States border, Garden City, Kansas, demonstrates the lure of agricultural jobs for Mexican immigrants in recent years. As in the Southwest, Mexican migrants came to Garden City in significant numbers between 1910 and 1930, finding work in the railroad and sugar beet industries.[232] Welcome for work but kept separated from white families, the Mexican residents were excluded from Garden City's famously large public swimming pool hand-dug in 1922.[233] Notwithstanding the Bracero Program drawing Mexican laborers to U.S. fields elsewhere, Garden City failed to attract additional Mexican workers until 1980, when the world's largest beef-packing plant opened near the city limits and helped spark, as one commentator put it, the "'Latinization' of the beef industry."[234] Soon, the local grocery stores were stocking Mexican food desired by immigrant workers and the Spanish language became commonplace in Garden City, along with the languages of other immigrant groups drawn to Garden City such as Vietnamese and other Southeast Asians—for example, a local meatpacking plant posts lunchroom signs in English,

---

[229] Eileen Diaz McConnell, "Latinos in the Rural Midwest: The Twentieth-Century Historical Context Leading to Contemporary Challenges," in *Apple Pie & Enchiladas: Latino Newcomers in the Rural Midwest*, ed. Ann V. Millard and Jorge Chapa (Austin: University of Texas Press, 2004), 26, 35-26.
[230] Of course, some of Kansas is part of Alto Mexico territory.
[231] McConnell, "Latinos in the Rural Midwest," 38.
[232] Tomás R. Jiménez, *Replenished Ethnicity: Mexican Americans, Immigration, and Identity* (Berkeley: University of California Press, 2010), 53-54.
[233] Oscar J. Martínez, *Mexican-Origin People in the United States: A Topical History* (Tucson, AZ: University of Arizona Press, 2001) 65.
[234] Ibid., 55.

Spanish, and Vietnamese. In Finney County, with its county seat of Garden City, Latina/os, most of them Mexican, now comprise almost half (45 percent) of the county population.

The Pacific Northwest too experienced a recent jump in its Latina/o population, with most newcomers of Mexican origin, primarily comprised of immigrants and California transplants. In the first decade of 2000, Oregon's Latina/o population grew 63 percent, in contrast to the state's overall growth rate of a more modest 12 percent (with just 5 percent growth among the state's Anglo population). Washington state saw a 71 percent increase among Latina/os, most of them Mexicans, in the same decade, following even larger gains in the 1990s. Idaho experienced 73 percent Latina/o growth in the first decade of the 2000s, again most of them Mexican, at a time when the state's non-Latina/o growth was only 17 percent.[235]

With job opportunities in the South, Midwest, and Pacific Northwest drawing hundreds of thousands of Mexican immigrants from the geographies of both Mexico and U.S.-governed Alto Mexico, no doubt some of the same lures of immigrants and consequent anti-immigrant tensions would have emerged in the United 44 States as within the United States today, particularly within its eight states bordering Alto Mexico—Oregon, Idaho, Wyoming, Colorado, Kansas, Oklahoma, Arkansas, and Louisiana. Foremost, assuming the same unduly restrictive federal immigration laws, the presence today of at least a few million undocumented residents in the United 44 States, many of them from Mexico, would likely prompt similar emphasis on federal immigration enforcement both at the border, as discussed in Chapter 7, and in the interior of the United 44 States. As they routinely occur today, federal ICE raids presumably would target workplaces from coast to coast, such as the 2008 Postville, Iowa factory raid. Similarly, federal immigration detentions centers would continue to dot the landscape. Within the United 44 States today, detention centers operate in Alabama, Colorado, Florida, Georgia, Illinois, Iowa, Kentucky, Louisiana, Maryland, Massachusetts, Michigan, Minnesota, Missouri, Nebraska, New Jersey, New York, Ohio, Pennsylvania, Virginia, Washington, and Wisconsin (as they do in the Alto Mexico states of Arizona, California, New Mexico, Texas, and Utah),[236] illustrating the broad reach of federal enforcement efforts against undocumented immigrants, and employer reliance on undocumented immigrant labor across the United States. The annual $18 billion

---

[235] Stephanie Zepelin, "Idaho's Hispanic Population Growing Faster Than Any Other Demographic," http://www.ktvb.com/news/Hispanic-population-in-Idaho-growing-205028091.html (posted April 29, 2013; last visited November 21, 2013).
[236] http://www.ice.gov/detention-facilities/ (last visited September 24, 2013).

cost of U.S. border enforcement[237] (alone more than the GDP of many countries such as Iceland) would likely be matched within the United 44 States. Although with its smaller size and presumably smaller economy the United 44 States should attract fewer undocumented immigrants than the entire United States does today, the much longer international border between Alto Mexico and the United 44 States would be even more expensive to fortify and police, particularly by means of a costly continuous wall touted by Donald Trump as a border security solution.

Anti-immigrant animus at the local level accompanied the changing U.S. demographics of recent decades, finding expression in state laws and local ordinances as fear of migrants took hold throughout the United States, but particularly in the four U.S.-Mexico border states and in the South given its jump in immigrant numbers. Fear of Mexican immigrants, in particular, fed animus in regions that experienced significant demographic change. In the South, Alabama enacted legislation in 2011, titled the Beason-Hammon Alabama Taxpayer and Citizen Protection Act, which, among other provisions, empowered police to check the immigration status of those reasonably suspected of being undocumented, barred undocumented students from public colleges, required school officials to determine the immigration status of schoolchildren, and prohibited landlords from renting to or employers from knowingly hiring undocumented immigrants.[238] Similarly, other Southern states such as Georgia legislated against undocumented immigrants, with Georgia's HB 87, the Illegal Immigration Reform and Enforcement Act of 2011, among other things, allowing police officers to ask for proof of lawful status and criminalizing transporting or harboring undocumented workers (without exceptions for ambulance drivers or church sanctuaries), or inciting someone to come unlawfully to Georgia.[239] South Carolina's 2011 anti-immigrant law prohibits harboring or transporting an undocumented person, being that harbored or transported undocumented immigrant, or failing to carry an alien registration card.[240] Anti-

---

[237] Josh Boak and Eric Pianin, "$10,000 to Nab One Illegal: Annual Cost—$18B," http://www.thefiscaltimes.com/Articles/2013/01/10/10000-to-Nab-One-Illegal-Annual-Cost-18-B (posted January 10, 2013; last visited November 21, 2013).

[238] See *Hispanic Interest Coalition of Alabama v. Governor of Alabama*, 691 F.3d 1236 (11th Cir. 2012) (enjoining the provision requiring school officials to determine the immigrant status of schoolchildren, as it impermissibly burdens the education of undocumented children as guaranteed in *Plyler v. Doe*, 457 U.S. 202 (1982)). A settlement agreement in 2013 permanently blocked much of the anti-immigration law, including the school verification provision and those criminalizing giving a ride or renting to undocumented immigrants.

[239] See *Georgia Latino Alliance for Human Rights v. Governor of Georgia*, 691 F.3d 1250 (11th Cir. 2012) (upholding preliminary injunction against the new crimes established of transporting, harboring, or inducing an undocumented immigrant).

[240] See *U.S. v. South Carolina*, 720 F.3d 518 (4th Cir. 2013) (affirming the preliminary injunction of these provisions on grounds of federal preemption).

immigrant sentiment took root within the Midwest too, as Indiana, for example, authorized its police in 2011 to make warrantless arrests of immigrants in specified circumstances.[241]

Evidencing the prevailing hostility toward Latina/o immigration in the South and Midwest coinciding with demographic change, in addition to enacting anti-immigrant laws, some state legislators in those regions began challenging the humanity of migrants and threatening or insinuating violence against them. For example, Southeastern Kansas Republican lawmaker Virgil Peck equated immigrants with hogs by suggesting in 2011 that "[I]f shooting these immigrating feral hogs [from helicopters] works [in Kansas], maybe we have found a solution to our illegal immigration problem."[242] Although explaining later he did not intend to advocate violence, Alabama state senator Scott Beason (architect of the 2011 Beason-Hammon Alabama Taxpayer and Citizen Protection Act) proposed that same year during a Republican Party breakfast that the best way to confront undocumented immigration was to "empty the [ammunition] clip, and do what has to be done."[243]

Local government jumped on the anti-immigrant bandwagon as well, with several U.S. counties and cities enacting ordinances targeting undocumented immigrants in their employment and housing, such as Hazleton, Pennsylvania's 2006 law, since invalidated in federal court, that prohibited rentals of housing to undocumented immigrants and outlawed their employment. In contrast, a federal court in 2013 upheld a similar ordinance enacted by residents of Fremont, Nebraska, near Omaha.[244] On the odd side of the anti-Latina/o immigrant backlash was the Alto Mexico city of Pahrump, Nevada, which passed an ordinance in 2006 outlawing the flying of a foreign (Mexican) flag without also displaying the U.S. flag above it, enacted in response to Mexican immigration advocates who marched in U.S. cities with the Mexican flag in protests seeking comprehensive immigration reform that never arrived.

The four U.S./Mexico border states led the way in the modern backlash against undocumented immigration, notably through California's Proposition 187, adopted by voters in 1994, and Arizona's multi-faceted assault on undocumented workers and their families. Propelled by media statements warning of "illegal-alien gangs" roaming the streets to "rob, rape, and in many cases, murder" innocent residents, Proposition

---

[241] See *Buquer v. City of Indianapolis*, 2013 WL 1332158 (S.D. Ind. 2013) (permanently enjoining enforcement of the law).

[242] Lynn Herrmann, "Kansas Lawmaker Compares Shooting Wild Hogs to Immigrants," March 15, 2011, http://digitaljournal.com/article/304685.

[243] Andrea Nill Sanchez, "On Immigration, Alabama State Senator Advises Politicians to 'Empty the Clip,'" February 8, 2011, http://thinkprogress.org/politics/2011/02/08/142922/scott-beason-immigration/.

[244] See *Keller v. City of Fremont*, 719 F.3d 931 (8th Cir. 2013). Fremont voters in 2014 reaffirmed the ordinance, with almost 60 percent supporting the measure.

187 was the first salvo from the four border states in the current U.S. legal onslaught targeting undocumented families. Excluding "illegal aliens" from state social services and heath care, as well as from public education, Proposition 187 faded from relevance once a federal court gutted most of its provisions.[245] But the border state attack on immigrants took up other fronts. Eventually, even Democratic governors of Arizona and New Mexico, Janet Napolitano and Bill Richardson, sent the National Guard to patrol and fortify their state borders with Mexico, as a prelude to Texas Republican governor, Rick Perry, who dispatched National Guard troops to the border in the summer of 2014 to protect against entry from undocumented youth, and successor Texas governor Greg Abbott, who in 2015 signed an $800 million border security package for positioning state troopers in place of the National Guard along the state's 1,200 mile border with Mexico. Abbott also signed a ban on sanctuary cities in 2017. Anti-immigrant ordinances at the local level within the four border states included Farmers Branch, Texas, which outlawed rentals to undocumented tenants,[246] and the California oceanfront community of Redondo Beach, which outlawed day laborers, most of them undocumented, from soliciting work on street corners, until a federal court invalidated the law as an unconstitutional violation of the workers' free speech rights.[247] Albuquerque, New Mexico, decided in 2010 to require, in partnership with federal ICE agents, immigration checks of everyone arrested.

Arizona, ultimately, claimed the mantle among the U.S. four border states, and the rest of the United States, as the unfriendliest to immigrants of color. Home to Sheriff Joe Arpaio, known as "America's Toughest Sheriff," whose reputation was built around capturing and humiliating undocumented immigrants using sweeps reminiscent of the infamous 1997 Chandler (a suburb of Phoenix) Roundup, Arizona laws cover the anti-immigrant gamut. Most prominent is Arizona's S.B. 1070—the Support Our Law Enforcement and Safe Neighborhoods Act, adopted in 2010, which, among its provisions, criminalized the presence of undocumented immigrants in that state, required police to determine the immigration status (known as "show me your papers") of persons they reasonably suspected of being undocumented, and criminalized sheltering or harboring an undocumented immigrant. Although the U.S. Supreme Court struck down much of S.B. 1070 in 2012, including its criminalization of undocumented immigrants, it left intact the core

---

[245] Steven W. Bender, *Greasers and Gringos: Latinos, Law, and the American Imagination* (New York: New York University Press, 2003), 77-78 (leaving intact the state crime of manufacturing or using false documents, already a crime under federal law).

[246] A decision by a federal judge striking down the city ordinance as preempted by federal law was upheld on appeal. *Villas at Parkside Partners v. City of Farmers Branch, Tex.*, 726 F.3d 524 (5th Cir. 2013).

[247] *Comite de Jornaleros de Redondo Beach v. Redondo Beach*, 657 F.3d 936 (2011).

"show me your papers" provision (Arizona ended the practice, however, as part of a legal settlement in 2016). Arizona voters joined the immigrant-bashing by approving initiatives denying undocumented immigrants any recovery of punitive damages in civil actions, such as for their personal injuries inflicted maliciously,[248] requiring proof of citizenship for voting[249] and, in the same vein as California's Proposition 187, proof of lawful immigration status to receive public benefits.[250] Voters also withdrew the possibility of release on bail to suspected undocumented immigrants charged with a felony crime,[251] and denied undocumented state residents the ability to pay in-state college tuition or receive financial aid subsidized with state funds. Additionally, Arizona enacted the Legal Arizona Workers Act in 2008, later upheld by the Supreme Court,[252] which penalizes employers who knowingly hire an undocumented immigrant or fail to use the federal e-verify system to ensure the lawful status of their employees. Finally, reaching beyond undocumented immigrants, Arizona adopted educational and cultural restrictions directed specifically at the local Latina/o population, notably an English-Only (anti-Spanish) law for government communications, Proposition 203 abolishing bilingual education programs in the manner of a similar California voter initiative (effectively repealed by California voters in 2016), and a law jeopardizing Mexican American studies (and other Ethnic Studies) curriculum in public schools. Overseeing Arizona's most populous county, until ousted by voters in 2016, Sheriff Joe exceeded lawful bounds of immigration enforcement in at least two respects—by wrongly charging border-crossing undocumented immigrants under a 2005 Arizona smuggling law with conspiring to smuggle themselves, and by racially profiling and targeting supposed undocumented Latina/o immigrants.[253] Reflecting the extremist anti-immigration views in the state, in 2014 an Arizona legislator proposed a law making it a misdemeanor for a first offense, and a felony for a repeat offense, if an undocumented immigrant avails herself of any public benefits, defined broadly to encompass everything from attending public school to driving on a public road, the latter leading to forfeiture of the

---

[248] Arizona Proposition 102 (2006).

[249] *Arizona v. Inter Tribal Council of Arizona, Inc.*, 133 S. Ct. 2247 (2013) (holding federal National Voter Registration Act preempts Arizona proof-of-citizenship requirement).

[250] In order to sidestep federal preemption issues, the Arizona Attorney General interpreted this law to apply only to discretionary state benefit programs and not to federally funded entitlements.

[251] See *Lopez-Valenzuela v. County of Maricopa*, 719 F.3d 1054 (9th Cir. 2013) (upholding constitutionality of measure).

[252] *Chamber of Commerce of U.S. v. Whiting*, 131 S.Ct. 1968 (2011).

[253] See *We Are America v. Maricopa County Board of Supervisors*, 2013 WL 5434158 (D. Ariz. 2013) (finding that charging non-smuggler immigrants with felony conspiracy to smuggle themselves is preempted by federal immigration law).

vehicle.[254] Overall, through its gauntlet of anti-immigrant measures already adopted by its legislature and voters, and by its enforcement at the hands of zealots, Arizona represents the most repressive state for Mexican migration. But Arizona is not alone in anti-immigrant ideals.

Anti-immigrant sentiment also percolates in the eight U.S. states along the Alto Mexico/United 44 States border. Of them, Oklahoma enacted the broadest single anti-immigrant law—the Oklahoma Taxpayer and Citizen Protection Act [of] 2007—initiated by a Republican legislator with strong party support but signed into law by a Democratic governor and approved by a majority of Democratic legislators. Among its provisions, the law criminalized harboring or transporting undocumented immigrants, denied driver's licenses and voter ID cards to undocumented immigrants, required verification of the citizenship status of those arrested for felonies or drunk driving, required verification of the lawful residency of welfare recipients, directed cooperation of local officials with federal immigration authorities, and denied resident tuition to undocumented college students.[255] Initially, the law prompted many undocumented immigrants to flee Oklahoma fearing its draconian application, exactly as the law's author intended.[256]

Among other oppressive anti-immigrant laws in the Alto Mexico/United 44 States border states, a Louisiana law enacted in 2002 criminalized anyone driving without documentation demonstrating their lawful presence in the United States, punishable as a felony by a maximum $1,000 fine and a maximum one-year jail term, with or without hard labor,[257] but in 2013 the state's supreme court invalidated the law.[258] A 2011 Louisiana law requires employers to e-verify their employees' lawful status as a condition to bidding on public contracts.[259] Idaho law requires verification of lawful presence in the United States as a condition to receiving state or local public benefits.[260]

In contrast, the Alto Mexico "border" states of Oregon, Idaho, Wyoming, and Kansas considered but did not enact laws modeled after Arizona's S.B. 1070 or Arizona's sanctions on employers hiring undocu-

---

[254] Of course, any prohibition of public education for undocumented children presumably would violate the federal Constitution. See *Plyler v. Doe*, 457 U.S. 202 (1982).

[255] See *Chamber of Commerce of U.S. v. Edmondson*, 594 F.3d 742 (10th Cir. 2010) (striking down various employment-related provisions of the Oklahoma Taxpayer and Citizen Protection Act).

[256] Emily Bazar, "Strict Immigration Law Rattles Okla. Businesses," http://usatoday30.usatoday.com/news/nation/2008-01-09-immigcover_N.htm (posted January 10, 2008; last visited November 21, 2013) (remarks of Republican legislator Randy Terrill, later convicted for political bribery).

[257] La. Rev. Stat. §14:100.13.

[258] *State v. Sarrabea*, 126 So. 3d 453 (La. 2013) (held preempted by federal immigration law).

[259] La. Rev. Code §38:2212.10.

[260] Idaho Code §67-7903.

mented immigrants. Proponents of an Arkansas ballot measure with a self-explanatory title, the Arkansas Illegal Immigrant Benefits Ban Amendment, failed to gather sufficient signatures to reach the 2010 or 2012 ballot, nor did a similar-minded bill to deny state benefits to un-documented immigrants pass the Arkansas legislature in 2011. Kansas successfully enacted a proof-of-citizenship requirement for voting, but in recent years rejected proposals to repeal favorable in-state tuition for resident undocumented immigrants and to require businesses to verify the immigration status of their employees.[261] At least one Alto Mexico border state reversed course on its existing anti-immigrant laws. Seen as the precursor to Arizona's S.B. 1070, Colorado enacted an immigration law in 2006 requiring police to notify federal immigration authorities if they arrested a person suspected of being undocumented. Colorado re-pealed the law in 2013, in part because the federal Secure Communities program (and its 2014 replacement, the Priority Enforcement Program) similarly monitors local arrests. Moreover, in 2013 Colorado joined the growing number of states offering driving privileges to undocumented immigrants.[262] Oregon's legislature extended driving privileges to un-documented residents, but voters invalidated the legislation in the fall 2014 election.

Illustrating how the eight Alto Mexico border states aren't ready to acknowledge immigrant labor contributions to their economies, howev-er, most of them (Idaho, Kansas, Louisiana, Oklahoma, and Wyoming) joined an amicus brief filed in the federal litigation that ultimately inval-idated most of Arizona's S.B. 1070 law in 2012, arguing that states were entitled to grab the reins and enforce restrictive federal immigration laws given selective or lax enforcement they claimed by federal officials. Although the Supreme Court rejected their urgings for state autonomy in establishing and enforcing immigration policy, the sentiment pre-sumably remains. Federal immigration law does permit state and local governments to enter into Memorandums of Understanding—so-called Section 287(g) agreements, to partner with ICE in enforcing federal im-migration laws away from the borders. Among the U.S. jurisdictions that have obtained 287(g) authority are some within the eight Alto Mexi-co/United 44 States border states—Arkansas' Benton and Washington (Fayetteville) Counties, Colorado's El Paso County (Colorado Springs), and Oklahoma's Tulsa County (Tulsa).[263] Moreover, most of the Alto

---

[261] John Eligon, "Kansas Official Holds Line Against Moderation in Debate on Immigration," *New York Times*, July 14, 2013, A17.

[262] These licenses, because of the federal REAL ID Act, are not valid for federal purposes of flying on airlines or entering federal buildings. Distancing itself from its Proposition 187-past, in 2013 California joined the list of states offering licenses to undocumented drivers (which includes the Alto Mexico states of Colorado, Nevada, New Mexico, and Utah), along with permitting undocu-mented lawyers to practice law.

[263] http://www.ice.gov/news/library/factsheets/287g.htm#signed-moa (last vis-ited November 21, 2013).

Mexico border states joined the legal challenge brought in 2014 by Texas against President Obama's executive action that year canceling the potential for deportation of millions of undocumented immigrants—Arkansas, Idaho, Kansas, Louisiana, and Oklahoma (joined by the states within Alto Mexico of Arizona, Nevada, Texas and Utah). In contrast, the Alto Mexico border state of Oregon supported the executive action in federal court (as did California and New Mexico).

With Arizona as the most hostile U.S. jurisdiction today for undocumented immigrants, the question is fairly posed of which of the eight Alto Mexico border states would assume Arizona's mantle of anti-immigrant policymaking if Arizona were within a Mexico-governed Alto Mexico? Relatedly, given the role of California in launching the modern-era of localized anti-immigrant legislation with Proposition 187 (but later reversing course in 2013 by offering driver's licenses to undocumented drivers and a license to practice law despite a lawyer's undocumented presence), of Arizona in sustaining and amplifying the pitch of state anti-immigrant laws, and of Texas in leading the challenge to then President Obama's compassionate deferral of immigration enforcement for some groups of undocumented immigrants, is there some unique immigration dynamic among border states that prompts especially stringent enforcement efforts in that borderlands geography?

Indeed, it seems clear that border states are the epicenter of reactionary anti-immigrant responses. The history of Mexican populations in the Southwest connected the Southwest culturally, economically, and otherwise to Mexico, ensuring significant cross-border movement and sustained immigration into the region. With more than 22 million Mexican residents in Alto Mexico today (albeit many of them U.S. born and of multiple generations), the vast majority of them living in the four border states of California, Arizona, New Mexico, and Texas, the Southwestern U.S. houses a disproportionately large number of recent documented immigrants, as well as undocumented migrants. Although this dynamic could be missing from the Alto Mexico/United 44 States border given the potentially lesser Mexican population in its eight border states such as Wyoming and Idaho, border-crossings would still occur in this terrain. Although almost half of undocumented immigrants entered the United States legally (often traveling through or into the border states) using visas for temporary visitation or residence, and then overstayed their visas,[264] the rest mostly crossed surreptitiously into the border states, primarily along the U.S.-Mexico border rather than the Canadian border.

Mexican border crossings along the U.S.-Mexico border sparked and galvanized much of the current anti-immigrant anger in the four U.S. border states. California's Proposition 187, and the concurrent reelection campaign in 1994 of then-Governor Pete Wilson, were buoyed by Wilson's campaign commercials showing grainy images of Mexicans

---

[264] Bender, *Run for the Border*, 134.

running through border traffic on Southern California's Interstate 5 with the ominous message, "They keep coming."[265] In Arizona and Texas, especially, borderlands ranchers began complaining of trespass and property damage by migrants crossing their property. Ranchers themselves, and vigilante groups such as the Minuteman Project and Ranch Rescue, took up arms to patrol the borderlands from both horseback and umbrellaed lawn chairs. The Minutemen in particular drew national media attention in their 2005 heyday and helped create the popular perception that undocumented immigrants (particularly Mexicans and other Latina/os) posed unchecked threats to border state resident safety and wellbeing. Eventually, fear transcended the four border states and reached the national psyche, leading Congressional lawmakers in December 2005 to propose the draconian Border Protection, Antiterrorism, and Illegal Immigration Control Act that would have made it a felony to assist an undocumented migrant, perhaps by merely supplying food and water to an imperiled crosser. Although the bill was defeated, its border-centric imperative for security led Congress the next year to enact the Secure Fence Act of 2006 to fortify the Mexican border. National Guard troops sent to the borderlands by Arizona and New Mexico governors fanned these nativist flames by creating the impression of a border gone wild with threats to the safety of local residents. A few years later, in 2010, Arizona's Governor Jan Brewer fueled those fears by contending that undocumented immigrants were beheading victims in the Arizona desert borderlands, later claiming she misspoke. In 2014, then Texas Governor Rick Perry weighed in by directing the Texas Department of Public Safety to "immediately begin law enforcement surge operations on the Texas-Mexico border to combat the flood of illegal immigration."[266] In the aggregate, then, it seems the epicenter for reactionary U.S. anti-immigrant rhetoric and enforcement is indeed the borderlands, a place where, as the late acclaimed writer Gloria Anzaldúa observed, "the Third World grates against the first and bleeds."[267]

Different dynamics are possible, however, along the Alto Mexico/United 44 States border. Foremost, that border is longer than the current U.S.-Mexico border of about 2,000 miles, and intersects with twice as many U.S. state borders, thus diluting the impact and number of entrants in any one state. Moreover, given the smaller U.S. territory and likely smaller economy of the United 44 States, fewer undocumented entries would occur in comparison to today's U.S.-Mexico border crossings. Given the Alto Mexico border's length, undocumented crossers likely would choose the location that best connects to their ultimate

---

[265] http://www.youtube.com/watch?v=lLIzzs2HHgY (last visited September 26, 2013).
[266] Bob Price, "Texas Approves Border Security Surge," http://www.breitbart.com/Breitbart-Texas/2014/06/18/BREAKING-Texas-Border-Security-Surge-Imminent (posted June 18, 2014; last visited June 23, 2014).
[267] Gloria Anzaldúa, *Borderlands/La Frontera: The New Mestiza* (San Francisco: Aunt Lute Books, 2d ed. 1999), 25.

destination in the United 44 States—presumably migrants headed for the Pacific Northwest would cross into Oregon or Idaho, those destined for the Midwest, into Wyoming, Colorado, or Kansas, and those aiming for the South, into Arkansas, Louisiana, or Oklahoma. Depending on the border securitization measures undertaken, undocumented entrants crossing the border on foot would likely enter in the same way as compelled by current U.S. border policy—away from urban entry points with a more visible presence of border security, and toward more desolate (and dangerous) entry points. The Alto Mexico/United 44 States border, generally, is no less desolate than the current U.S.-Mexico border. Although population and density of a Mexico-governed Alto Mexico are a matter of speculation, the Alto Mexico borderlands region today offers wide swaths of open space, much of it uninterrupted ranchland, particularly along the Nevada/Oregon-Idaho border. Similarly, a long stretch of highway following the Arkansas River and thus the old U.S.-Mexico border, near the Santa Fe Trail, from La Junta, Colorado, to and beyond the Kansas state line, is so desolate that one long-time resident cautioned me to carry sandwiches before attempting its travel. Little of the rest of the Alto Mexico/United 44 States border today is demarcated by a highway or road of any kind following its length, aside from occasional roads along boundary rivers such as the Arkansas, and highways that traverse the border, themselves far between in regions such as the southern reaches of the Pacific Northwest.

Of the eight Alto Mexico/United 44 States border states, consider which is the most likely to assume Arizona's current stance as the hub of sub-national anti-immigration policy designed to deter additional undocumented immigrant entry and to cause existing undocumented state residents to, borrowing 2012 Republican presidential candidate Mitt Romney's proffered immigration strategy, self-deport? Given the votes on such measures that often break along political party lines, one factor in identifying that nativist state would be the current party affiliation of the border state governors, with just Oregon and Colorado led by Democrats in mid-2015. Relatedly, Democrats control the state legislature of only one Alto Mexico/United 44 States border state, Oregon (and Colorado's House).[268] Similarly, they control one of the four present border states—California (and New Mexico's Senate), and as of 2015 only California had a Democratic governor. Yet Oklahoma's draconian anti-immigrant law was signed by a Democratic governor, signaling that party affiliation may not fully predict sentiment and policies toward immigrants.

History is also a guide. Through this lens, all the eight Alto Mexico border states are at risk for xenophobic backlash. For example, although Oregon seems benign and even progressive today on the presence of

---

[268] Eastern Colorado, the state's population center, includes liberal (Boulder, Denver) and conservative (Colorado Springs, south suburbs of Denver) enclaves, and presumably would be tilted Democrat as with the entire state today.

newcomers within its boundaries, its startling history of racism speaks otherwise. As examples, 1849 and 1857 Oregon laws forbade blacks from settling in the (then) territory. Oregon's 1857 Constitution authorized the legislature to restrain entry of nonwhites, and provided no "Chinaman" could own property in the state, while protecting the immigration of "white foreigners."[269] Eventually, the Ku Klux Klan took firm root in the state's geography and racial history, with Klan members serving in the Oregon legislature, enabling the election of the state's governor in 1922, and helping enact a broader prohibition, the Alien Property Act of 1923, barring all Asians from owning land or businesses.[270] Oregon's Supreme Court, as had the U.S. Supreme Court, validated the segregation of black and white residents in public places.[271] Even vital wartime bracero workers from Mexico encountered racial animosity in Oregon,[272] with some Oregon businesses, particularly taverns, posting "No Mexicans, White Trade Only" signs.[273] Vestiges of overt racial discrimination survived well into the twentieth century, as evidenced by a sign at a popular 1950s era Portland coffee shop, "White Trade Only," and a Noti, Oregon tavern whose door in the 1980s read "No Niggers." Although of late Oregon generally has resisted enacting anti-immigrant laws, in 2014 its voters overwhelmingly rejected a legislative allowance of driver's licenses for undocumented immigrants following a rancorous campaign.

Of the eight Alto Mexico border states, Oklahoma enacted the most draconian anti-immigrant law during the last few decades targeting Mexican and other Latina/o immigrants. But Idaho might be best positioned among the eight Alto Mexico border states to set the tone for restrictive immigration policy in the United 44 States. Despite the absence of Arizona S.B. 1070 copycat legislation there, Idaho holds a critical ingredient for a border stronghold state—its attraction of paranoia-fueled residents

---

[269] Gordon B. Dodds, *Oregon: A Bicentennial History* (New York: W.W. Norton, 1977), 100-101; "Alien Land Laws," http://encyclopedia.densho.org/ Alien_land_laws/ (last visited September 26, 2013). Article XV, section 8 of the 1857 Constitution provided that "No Chinaman not a resident of the State at the adoption of this Constitution shall ever hold any real estate or mining claim or work any mining claim therein." http://bluebook.state.or.us/state/constitution/ orig/article_XV_02.htm (last visited January 22, 2014).
[270] John Shuford, "'The Tale of the Tribe and the Company Town,': What We Can Learn About the Workings of Whiteness in the Pacific Northwest," *Oregon Law Review* 90 (2012): 1273, 1300-1301.
[271] *Taylor v. Cohn*, 47 Or. 538, 84 P. 388 (1906) (allowing segregation in theater that told black patrons "You are colored people, and it is a rule of this house not to allow negroes to occupy box[seats].").
[272] Erasmo Gamboa, "The Bracero Program," in *Nosotros: The Hispanic People of Oregon, Essays and Recollections*, ed. Erasmo Gamboa and Carolyn M. Buan (Portland, OR: Oregon Council for the Humanities, 1995), 41, 44; Erlinda Gonzales-Berry and Marcela Mendoza, *Mexicanos in Oregon: Their Stories, Their Lives* (Corvallis, OR: Oregon State University Press, 2010).
[273] Gamboa, *Mexican Labor*, 112 (describing signs in beer parlors and pool halls).

who disdain the federal government and its exclusive jurisdiction to enforce national borders, and whose vision of security and extremism includes a racialized bent. Even more so than Arizona, Idaho is a Minuteman Project dream. Replete with extremist groups such as the white supremacist Aryan Nations that once thrived in its Kootenai County (with county seat Coeur d'Alene still 95 percent white), Idaho is overrun with gun-loving patriots in the mold of infamous Idahoan survivalist Randy Weaver, such as those seeking the "purge" of Latina/os and Muslims, and "blue voters," from within a walled separatist city envisioned in Benewah County in northern Idaho.[274] Aryan Nations once even contemplated a homeland seizure, forming the Confederate Northwest comprised of five states—Washington, Oregon, Idaho, Wyoming, and Montana.[275] Outside of the agricultural counties encompassing the Twin Falls region, Idaho boosts a surfeit of "whiteopia" towns.[276] Discrimination against Mexicans in Idaho dates to wartime Mexican bracero workers barred from businesses in Caldwell and Nampa, Idaho by signs reading "No Japs or Mexicans Allowed," and subjected to such extreme prejudice that the Mexican government eventually blacklisted Idaho (and Texas) as a destination for braceros.[277] As a countervailing factor, Idaho relies on immigrants, including undocumented migrants, in its critical agricultural industry, once prompting Larry Craig, a long-time (1991 to 2009) Republican U.S. Senator from Idaho, to champion the federal Agricultural Job Opportunity, Benefits and Security Act (AgJOBS) that would have supplied undocumented farm workers with a temporary lawful immigration status and the possibility of U.S. citizenship over time.

Idaho's need-hate relationship with Mexican immigrants reflects the national psyche which tends to welcome immigrants in times of labor need, such as through the Bracero Program, and deport them, such as through the 1950s Operation Wetback described in Chapter 6, or legislate against them, such as under Arizona's SB 1070, in times of economic downturn. This dynamic of invitation and exile defines the U.S. relationship with Mexican workers during the last 100 years, in both the U.S.-governed Alto Mexico and the United 44 States, meaning that the likelihood of draconian laws and enforcement along the Alto Mexico/United 44 States border would turn largely on the economic fortunes of the United States, which has never fully embraced Mexicans aside from accepting and benefitting from their vital labor contributions.

---

[274] Bill Morlin, "7000 Gun-Loving 'Patriots' Living in a Walled Citadel Built Around an Arms Factory in Idaho—What Could Possibly Go Wrong?," http://www.alternet.org/tea-party-and-right/7000-patriots-living-walled-citadel-built-around-arms-factory-idaho-what-could (posted August 15, 2013; last visited September 26, 2013).

[275] Rich Benjamin, *Searching for Whitopia: An Improbable Journey to the Heart of White America* (New York: Hyperion, 2009), 114.

[276] Shuford, "Tale of the Tribe," 1289.

[277] Gamboa, *Mexican Labor*, 112.

5. ANGLO MIGRATION TO MEXICO AND ALTO MEXICO

> Everyone seems to agree: the quality of your [Anglo] life improves in Mexico. . . . [Y]ou can afford the kinds of luxuries only the very wealthy enjoy up north—like a maid, a cook, and a gardener.
>
> —*Gringos in Paradise*[278]

Having just discussed the migration of Mexicans to the United 44 States, here I examine a reverse flow—the migration of Anglos to a U.S.-governed Alto Mexico after the U.S.-Mexican War and their cultural and numerical dominance in that region's history during the last 170 years. Yet the growth in recent decades of the region's Mexican and other Latina/o population challenges that status, transforming the Alto Mexico terrain into a cultural convergence zone as later chapters develop. Relatedly, this chapter considers the potential differences in Anglo migration to a Mexico-governed Alto Mexico as a predictor of how the Southwestern U.S. might look today under Mexican ownership. The materials below also engage the history of the U.S. Anglo migration south to Mexico as an indicator of Anglo migration to Mexican-governed turf. Overall, at the same time that Mexican immigrants are making the United States more Mexican, Anglos and other U.S. residents, and U.S. businesses, are making inroads in Mexico, which increasingly elevates the Alto Mexico terrain as a convergence zone for this vibrant melding of cultures in the Americas.

Although Mexicans (primarily through their residence in New Mexico) once outnumbered Anglos in the Southwest at the time of the U.S.-Mexican War and before, Anglos soon arrived in successive waves in search of economic opportunity. Defining episodes of Anglo migration to the U.S.-governed Alto Mexico include, chronologically, California's Gold Rush and the allure of Colorado mining towns,[279] migration following the completion of rail lines into the Southwest (particularly in 1880s Southern California), the Dust Bowl migration of "Okies" and residents of other Great Plains states to California in the 1930s and, most recently, the Sun Belt migration to Southwestern states (and to Southern states

---

[278] "Gringos in Paradise: Live & Work in Paradise,"http://www.gringosinparadise.com.mx/sample-budgets-cost-of-living-in-mexico/ (last visited June 4, 2014).

[279] http://history.fcgov.com/archive/contexts/colorado.php (last visited September 5, 2013) (estimating 100,000 settlers headed for Colorado in 1859, and that although some didn't make it, those who did established Denver as a major regional center).

such as Florida outside of Alto Mexico) in the latter part of the twentieth century as Anglos followed jobs and the sun from the Rust Belt and other northern states.

Anglos have long been the dominant group in the Southwest in number, political power, and cultural influence—a dominance vital in explaining and predicting U.S. immigration policy toward Mexicans, as well as for imagining the contrast in demographics and culture of a Mexico-governed Alto Mexico. As detailed in Chapter 2, the ascendancy in number of Anglos over Mexican residents in the post-War Southwest took longest in New Mexico, home to an estimated 60,000 Spanish-speaking residents and only about 1,000 Anglos at the end of the U.S.-Mexican War (still, indigenous peoples outnumbered even the Spanish-speaking residents of New Mexico, with about 60,000 nomadic and semi-nomadic Indians including Apache, Comanche, Kiowa, Navajo, and Ute tribal members, and another 15,000 Pueblo Indians at the time of the War).[280] By the time joint statehood of New Mexico and Arizona was considered in 1906 (New Mexico finally obtained statehood separately in 1912), New Mexico's population was still about 50 percent Spanish-speaking,[281] a number that held up at least into the 1930s.[282] Eventually Anglos outnumbered Latina/o residents there, but by the 2010 Census, Latina/os in New Mexico surpassed Anglo residents to become the state's largest group, a trend that continued through 2012 with Anglos constituting just 39.8 percent and Latina/os (most of them of Mexican origin) 47 percent of New Mexican residents.

In other regions of Alto Mexico thinly settled by Mexican residents at the time of the U.S.-Mexican War, Anglos more quickly outnumbered Spanish-speaking ranchers and laborers. As detailed in Chapter 1, Anglo immigrants in present-day Texas surpassed Mexicans in number while the region was still part of Mexico. Elsewhere in Alto Mexico, the Anglo influx came after the War. Gold Rush settlers flooded California in particular, quickly diluting the once dominant Mexican population in California to just 4 percent by 1870.[283] For the most part, Anglos still outnumber Mexican residents in the Southwest, at least for another few decades. Today, despite significant recent growth in Latina/o population, as of 2012 Anglos still account for 8 of 10 Utah residents, with Latina/os constituting just 13.3 percent of Utah's population. As of 2015, Arizona, Texas, and Nevada maintained an Anglo majority. Although Latina/os

[280] Laura E. Goméz, "Off-White in an Age of White Supremacy: Mexican Elites and the Rights of Indians and Blacks in Nineteenth-Century New Mexico," *UCLA Chicano-Latino Law Review* 25 (2005): 9, 13.
[281] http://www.ped.state.nm.us/BilingualMulticultural/dl09/Language%20Rights%20and%20New%20Mexico%20Statehood.pdf (last visited September 5, 2013).
[282] James I. Culbert, "Distribution of Spanish-American Population in New Mexico," *Economic Geography* 19 (1943): 171.
[283] Weber, *Foreigners in Their Native Land*, 148 (Editor's Introduction).

(most of them Mexican) ultimately surpassed Anglo residents in California in 2014, the 2010 Census counted some 15 million Anglos living in California.[284] That 2010 Census also found 11.4 million Anglos residing in Texas (where Latina/o residents, most of them Mexican, might eclipse Anglos by as early as 2020), 3.7 million in Arizona, 3.5 million in Colorado (although most live outside Alto Mexico's boundaries in population centers such as Denver), 2.2 million in Utah, 1.4 million in Nevada, and slightly more than 800,000 in New Mexico—a total in these regions alone of about 38 million Anglo residents, well exceeding the current Mexican (and other Latina/o) population in Alto Mexico.

Whether Anglos would have the same numerical dominance within a Mexico-governed Alto Mexico, despite the inherent speculation of the answer, is informed by the Mexican experience of mostly welcoming and, only occasionally, resisting Anglo immigration to Mexico. Apart from its attempted exclusion of U.S. immigrants into the Texas region in the 1830s, discussed in Chapter 1, its exclusion from Mexico of Anglo immigrants in the wake of the U.S.-Mexican War, its harassment and exclusion of long-haired U.S. hippies in the late 1960s and early 1970s thought to bring a culture of psychedelic drugs and flawed values to Mexican youth, and restrictive policies against foreign workers prevailing during Mexico's economic woes as reflected in a 1974 law,[285] Mexico generally has tolerated and even encouraged foreign entrants, whether as tourists, part-time residents, or permanent residents, at least if they are well-to-do Anglos rather than poor Central American migrants.[286] Today, perhaps as many as one million U.S. citizens live in Mexico. Although some reside part-time in Mexican vacation homes and others come from different racial-ethnic backgrounds, most of these U.S. immigrants to Mexico are Anglos who work or have retired south of the border.

As detailed in Chapter 1, before the U.S.-Mexican War, Mexico had opened the Texas region (then mostly part of the Mexican state of Coahuila y Tejas) to Anglo immigrants, allowing these immigrants to become Mexican citizens in the hopes of defending the region against tribal inhabitants and the expansionist ideals of the United States. When Mexico closed the door to Anglo migration into Tejas in 1830, enforcing the prohibition with military garrisons, Anglo immigrants still came from the U.S. East and South into Tejas as undocumented immi-

---

[284] http://factfinder2.census.gov/bkmk/table/1.0/en/DEC/10_DP/DPDP1/0400000US06 (last visited September 5, 2013).
[285] Laura Valeria González-Murphy, *Protecting Immigrant Rights in Mexico: Understanding the State-Civil Society Nexus* (New York: Routledge, 2013), 148-149.
[286] See Hernández, *Mexican American Colonization*, 34 (stating that Mexico issued an 1848 decree after the U.S.-Mexican War barring European American colonists from immigrating to Mexico).

grants, ignoring Mexico's restriction.[287] Soon, they outnumbered Mexican residents ten to one and the secession led by Anglo immigrants swiftly followed to establish the Republic of Texas, and a decade later came the loss of the entirety of Alto Mexico to the United States.

Probably the first significant post-War migration of U.S. residents to a now much smaller Mexico was of Mexicans living in Alto Mexico who returned south of the border after both countries ratified the Treaty of Guadalupe Hidalgo in 1848. Seeking to protect its newly drawn border with the United States, Mexico's government lured some Mexicans living north of the border to migrate into the Mexican borderlands, offering them land and compensation.[288]

Anglos came to Mexico too, first as refugees and later to exploit its natural resources. Migrations of Anglos to Mexico included Confederates at the conclusion of the Civil War in 1865, who fled to Mexico at the invitation of Maximilian, Mexico's Emperor from 1864 to his execution in 1867 when France's brief control of Mexico ended. Although whole families of Confederates came south—an estimated 1,000 migrants by summer 1865, their affiliation with the vanquished Maximilian, among other factors, led many to depart Mexico for other countries.[289] Just a couple decades later, Anglo Mormon polygamists migrated from the Utah region to northern Mexico, particularly the Mexican state of Chihuahua bordering New Mexico and Texas. Once the U.S. Congress passed the Edmunds Act of 1882, establishing polygamy as a felony, these Mormons fled south to escape potential prosecution, forming colonies to farm Mexican land. Surely the most famous descendent of those colonies, 2012 presidential candidate Mitt Romney, is the son of George Romney, who was born in a Chihuahua Mormon colony in 1907. Earlier, coinciding with the U.S.-Mexican War, Mormons had migrated westward to the Great Salt Lake region of present-day Utah, where they still dominate local culture and politics, with almost two-thirds of the Utah population today of the Mormon faith, albeit in declining proportion.[290]

---

[287] Jay Root, "Back When Americans Were the 'Illegals,'" *New York Times* http://www.nytimes.com/2012/12/14/us/when-americans-were-illegal-immigrants-in-mexico.html (posted December 13, 2012; last visited September 11, 2013); U.S. Mexican War 1846-1848 (PBS, 1998), prt. 1.

[288] Richard Griswold del Castillo, *The Treaty of Guadalupe Hidalgo: A Legacy of Conflict* (Norman: University of Oklahoma Press, 1990), 64 (discussing that although few Californios—Californians of Spanish/Mexican heritage left, between 1,500 and 2,000 New Mexican residents repatriated to Mexico).

[289] Bender, *Run for the Border*, 14.

[290] Matt Canham, "Mormon Portion of Utah Population Steadily Shrinking," *Salt Lake Tribune*, July 24, 2005 (speculating Mormon residents may not constitute a majority by 2030). For background on the history of Mexican settlement in and immigration to Utah, see Armando Solórzano, *We Remember, We Celebrate, We Believe, Recuerdo, Celebración, y Esperanza: Latinos in Utah* (Salt Lake City: University of Utah Press, 2014).

During Spanish rule of Mexico, Spain generally had excluded foreign entrants (other than Spaniards and black slaves) from Mexico's terrain,[291] making an exception on the verge of Mexican independence to allow U.S. Anglos to help settle the Tejas region, a policy the Mexican government furthered, with disastrous consequences. Mexico was never a big draw for European immigrants after the U.S.-Mexican War. Even Spanish immigrants typically headed to Argentina over Mexico, and the United States and Canada received most other European immigrants. In one study encompassing 100 years from 1824 to 1924, 72 percent of European immigrants went to the United States, and another study spanning from 1820 to 1932 found only 270,000 European immigrants came to Mexico during that considerable time.[292] As one Latino historian explained, the lure of the United States for these immigrants derived from "its geographical location, fertile lands, liberal land and immigration policies, higher wages, and a relatively low population density of indigenous peoples—a population that usually served to compete with incoming immigrants for wage labor." In contrast, Mexico would neither subsidize the travel of European immigrants nor raise wages to attract them.[293] Not until recent decades did Mexico receive significant immigrants of European background, and this influx, as described below, came in the form of U.S. citizen Anglo retirees rather than as immigrants directly from Europe. Despite these entries, immigrants today account for only about one percent of Mexico's total population.[294]

The entry into Mexico of U.S. entrepreneurs (if not physically, at least their capital) in the late 1800s and early 1900s eventually prompted Mexican laws that displayed some hostility to foreign entrants and investment. In the late 1800s, U.S. entrepreneurs built railroads connecting Mexico to the United States. Those U.S.-owned rail lines came in handy to extract Mexico's extensive deposits of silver, coal, oil, copper, and iron for U.S. purposes—by the early 1900s U.S. entrepreneurs owned 81 percent of the Mexican mining industry and a majority stake (61 percent) in its oil fields development,[295] the latter of great value at a time when ships went from coal power to fuel oil and the automobile began to replace the horse. U.S. land barons also amassed huge tracts in Mexico operated as cattle ranches and sugar plantations. One of these Anglo ranchers, publishing magnate William Randolph Hearst, born in San Francisco, oversaw vast family ranch and farmland in Mexi-

---

[291] Weber, *Mexican Frontier*, 159-160 (describing how Spain anticipated the open door immigration policy of an independent Mexico in the Tejas region).

[292] Hernández, *Mexican American Colonization*, 42-43. Still, after the Spanish Civil War considerable numbers of vanquished Spanish republican refugees came to Mexico beginning in 1939.

[293] Ibid., 43, 65 (posits that despite Mexico liberalizing its immigration policies throughout the nineteenth century, European immigration was deterred by factors such as unfertile lands, intolerance of non-Catholics, and low wages).

[294] González-Murphy, *Protecting Immigrant Rights*, 148.

[295] Bender, *Run for the Border*, 41.

co, with one Hearst family ranch in Chihuahua alone encompassing 1,192,000 acres.[296] Expressing his arrogant assumption that Anglos would eventually control Mexico as they did the U.S. Southwest, Hearst once boasted, "I really don't see what is to prevent us [U.S. entrepreneurs] from owning all of Mexico and running it to suit ourselves."[297] Hearst's father, born in Missouri, made his own fortune in silver, copper, and gold mines throughout the U.S. West and Southwest, including those in Nevada, Utah, and New Mexico, and had acquired the Mexican ranchland his son managed from afar.[298] Presumably Mexico would have allowed these Anglo tycoon entries and acquisitions in a Mexico-governed Alto Mexico as it did in Northern Mexico—previously, Mexico allowed Anglos to acquire substantial land in Tejas for their lucrative cotton plantations predating the industrialization era. But the Mexican Revolution brought significant changes to Mexico's receptivity to foreign (particularly U.S.-citizen) investment.

Following the Revolution, Mexico law became more hostile to foreign ownership of its land and other resources. The resultant 1917 Constitution limited mining concessions to Mexicans by birth or naturalization, or to Mexican companies. The government nationalized Mexican petroleum and its railroads, and agrarian reform took 6.2 million acres, some without compensation or with inadequate compensation, from large U.S. property owners from 1927 to 1940,[299] even prompting some in the United States to urge war with Mexico[300] and U.S. oil companies to demand a boycott of Mexican goods to no avail. Significantly for future entrants, Mexico's 1917 Constitution imposed restrictions on foreign ownership of Mexico's border and coastline property, stating: "Within a zone of one hundred kilometers [sixty-two

---

[296] Ibid.
[297] John Mason Hart, *Empire and Revolution: The Americans in Mexico since the Civil War* (Berkeley: University of California Press, 2002), 167. Some of Hearst's ranchland was expropriated by the Mexican government, with payment by long-term bonds, and divided among small farmers after his death. "Mexico to Take Over Former Hearst's Ranch," *Prescott Evening Courier*, August 4, 1953.
[298] For additional detail on the Hearst holdings in Mexico, see Raymond Caballero, *Lynching Pascual Orozco: Mexican Revolutionary Hero and Paradox* (CreateSpace, 2015), 39, 244-245.
[299] Bender, *Run for the Border*, 42.
[300] John A. Britton, "From Antagonism to Accord: The Controversy over the Mexican Revolution in the Political Culture of the United States," in *Open Borders to a Revolution: Culture, Politics, and Migration*, ed. Jaime Marroquín, Adela Pineda Franco, and Magdalena Mieri (Washington D.C.: Smithsonian Institution Scholarly Press, 2013), 25 (discussing a public opinion poll on the use of force in Mexico, revealing a divided response, and also providing that Mexico agreed to pay U.S. and British oil companies just $30,000,000 of their compensation claims of between $250 million and $400 million; similarly, Mexico paid just $22 million of compensation to agricultural landowners, despite their claims for $136 million).

miles] along the borders and fifty [thirty-one miles] of the shores, for no reason may foreigners acquire legal title to the lands and waters."[301] Although U.S. residents could still enter Mexico and rent coastal and borderlands property, they could not own it directly. Applied to a Mexico-governed Alto Mexico, this ownership restriction would encompass the California coastal cities of San Francisco, Oakland, Los Angeles, San Diego, and the Texas coastal cities of Beaumont-Port Arthur, Houston, and Corpus Christi, as well as inland Alto Mexico/United 44 States borderlands cities such as Ogden, Utah, Pueblo, Colorado, and Wichita Falls, Texas and some suburbs of Dallas-Fort Worth. It would include the wealthy towns of Aspen, Colorado and Carmel, California, and vineyards and rich farmland along the California coast, as well as the terrain of Hearst Castle,[302] Disneyland, and the renowned Pebble Beach Golf Links.

In recent decades, however, the Mexican government eased these foreign ownership restrictions. First, Mexico enacted legislation in 1973 that allows U.S. citizens (and other foreigners) to purchase coastal and borderland restricted zone property using trusts (known as fideicomisos) in which Mexican banks, for initial and ongoing fees, hold legal title to the desired real estate for the benefit of the U.S. citizen, who may occupy the property as an owner would. Instead of an outright deed, selling the trust property involves transferring the beneficial interest in the trust while the trustee bank remains the owner. At their inception, fideicomiso trusts lasted only 30 years, and presumably before the trust termination the U.S. citizen would need to sell her interest to a Mexican national, thereby diminishing the attractiveness of this short-term property interest. But in 1989, the Mexican government authorized a 50-year initial term for fideicomiso trusts, with subsequent renewals for 50-year terms.[303] Prompting commercial development of Mexican coastal hotels and restaurants by U.S. investors, Mexico's 1993 Federal Investment Act allowed foreign investors to form a Mexican corporation and own direct title to restricted zone property used only for nonresidential purposes.[304]

---

[301] Translation derived from John De La Vega, *Mexican Real Estate: Laws and Practices Affecting Private U.S. Ownership* (Tucson: University of Arizona Press, 1976). Outside the so-called coastal and borderlands restricted zone, foreigners can purchase property upon signing an agreement with the Mexican Ministry of Foreign Affairs in which the U.S. citizen agrees to refrain from invoking U.S. government protection in disputes relating to the land.

[302] William Randolph Hearst's father purchased the underlying acreage, 40,000 acres, in 1865, and the holdings later ballooned to a 250,000 acre inheritance.

[303] Signet, *Mexican Real Estate System*, 109.

[304] Michael T. Madison, Jeffry R. Dwyer, and Steven W. Bender, *The Law of Real Estate Financing* (Eagan, MN: West, rev. ed. 2014), 2:78 (the corporate charter must contain the clause by which the corporation agrees to refrain from invoking the protection of the foreign government in matters relating to the property). The likelihood of Mexican government seizure of the foreign-owned real estate was eased by the inclusion in the North American Free Trade

Spurred by the adoption of the North American Free Trade Agreement, Mexico law now allows foreigners to wholly own companies in Mexico (under a 1944 law they could only own a minority stake in Mexican companies) except for certain sectors reserved for government or Mexican national control, such as petroleum,[305] and U.S. foreign direct investment in Mexico spiked in the 1990s.[306] Today, in a Mexican resort, beachgoers and residents can choose from a variety of familiar U.S.-owned hotel and restaurant chains, from Hiltons, Hyatts, and Marriotts, to Planet Hollywoods, Subways, Hard Rock Cafes, and Burger Kings. Shopping choices in Mexico include familiar U.S. retailers such as Walmart and Home Depot, accompanied by a variety of U.S.-based insurance companies and banks. Walmart now dominates the Mexican retail sector, becoming Mexico's largest private-sector employer with more than 1,000 stores and 150,000 employees.

Further legal reform to attract additional U.S. residents to Mexico may be forthcoming. Despite the ability to own and occupy coastal condos through the fideicomiso trust, many U.S. buyers (and banks financing them) are reluctant to undertake an acquisition that does not involve a property deed in their name. Given the scarcity of credit and onerous interest rates and down payment requirements of mortgage loans on Mexican property, most U.S. citizen purchasers tend to use cash or to obtain loans against U.S. property to finance their Mexico residence. Responding to this apparent distrust of Mexican bank trusts, Mexican legislators in 2013 were considering a constitutional amendment (that a majority of Mexican state legislatures would also need to approve) to allow direct ownership of coastal residences by foreigners. Aiming to compete with the U.S. South (particularly Florida) and Central American beaches luring U.S. retirees, advocates for the change contended it would significantly boost sales to U.S. citizens for whom the trust device may prove confusing and alarming.[307] Even without the change, Mexican officials estimate as many as 5 million U.S. citizens

---

Agreement of a provision that neither the United States nor Mexico could "nationalize or expropriate an investment of an investor of another Party [nation] in its territory . . . except (a) for a public purpose . . . (c) in accordance with due process of law . . . [and on payment of fair market value]." NAFTA, art. 1110.

[305] But see Chapter 3 for discussion of reforms opening Mexican oil fields to foreign investment.

[306] See Edward M. Graham and Erika Wada, "Domestic Reform, Trade and Investment Liberalization, Financial Crisis, and Foreign Direct Investment in Mexico," http://www.iie.com/publications/papers/print.cfm?ResearchId =360&doc=pub (last visited September 21, 2014) (1999 article published in *The World Economy*).

[307] Tim Johnson, "Mexico, To Attract U.S. Retirees, May Ease Limits on Land-ownership," http://www.mcclatchydc.com/2013/05/09/190819/ mexico-to-attract-us-retirees.html (May 9, 2013, last visited September 5, 2013).

may be living in Mexico by 2025, as baby-boomer Anglos age and seek sunny, cheap places to retire.[308]

Although U.S. residents frequented Mexican bordertowns, such as Tijuana and Ciudad Juárez, during the Prohibition era seeking free-flowing booze and gambling winnings, it wasn't until the 1950s that the availability of commercial airline flights brought U.S. residents en masse to visit Mexican beach resorts away from the borderlands. Famously, Frank Sinatra's 1957 hit song "Come Fly with Me" touted Acapulco for romantic Anglo honeymoons in that era. Eventually, other Mexican beach resorts such as Cabo San Lucas, Puerto Vallarta (launched by the 1964 film *Night of the Iguana*), and Cancún became staples for U.S. vacationers, the latter particularly popular among tens of thousands of young Anglo Spring breakers who annually visit. In 2012, almost 6 million U.S. residents visited Mexico (among the 24 million international visitors), supplying employment to about 7 million Mexican workers in the tourism industry and constituting Mexico's fifth largest revenue source.[309]

Once introduced to Mexico as vacationers, many Anglos wanted more. Especially in recent decades, and with the vehicle of the fideicomiso trust for coastal properties, U.S. residents, particularly Anglos, began purchasing Mexican homes and condominiums for retirement, telecommuting, or as vacation residences. Four Mexican coastal regions emerged as gringo[310] favorites—southern Baja in the Cabo San Lucas area, Puerto Vallarta, Sonora on the northern Sea of Cortez from San Felipe to Puerto Penasco, and Cancún. Popular inland locations include the Lake Chapala region near Guadalajara. The *Dallas Morning News* reported in 2005 that more than one million U.S. citizens, most of them retirees, were living at least part-time in Mexico, an astounding fivefold increase during the decade.[311] Mexico is therefore home to the largest U.S. community living abroad anywhere in the world. Another report put the number somewhat lower, with U.S. citizens comprising three-quarters of about one million documented foreigners living in Mexico, an increase from two-thirds in 2000, but presumably not counting those

---

[308] Andres Oppenheimer, "Mexico's Big Hope: Get 5 Million U.S. Retirees," http://www.rosaritoproperties.net/tag/real-estate-in-mexico/ (last visited September 11, 2013).

[309] Jose Enrique Arrioja, "Tourism Seen Jumping to No. 3 Mexico Cash Source by 2018," http://www.bloomberg.com/news/2013-06-25/tourism-seen-jumping-to-mexico-s-3rd-biggest-cash-source-by-2018.html (June 24, 2013; last visited September 11, 2013) (behind manufacturing, oil, remittances, and foreign direct investments, but expected to rise to third place).

[310] For origins of the term gringo, see Bender, *Greasers and Gringos*, 156.

[311] Les Christie, "Retire in Style South of the Border," http://money.cnn.com/2006/02/13/real_estate/acapulco_alternatives/ (February 14, 2006, last visited February 12, 2014).

who sought and had obtained Mexican citizenship.[312] Remarkably, the boost in U.S. residents moving south to Mexico is substantial enough that their numbers in recent years eclipsed the net number of Mexican migrants coming to the United States (in relation to those Mexican migrants returning to Mexico),[313] an astounding statistic for U.S. xenophobes to consider.

Several factors drive Mexican "gringo" retirements, including sunny climate and scenic beaches, but the primary factor is surely the cheaper cost of living. Despite gated beach resort enclaves carrying high sticker prices, Mexican real property taxes and maintenance costs (given the low wages of landscapers, housekeepers, and other workers) tend to be dramatically lower than in the United States—with taxes as little as $30 annually on a $200,000 property. Healthcare is less expensive as well.[314] Thus, in the same way that economic opportunity lures Mexican residents north, financial aspirations of cheaper living in Mexico draw Anglo residents south, yet without the legal impediments Mexican laborers face in their journey to U.S. employers.

Mexican officials enthusiastically encourage U.S. retirees, evident in substantial government investments in infrastructure for tourists and transplants such as the capital infusions that transformed Cancún from a small fishing village before the 1970s into an international resort city and may do the same for Baja's coastal Loreto. Mexican immigration law also facilitates the entry of U.S. retirees and second-home owners. In contrast to strict numerical limits imposed on Mexican immigrants coming to the United States that tend to require some familial connection and a long wait as a condition to entry beyond a short visit, Mexico provides unlimited visas to foreign retirees based on relatively modest retirement income and assets. Resultantly, the United States is the largest county of origin of immigrants living in Mexico, followed by Guatemala and Spain.[315] Under the most recent immigration rules implemented in 2012 under Mexico's 2011 Migratory Act, retirees in Mexico can obtain a visa for temporary residence or a permanent resident visa, the latter on proof of either a minimum monthly retirement pension of $2,300, or a bank balance of $119,000,[316] and after having held a temporary resident visa for four years.[317] Visas are also available for foreigners

---

[312] Damien Cave, "For Migrants, New Land of Opportunity is Mexico," *New York Times*, September 22, 2013, A1 (the total appears to include U.S. born children, and therefore U.S. citizens, of Mexican citizen parents).

[313] Ibid.

[314] Bender, *Run for the Border*, 32.

[315] González-Murphy, *Protecting Immigrant Rights*, 146.

[316] http://consulmex.sre.gob.mx/detroit/index.php/info-english (last visited September 5, 2013) (the minimum retirement income must be shown for the previous six months, alternatively, the minimum bank balance must be an average balance during the preceding twelve months).

[317] Article 57 of Mexico's Migratory Act, adopted in 2011, also authorizes a point system based on factors such as education and work experience that allows for

coming to work and live in Mexico, yet generally these U.S. workers are few, outside of high-level management and telecommuters, given the substantially lower wages paid in Mexico than in the United States. Mexico's welcome of U.S. immigrants was evident in a 2015 calendar year policy supplying a grace period to Mexican residents, most of them from the United States, who failed to obtain the necessary documentation for a permanent stay and who, under the amnesty program, can avoid paying any fine.

Consider the conditions for a similar influx of Anglo retirees and vacation home owners to a Mexico-governed Alto Mexico. During the last several decades, Anglo retirees and "snowbird" winter visitors from colder northern U.S. states flocked to temperate cities within Alto Mexico such as Las Vegas, Phoenix, and San Diego. Migration to Alto Mexico of both Anglo retirees and younger job-seekers began in earnest in the 1950s, coinciding with the mass production of air conditioners in the 1950s opening the desert to year-round living—in the 1950s decade, for example, Phoenix's population surged 311 percent from 106,818 to 439,170 residents,[318] the vast majority of them Anglo. Presumably most Anglo transplants to Alto Mexico would qualify under the new Mexican financial standards for immigration, making their move across an international border not demonstrably different than a move across current U.S. state lines. Further facilitating that entry of U.S. residents into a Mexico-governed Alto Mexico would be the presumably cheaper cost of maintaining residences there—of course dependent on the prevailing economy—albeit with the lesser government/social services that retirees and other transplants receive from the Mexican government.

Still, no doubt the Anglo population of a Mexico-governed Alto Mexico would be far less than the roughly 38 million Anglos that reside today in this region. Among the indicators suggesting this lower number is that, as noted previously, the southward migration of large numbers of U.S. retirees and vacation homeowners to Mexico is a relatively recent phenomenon. Reasons for the historical delay in southward migration to Mexico include the recent advent of telecommuting jobs with U.S. salaries. Further, until recently, U.S. home prices and health care costs were relatively affordable, allowing retirees a better chance of retiring comfortably within the United States. Also, until the 1950s, the absence of regularized speedy travel aboard commercial airline flights dampened the prospect of retiring far away from U.S. resident children and grandchildren.

But probably the biggest historical impediments to mass migration to Mexico for Anglos, whether as retirees, telecommuters, vacation

---

potentially speedier issuance of permanent residency without complying with the four years requirement.
[318] Bradford Luckingham, "Phoenix: The Desert Metropolis," in *Sunbelt Cities: Politics and Growth Since World War II*, ed. Richard M. Bernard and Bradley R. Rice (Austin, TX: University of Texas Press, 1983), 309, 314-315.

home occupants, or workers in search of gainful employment, are the perceived cultural differences between the two countries and the absence, until recently, of a critical mass of U.S. settlements within Mexico equivalent to Mexican barrio enclaves in the United States that beckon and nurture newcomers. Today, Anglo settlements in Mexico tend to be clustered and cloistered within walls and gates of newly constructed resort developments that target Anglo buyers to come live with Anglo neighbors. Signaling its desired buyers, one representative Cancún resort, the Residencial Bay View Grand condominiums, featured in its promotions "a blue-eyed family of Nordic appearance frolicking in the sands of the world famous resort."[319] Proximate to these settlements, U.S. stores like Walmart and Costco, and restaurant chains such as Starbucks and Chili's, serve Anglo residents' needs. With today's technology, Anglos living in Mexico can remain readily connected to Anglo culture within the United States. Satellite television can deliver any English language programs, sports, and movies, and the Internet allows transplants to read their favorite U.S. morning paper in English. This recent solicitation of Anglo buyers, their critical mass within these resort settlements, and the potential connectedness of expatriates to U.S. culture through technological advances, all help explain why only in the last few decades has there been such a push of south-of-the-border Anglo migration, particularly among retirees or those with means to draw significant salaries while working abroad.

Different historical factors within Alto Mexico suggest that, although no doubt its Anglo population would not approach 38 million, the numbers might far exceed the 1 million or so U.S. transplants in the entirety of Mexico today. Particularly the Gold Rush drawing Anglo settlers into California, and the subsequent push of migrants toward the Colorado and Nevada silver mines in the late 1800s suggest a substantial, early influx of Anglos into a Mexico-governed Alto Mexico that would have laid the foundation for additional settlements. Mexico's encouragement of Anglo immigrants to enter Tejas brought thousands who created an English language-based culture (as Chapter 8 discusses) and might have lured significant numbers of additional Anglos to the region. As evidenced by the migration of Mormons to Mexico described above, Mormons likely would have continued their settlements in a Mexico-governed Utah. On the verge of the U.S.-Mexican War, Anglo immigrants began receiving land grants in California from the Mexican government, further suggesting the potential for ongoing and substantial Anglo settlements in that region.

Vacation home magnets within Alto Mexico would have drawn additional Anglo migrants for seasonal frolics. Aspen and Park City, for example, swell with affluent wintertime residents, while beach communities along the Southern California coastline attract transitory residents

---

[319] Joseph Contreras, *In the Shadow of the Giant: The Americanization of Mexico* (New Brunswick, NJ: Rutgers University Press, 2009), 141.

from throughout the United States. Less costly locales near the border, such as Yuma, Arizona, and San Benito, Texas, draw tens of thousands of winter visitors living in their recreational vehicles. Regions like Lake Tahoe, California's Palm Springs and Lake Arrowhead, and Arizona's Sedona, lure more wealthy vacation home residents year-round. The Los Angeles area, home to entertainment industry stars, might hold a similar attraction within a Mexico-governed Alto Mexico. Overall, the potential exists for considerably more Anglo residency, full-or part-time, in a Mexico-governed Alto Mexico than seen in the rest of Mexico today.

* * *

Meanwhile in Mexico, U.S. transplants arriving of late in resort enclaves on Mexican beaches have driven up prices there, contrasting with the shacks of the impoverished Mexicans who service their newly built luxury homes, thereby replicating the dynamic of cheap Mexican labor for the wealthy prevailing in Alto Mexico locations such as Aspen. Preferring to live within gate-guarded communities, these Anglo retirees in Mexico insulate themselves from perceived risks of crime but, intentionally or not, also from the reach of Mexican culture percolating outside their condominium gates. Within the U.S. Sun Belt, a similar dynamic occurred of Anglo transplants opting for gate-guarded subdivisions that insulate them from multicultural influences and neighbors of color that reside outside those walls. Whether within the U.S. Southwest, or in Mexico, despite the increasing number of Anglos migrating to Mexico and the rising number of Mexicans coming to the United States, their worlds do not always synthesize. Rather, through the means of de facto residential segregation, private schools, income inequalities, and restrictive U.S. immigration laws keeping many migrants in the shadows, these groups rub elbows and forge the ties of good neighbors far less often than the sheer population numbers would suggest. Chapter 9 argues for a more meaningful melding of cultures in the recognition and furtherance of the shared destinies of the United States and Mexico—increasingly we are neighbors not just of bordering countries, but of Anglos and Mexicans living in the same cities, whether in the United States or Mexico. Only through the proximity of shared experiences in workplaces, neighborhoods, schools, and community involvement will Anglos realize the commonality of mutual aspirations with Mexican residents, who want the same thing as other Americans—opportunity for economic advancement, good health, freedom from violence, and adequate education for their children.

6. MEXICAN MIGRATION TO ALTO MEXICO

> As long as everything remains this way, we will keep crossing. If they throw out two by Nogales, ten will enter by Mexicali. And if they deport five by Juárez, seven will come through Laredo. If today they throw me out, tomorrow I'll come back.
>
> —Remarks of undocumented Mexican immigrant[320]

> You show me a 50-foot wall, I'll show you a 51-foot ladder.
>
> —Then Arizona Governor Janet Napolitano (2005)

Home to a large majority of the U.S. Mexican population, Alto Mexico is the epicenter of much of the current focus and debate on undocumented and unwanted immigration, particularly in the four U.S.-Mexico border states. In recent decades, especially, Mexicans have come to represent the face of both undocumented, and unwanted, immigration. Despite the inroads of Mexican immigrants to the United 44 States in past decades, Alto Mexico remains the hub of Mexican immigration to the United States. Of equal relevance to Chapter 5's speculation on how many Anglo residents would populate a Mexico-governed Alto Mexico is the question of its potential Mexican composition explored in this chapter. Well in excess of 22 million U.S. residents of Mexican background reside in today's Alto Mexico, a vast increase in relation to the sparse Mexican population of the region at the time of the U.S.-Mexican War, estimated at only 75,000—60,000 of those Spanish-speaking residents living in what is now New Mexico, 7,500 in California, 5,000 in Texas, 1,500 in Colorado, and 1,000 in Arizona,[321] with no Mexican residents in the rest of Alto Mexico—today's Utah, Nevada, and parts of Wyoming, Kansas, and Oklahoma—before the War. As measured by the 2010 Census, approximately 11.4 million residents of Mexican background now live in California, followed by 8 million in Texas, 1.7 million in Arizona, 591,000 in New Mexico,[322] 541,000 in Nevada, and 259,000 in Utah, cu-

---

[320] Rudy Adler, Victoria Criado, and Brett Huneycutt, *Border Film Project: Photos by Migrants & Minutemen on the U.S.-Mexico Border* (New York: Harry N. Abrams, 2007), n.p.

[321] http://www.ped.state.nm.us/BilingualMulticultural/dl09/Language%20Rights%20and%20New%20Mexico%20Statehood.pdf (last visited September 5, 2013) (noting these estimates are now considered conservative).

[322] In addition to Mexican, Cuban, and Puerto Rican designations, the Census also counted the category of Other Hispanic or Latino, which includes self-

mulatively exceeding 22 million Mexican residents today in the Alto Mexico region and likely not including potentially millions of Mexican undocumented immigrants escaping count but laboring in the Southwest, nor including Mexican residents—both U.S. citizens and documented immigrants—living within the once Alto Mexico terrain of western and southeastern Colorado, southern Wyoming, southwestern Kansas, and far western Oklahoma. As discussed below, most of these 22 million Mexican residents were drawn to, or remain in, the Alto Mexico region for its economic opportunities. The question can fairly be asked whether the number of Mexican residents would be much different in a Mexico-controlled Alto Mexico given that Mexican immigrants have shown that no border impediment or risk will stop their entry toward economic opportunity and survival.

Speculating on the Mexican population of a Mexico-controlled Alto Mexico, and their economic status, is informed by history. Initially, consider the different fortunes of Mexican landowners in a Mexico-governed Alto Mexico in contrast to the mass divestment of land that followed the U.S.-Mexican War. At the end of that war, the some 75,000 Mexicans in Alto Mexico resided mostly on individual or community (ejido) land grants from either the Spanish or, later, the Mexican government after its independence from Spain in 1821.[323] Intended both to reward for military service and to help populate and thereby protect Alto Mexico from hostile tribes and the U.S. government,[324] large land grants were common. As estimated in 1849, two hundred families in California owned fourteen million acres acquired through Spanish/Mexico land grants, and just 295 land grants conveyed significant New Mexico real estate, 141 of them to individuals and the rest to community ownership.[325] Community grants usually included individual plots to families

---

identified residents with origins in the Dominican Republic, Spain, or Spanish-speaking Central or South American countries. In New Mexico the Other Hispanic or Latino total was 350,000. Given the longstanding identification of Latina/os in New Mexico with Spain rather than Mexico (see Rodolfo F. Acuña, *Anything But Mexican: Chicanos in Contemporary Los Angeles* (New York: Verso, 1996)), it is likely that much of that total is residents of Mexican origin.

The above statistics also don't include Latina/o residents of western Colorado, southern Wyoming, and other slices of Alto Mexico.

[323] Of course, some pre-War Mexicans in the Southwest were laborers for the landed Mexican class.

[324] Aside from tribes who were already there, presumably the Mexico government feared settlers loyal to the United States occupying and following the same course as Texas by declaring independence and then seeking annexation by the U.S. government.

[325] U.S. General Accounting Office, "Treaty of Guadalupe Hidalgo: Findings and Possible Options Regarding Longstanding Community Land Grants in New Mexico" (June 2004): 14. But see Armando C. Alonzo, *Tejano Legacy: Rancheros and Settlers in South Texas, 1734-1900* (Albuquerque: University of New Mexico

for their private homes and vegetable gardens, augmented by substantial common lands not subject to individual sale, often comprising 90 percent of the total land grant, for grazing, hunting, fishing, drinking water, and timber for firewood and home construction by the individual grantees. In the aggregate, the Spanish and Mexican land grants in Alto Mexico formed a land area "nearly as big as Vermont and New Hampshire combined."[326] As initially written, the Treaty of Guadalupe Hidalgo well protected these land grants: "All grants of land made by the Mexican government or by the competent authorities, in the territories previously appertaining to Mexico, and remaining for the future within the limits of the United States, shall be respected as valid, to the same extent that the same grants would be valid, if the said territories had remained within the limits of Mexico." But in ratifying the treaty, the U.S. Senate struck out this language, leaving only an assurance that: "Mexicans now established in territories previously belonging to Mexico . . . shall be free to continue where they now reside, or to remove at any time to the Mexican Republic, retaining the property which they possess in the said territories, or disposing thereof and removing the proceeds wherever they please . . . ."[327]

Despite the supposed protection that remained in the treaty, most of the Spanish/Mexican land grant acreage found its way to Anglo hands within a few decades as Mexicans regressed in the U.S.-governed Southwest from a landholding class into mostly servants of the land.[328] Although several factors contributed to their divestment, the most significant tool was the confirmation process the U.S. Congress demanded of Spanish/Mexican land grant holders. Differing by region, the confirmation procedures proved disastrous to most of these owners. In New Mexico, for example, Congress initially established the Office of the Surveyor General in 1854 to investigate the local land grants and recommend to Congress their approval or rejection, but Congress replaced this unwieldy procedure in 1891 with the Court of Private Claims holding jurisdiction to adjudicate the validity of New Mexico's land

---

Press, 1998), 260 (contending that about 1,000 land grants were made in New Mexico during Spanish/Mexican rule).

[326] Phillip B. Gonzales, "Struggle for Survival: The Hispanic Land Grants of New Mexico, 1848-2001," *Agricultural History* 77(Spring 2003): 293, 298.

[327] Treaty of Guadalupe Hidalgo, art. VIII (also providing that "Those who shall prefer to remain in the said territories, may either retain the title and rights of Mexican citizens, or acquire those of citizens of the United States. . . . . In the said territories, property of every kind, now belonging to Mexicans not established here, shall be inviolably respected. The present owners, the heirs of these, and all Mexicans who may hereafter acquire said property by contract, shall enjoy with respect to it, guaranties equally ample as if the same belonged to citizens of the United States.").

[328] Some of the Spanish/Mexican land grants were made to Anglo immigrants within Alto Mexico, but the bulk of the acreage of the grants went to those of Spanish/Mexican heritage.

grants. For California grants, Congress created the California Land Claims Commission in 1851. The upshot of these federally mandated confirmation procedures was that land grant owners were forced to hire expensive lawyers to initiate court proceedings in order to prove the validity of their land grants from the Spanish or Mexican governments. The U.S. Supreme Court concluded that even those California landowners with perfect title needed to hire lawyers and land surveyors and file their claim with the California Land Claims Commission for confirmation within a two-year deadline or lose their land.[329] Claims were readily denied if paperwork (before the days of local recording offices for property deeds) was destroyed in the U.S.-Mexican War, or if that War prevented completion of the granting process. Contrary to Spanish and Mexican law, claims were denied for grants not issued by governors, such as when Spanish municipal magistrates (*alcaldes*) or lieutenant governors dispensed grants.[330] U.S. officials found land descriptions in the written grants too imprecise when they used ephemeral geographic points of measurement such as rocks and tree stumps. Lawyers for the Mexican landowners took a whopping cut of one-fourth to one-half of the acreage successfully confirmed, and some even sought judicial partition of land awarded them as co-tenants with the Mexican grantee, leading to a sale at which a cash-rich (Anglo) lawyer could outbid the Mexican landowner and acquire the entire parcel on the cheap. In an 1897 case involving New Mexico real estate, the U.S. Supreme Court ignored the proper structure of the ejido/community land grant under Mexican law, and ruled that the common lands, rather than owned by the collective of individual owners, were owned by the sovereign.[331] This meant that extensive common ejido lands passed post-treaty to U.S. government ownership—lands that now encompass most of the Carson and Santa Fe National Forests in New Mexico—and could not be sold or even occupied by the collective of private Mexican owners.

Lands in the Southwest surviving the confirmation process that wrested away millions of acres were still vulnerable to other more aggressive tactics of divestment. Some Anglo settlers defrauded Mexican landowners into signing away a deed by exploiting the language barrier (for example, what the Spanish-speaking Mexican owner understood orally as a mere land lease was written in English as a conveyance deed), while others squatted on the land and harassed the Mexican owners, with some resorting to outright violence to steal the land in the often lawless West. Squatters were especially thick in California where the Gold Rush lured 100,000 entrants in 1849 alone.[332] Desperate for cash to

---

[329] *Botiller v. Dominguez*, 130 U.S. 238 (1889).

[330] Gonzales, "Struggle for Survival," 306.

[331] *United States v. Sandoval*, 167 U.S. 278 (1897) (leading to confirmation of only 5,207 acres of 315,300 acre land grant parcel).

[332] Steven W. Bender, *Tierra y Libertad: Land, Liberty, and Latino Housing* (New York: New York University, 2010), 22. As with the potential for acquisition of

navigate the mandatory land confirmation process, fight squatters, and pay real estate taxes, Mexican landowners in the Southwest borrowed from Anglo lenders at outrageous rates, and sometimes lost their lands in foreclosure sales. Tax auctions took other Mexican lands, now taxed on their assessed market value for resale rather than under the Mexican system of their production value, leaving Mexican landowners who grazed cattle and raised crops for family subsistence rather than for profit unable to pay their newly imposed land taxes. Floods and drought variously took their toll on remaining lands. By the time the railroads arrived in the 1870s and 1880s, most of the Spanish-Mexican land grants were in other, mostly Anglo, hands, and the West was truly won. Although the Mexican Revolution of the early 1900s might have threatened a similar divestment of massive rancho titles in the hands of Mexican landowners in a Mexico-controlled Alto Mexico, some countervailing factors likely would have produced a different script from the divestment outlined above. The roots of the Mexican Revolution extended to hostility over mass holdings of Mexican land and natural resources by U.S. residents and other foreign nationals, as detailed in Chapter 5. Query if the same dynamic would have emerged in a Mexico-controlled Alto Mexico. Moreover, in the aftermath of the Revolution some of the lands appropriated were distributed toward Mexican collective farming uses, which in a Mexico-controlled Alto Mexico would have kept the lands in (more) Mexican hands.

In the U.S. controlled Southwest, however, the divestment of Mexican rancho lands fundamentally altered the fortunes of Mexican residents. Perhaps the most valuable Alto Mexico acreage lost from today's vantage point was in Southern California, where Mexican ranchos were hit particularly hard by real estate taxes levied to pay for infrastructure needed in northern Gold Rush country—the lucrative Anglo-owned gold mines, in contrast, weren't taxed.[333] Moreover, tax rates were sometimes discriminatorily levied more heavily on Mexican than Anglo landowners.[334] Most of Southern California's now pricey real estate was once held in vast Mexican ranchos. Today's astounding value for just a sliver of land underlying each home in areas once subject to ranchos, such as Laguna Beach (part of the Niguel land grant),[335] which in summer 2015 carried a Zillow estimated median home value of nearly $1.5 million, suggests that Mexican landowners in a Mexico-governed Alto

---

land title through adverse occupation in the United States, Mexico also recognizes the concept of acquiring land title by adverse possession. Signet, *Mexican Real Estate System*, 165.

[333] Bender, *Tierra y Libertad*, 23.

[334] Ibid. (stating some Mexican owners were taxed at $1.50 an acre but Anglos acquiring that same property were taxed at 20 cents per acre).

[335] Although the Niguel land grant survived confirmation, its Mexican owner sold to an Anglo buyer following the drought of 1863-1864. "Rancho Niguel," http://en.wikipedia.org/wiki/Rancho_Niguel (last visited September 6, 2013).

Mexico as a class, not forced to undergo judicial confirmation and a divestment gauntlet, may have prospered and established a financial legacy and identity as wealthy landowners or land developers instead of as California's long-abused migrant farm workers and low-income laborers. Presumably the Mexican government would have continued to dole out land grants to additional Mexican settlers, and the Southwest might have a vastly different economic hierarchy. Although the United States offered its own land grant program, through the Homestead Act of 1862, supplying 160 acres of federal land (often appropriated from tribes) to each settler who agreed to cultivate it for five years, Anglos were the primary beneficiaries of this U.S. program. Among other explanations, the U.S. land grant program came at a time when holders of Spanish and Mexican land grants were being divested of their larger landholdings, and Mexican migration to Alto Mexico slowed awaiting the Mexican Revolution decades later. Also, because of its arid climate and sparse vegetation, some parts of the U.S. Southwest, where Mexicans were settled at the time, were unsuited for 160-acre homestead ranches; ranchers needed several thousand acres, which they had received in Spanish/Mexican land grants, to effectively graze livestock. Mexicans, then, found themselves largely landless in the U.S.-governed Alto Mexico, the epicenter of Mexican population in the United States then and now.

Even today, given the high cost of coastal real estate, beach towns of California are at least de facto restricted zones for Mexican immigrant ownership, relegating many of California's Mexican residents to live in cheaper inland areas such as East Los Angeles, with a summer 2015 Zillow median value estimate of only $340,900 and Riverside, California, with a summer 2015 Zillow home value of $300,800. Similarly, the San Francisco area is exorbitantly expensive for most Mexican immigrants, and for anyone who earns less than a six figure annual salary. Currently, more than twelve times the median Latina/o household income is needed to purchase a home in the San Francisco Bay Area, and more than nine times in the Los Angeles-Orange County region.[336] Priced out of home- and land ownership in many regions of Alto Mexico, many low-wage Mexican residents in Alto Mexico have opted for substandard colonia housing—self-built communities in U.S. rural and borderlands areas, that lack basic utilities and services such as clean water and paved streets. Found primarily near the U.S.-Mexico border, and also scattered in Central California, Texas alone hosts more than 2,000 of these colonia communities, populated by more than 400,000 residents who are almost entirely Mexican or other Latina/os, many of them farm workers or industrial workers.[337] Even residents of these substandard houses, largely

---

[336] Joel Kotkin, "What Will Our Latino Future Look Like," http://www.ocregister.com/articles/latino-643803-california-state.html (posted November 30, 2014; last visited December 14, 2014).
[337] Bender, *Tierra y Libertad*, 33-34.

self-built, are more fortunate than many underpaid Mexican laborers in the United States who are not merely landless, but homeless as well, living in cars or sleeping on the ground.

Yet Mexican immigration to the United States is not all low-wage laborers. For example, propelled by spiraling narcoviolence that targets wealthy Mexican families for extortionate kidnappings, wealthy Mexican immigrants in recent years have come to such U.S. cities as El Paso, San Antonio, Houston, and San Diego. Here, many have started businesses in order to qualify for special visa admission granted to wealthy immigrants investing considerable funds in U.S. enterprises. In contrast to U.S. residents migrating to Mexico to take advantage of cheaper living and scenic locations, these wealthy expatriates are seeking safety for their families in a home and business away from the bloody Mexican drug violence addressed in Chapter 7.

* * *

Despite their loss of Southwest land, and the postwar migration of some Mexicans from the Southwest to Mexico described below, we nonetheless went from a Southwest with about 75,000 Mexicans at the time of the 1846-1848 U.S.-Mexican War to more than 22 million Mexican residents today. A key ingredient for this growth, particularly in the last few decades, has been ongoing immigration.[338] Interestingly, much of the growth came recently during a time when U.S. law severely limited annual Mexican migration. In contrast, after the U.S.-Mexican War, and indeed until 1965, no formal numerical limits existed on migration from Mexico to the United States. Rather, Mexicans tended to come, as they still do, when U.S. job opportunities beckoned. A brief history of Mexican migration to the Alto Mexico region confirms this economic draw and its consequences for a Mexico-governed Alto Mexico.

Following the Treaty of Guadalupe Hidalgo at the conclusion of the U.S.-Mexican War in 1848, migration from Mexico to the Southwest was insubstantial and if anything flowed in reverse as some Mexicans returned south of the newly located border, lured by land and compensation to protect that border for Mexico. Around the turn of the century, those crossing the U.S.-Mexico border headed north were more likely to be smuggled Chinese immigrants than Mexican migrants, the former sidestepping the federal Chinese Exclusion Act of 1882 denying their U.S. entry by crossing from the south by stagecoaches, railcars, and burros toward Chinese settlements in Los Angeles or San Francisco. Alt-

---

[338] Jens Manuel Krogstad and Mark Hugo Lopez, "Hispanic Nativity Shift: U.S. Births Drive Population Growth as Immigration Stalls," Pew Research Center, http://www.pewhispanic.org/2014/04/29/hispanic-nativity-shift/ (posted April 29, 2014; last visited June 10, 2014) (noting that immigration outpaced native births from 1980 to 2000 in the United States, but since then the foreign-born percentage of the Latina/o population has been declining).

hough the U.S. Immigration Act of 1924 imposed restrictions on immigration from southern and eastern Europe, and Asians had previously been excluded outright from U.S. entry, labor demands of bustling U.S. industrialism ensured leeway for Mexican workers to enter as needed. Shielded from direct immigration restrictions by Southwestern agriculture and transportation interests, as well as other industrialists, Mexicans benefitted from the so-called Western Hemisphere exemption in the 1924 Act that, in theory, allowed unlimited immigration to the United States from Mexico and other Western Hemisphere countries in furtherance of a good neighbor ethos. The reality was much more restrictive, however, as a variety of discretionary or nebulous administrative controls, such as a head tax, literacy test, and a prohibition on migrants likely to become public charges, were enforced as needed by U.S. officials to exclude Mexicans during times of economic downturn.

Against this regulatory backdrop, the first significant arrival of Mexicans to the United States, primarily destined for the U.S.-governed Alto Mexico region, came during the 1910 decade as U.S. laws excluding Asians; labor demand in agriculture, railroads, meat packing plants, steel mills, and mining; labor shortages during World War I; and the bloody Mexican Revolution, all combined to push and pull Mexicans northward. Opportunities in the Alto Mexican terrain were diverse, and included the sugar beet farms and mills of the Arkansas River Valley in southeastern Colorado which came to rely on Mexican labor by the 1920s.[339] Overall, some 200,000 Mexicans immigrants arrived in the United States during the 1910 decade, with almost 500,000 coming during the 1920s, most of them settling in Alto Mexico with its proximity to Mexico and its long-established Mexican presence.[340] Still, when economic downturns occurred in 1921-1922 and later during the Great Depression, it wasn't enough to merely shut off the administrative faucet to halt further Mexican entry. Public mobs, police, and government officials allied to physically oust Mexicans, even U.S. citizens of Mexican heritage, from the United States when their labor became unneeded and unwelcome. Scholarly estimates of those removed during the Great Depression differ but some 20 percent of the U.S. Mexican population was ousted.[341] Although the repatriation efforts were centered in the more populated areas, particularly Southern California, no reaches of Mexican settlement were unscathed. In Colorado's Arkansas River Valley, for example, Mexican migrant workers in the sugar beet fields were scapegoated when the economy soured in the 1930s. While trying to

---

[339] Tanya W. Kulkosky, "Mexican Migrant Workers in Depression-era Colorado," in *La Gente: Hispano History and Life in Colorado*, ed. Vincent C. De Baca (Denver: Colorado Historical Society, 1998), 122-123.
[340] Bender, *Run for the Border*, 120.
[341] Ibid., 122. Estimates of the number removed range from 350,000 to 600,000. Ibid.

eject Mexican migrant workers, some states concurrently blocked their entry, with Colorado's governor, "Big" Ed Johnson, declaring martial law in 1936 to briefly seal the New Mexico border with National Guard troops in order to "prevent and repel the further invasion of . . . aliens, indigent persons, or invaders," which was apparently directed at migrant workers originating in Mexico and longstanding New Mexican residents of Mexican heritage.[342] Further illustrating the prevailing anti-Mexican sentiment in the region were orange placards posted throughout Colorado warning Mexicans to leave the state at once, "by order of Colorado state vigilantes."[343]

Of course, when labor demand returned within the United States during World War II, Mexicans once again were summoned north, this time under a formal labor recruitment program negotiated by the U.S. and Mexican governments—the Bracero Program—given the imperative for wartime manual labor.[344] Operative until Congress terminated this guest worker program in late 1964, the labor accord drew some 4.8 million Mexican laborers to U.S. employment, often in Southwestern U.S. agriculture or railroad maintenance. Yet even during the pendency of the Bracero Program that U.S. employers relied upon to supply low-wage workers during times of labor demand, a massive scale deportation of undocumented Mexican workers, known as Operation Wetback, coinciding with the so-called Recession of 1953,[345] removed some 3.7 million Latina/os from the United States, most of them Mexican, including U.S. citizens of Mexican origin caught in the military-like deportation sweeps.[346]

In the 1965 Immigration and Nationality Act, for the first time, the United States formally limited migration from Mexico, removing the Western Hemisphere exemption and imposing an overall 120,000 annual hemisphere limit, later restricted in 1976 to just 20,000 permanent visas

---

[342] Kulkosky, "Mexican Migrant Workers," 128; see also Tom I. Romero II, "'A War to Keep Alien Labor Out of Colorado:' The 'Mexican Menace' and the Historical Origins of Local and State Anti-Immigrant Initiatives," in *Strange Neighbors: The Role of States in Immigration Policy*, ed. Carissa Byrne Hessick and Gabriel J. Chin (New York: New York University Press, 2014), 63.
[343] Romero, "Alien Labor," 83.
[344] Bender, *Run for the Border*, 122-123 (suggesting how the agricultural labor shortage may have been contrived by growers to avoid unionization and the payment of fair wages).
[345] "Recession of 1953," http://en.wikipedia.org/wiki/Recession_of_1953 (last visited November 21, 2013).
[346] Despite the existence of the Western Hemisphere exemption at the time that allowed unlimited migration from Mexico, given the lax border enforcement many Mexicans came as undocumented migrants either to avoid the administrative requirements of entry such as the head tax or, with the complicity of border guards, to enter the United States freed from the wage and other protections, albeit minimal, of the Bracero Program and thus more desirable to employers. See Bender, *Run for the Border*, 124.

annually per-country (including Mexico), together with the possibility of reunification with immediate relatives and various temporary entry programs such as those for farm workers, themselves subject to limits. With the Bracero Program terminated and the new Mexican entry restrictions operative at the same time, but with U.S. employers continuing to demand cheap labor, Mexican workers still came north, only now as vulnerable, undocumented workers. The U.S. workforce, particularly in agriculture, swelled with undocumented workers living in the shadows. Signed by President Reagan, the Immigration Reform and Control Act of 1986 made possible the permanent residency, and potentially the U.S. citizenship, of between 2.7 and 3.1 million undocumented workers, most of them from Mexico.[347] But despite expensive efforts to fortify the U.S.-Mexico border against further undocumented entry, millions of undocumented Mexican workers crossed in the 1990s and 2000s to their U.S. field of dreams and other U.S. employment opportunities.

In sum, at least 22 million residents of Mexican descent—the clear majority of them noncitizen immigrants with proper authorization or U.S. citizens, including descendants of the original Spanish and Mexican settlers in Alto Mexico before the U.S.-Mexican War, now live in the U.S. Southwest, not counting possibly a few million undocumented Mexican immigrants. A Mexico-governed Alto Mexico, surely, would have at least that many Mexican residents. The touchstone, of course, is jobs, as Mexican immigrants have always come to the United States to pursue economic opportunity, not welfare handouts, and Mexico generally does not offer such financial assistance.[348] Although it is hard to predict the economic climate of Alto Mexico, as Chapter 3 revealed, a number of factors suggest that jobs would have been plentiful and thus migration within Mexico toward a Mexico-governed Alto Mexico would be similar to, if not eclipse, the current historical record of Mexican migration north to the U.S.-governed Southwest.[349] Rich agricultural land, better

---

[347] Ibid., 128 (about 750,000 of these workers were farm workers).

[348] Mexico City offers unemployment benefits to those having worked in Mexico City for at least six months.

[349] One variable suggesting a lower Mexican population in the region is the potential Anglo population of the region, as a number of Mexican jobs in Alto Mexico today are those servicing the millions of Anglo residences and residents.

Also worth considering is the potential impact on the rest of Mexico of an increased Mexican population in a Mexico-governed Alto Mexico. Presumably that would mean fewer Mexicans living in the rest of Mexico, which prompts interesting speculation about where in Mexico the population numbers might be lower. One possibility is along the current U.S.-Mexico border, with several cities boosted by the maquiladora economy, and previously the sin economy as discussed in Chapter 7. As Chapter 7 suggests, if the maquiladora economy simply moved north along the Alto Mexico/United 44 States border, then the current northern Mexico border states and cities such as Tijuana, Mexicali, and Ciudad Juárez presumably would have less of an employment draw without the dominant maquila economy, and would be much smaller in size. Of equal note,

access to water than in northern Mexico, tourist havens from ski resorts to the Grand Canyon reliant on low-wage labor, temperate climate drawing Anglo retirees needing homes and ongoing services and extensive petroleum and mineral reserves, all signal the potential for significant Mexican migration. As explained in Chapter 7, in recent decades significant migration occurred within Mexico to its northern border states to take advantage of borderlands factories paying higher wages than many jobs elsewhere in Mexico. Mexican residents, in the interest of survival and opportunity, have demonstrated their willingness to migrate, whether to these borderlands or further to the U.S. interior, and no doubt they would have come in significant numbers to a Mexico-governed Alto Mexico.

In contrast to the harrowing immigration experience of many Mexicans entering the Southwest under current restrictive U.S. law, Mexicans migrating to and staying within a Mexico-governed Alto Mexico would have faced none of the restrictions and upheaval endured by today's Mexican entrants. Particularly, Mexicans in Alto Mexico would have avoided abusive repatriation campaigns such as those during the Great Depression and Operation Wetback, which focused on ousting Mexicans from the Southwest. But most important, after 1965 when almost every migration from Mexico became unlawful and even family reunifications faced decade waits or longer, Alto Mexico migrations would not have put Mexican migrant lives in peril when they merely sought a chance at economic survival. As explained in Chapter 7, after the United States fortified the border in the mid-1990s, undocumented entrants from Mexico no longer crossed in or near urban areas. Rather, they undertook perilous crossings in remote deserts and mountainous terrain of California, Arizona, New Mexico, and Texas. As revealed in a 2009 ACLU report, an estimated 5,600 migrants died during their Mexican border crossing since the mid-1990s build-up redirected their routes.[350] Even more disturbingly, for every one of the bodies discovered, countless others are never found, as they are literally swallowed by the desert and uncounted in the already substantial death toll. Migrant crossers died every imaginable, heartbreaking way. Most died from the harsh elements of scorching heat in isolated desert crossings where guides (known as coyotes) can lose their way. Others fell victim to surprise snowstorms and accompanying freezing temperatures on mountainous

---

many Mexico bordertown residents work in the United States with daily commuter visas, servicing homes and businesses in U.S. bordertowns. These jobs too would migrate to the Alto Mexico/United 44 States border, assuming the similar dynamic of significant cities located on the U.S.-side of the border, as in the case of such current U.S. bordertowns as San Diego and El Paso.

[350] Of course, some of these migrants who perished might have been Central Americans, but having successfully navigated the southern Mexico border, they would not have encountered additional obstacles akin to the U.S.-Mexico border in reaching jobs in Alto Mexico.

routes. Some drowned while crossing swift border channels such as the All-American Canal that runs along the California-Mexico border. Others perished in flash floods after desert downpours on unyielding ground. Still others died in wildfires, or when smuggled in suffocating railcars (for example, in 2002 when 11 migrants were discovered dead in Iowa inside a sealed railcar from Mexico) or trucks (as when 19 immigrants died in 2003 while transported in a stifling 18-wheeler within Texas). Many others died in transport within the Southwest, as when nine migrants perished in a 2006 crash when a Chevy Suburban in the Arizona borderlands with 22 migrants crammed inside, chased by the Border Patrol, overturned after speeding across a spike strip positioned to blow its tires. Advocates for human rights, myself included, lament each of these thousands of deaths as needless loss against the reality that U.S. jobs await those who survive the deadly gauntlet of undocumented entry.[351] In a Mexico-governed Alto Mexico, at least, no Mexican migrant would have to die during his or her journey to a job.[352]

* * *

Alto Mexico, today, is home to other racial and ethnic groups than Anglos and Mexicans. In addition to considering the Mexican composition of a Mexico-governed Alto Mexico, this chapter addresses the likely status of some of these other groups (indigenous peoples, black and Chinese residents, and so-called trans-migrants emigrating from Central and South American countries such as Guatemala and Honduras) in today's Alto Mexico terrain. Overall, as revealed by the discussion below, the differences for the presence and prosperity of these groups between a U.S.- and a Mexico-governed Alto Mexico are more subtle than stark.

Indigenous peoples of the Americas predated Spanish and other European entry and conquests in the region by many thousand years, migrating into North and South America during the Ice Age through the frozen Bering Strait. Archeology sites within Alto Mexico have dated tribal presence to at least 9000 B.C. in California's Mohave Desert, and between 11,000 and 8,000 B.C. for a Lewisville, Texas site, near Dallas, as

---

[351] Of course, almost half (45 percent in a 2006 study) of unauthorized migrants entered the United States lawfully and then overstayed their visas, or entered at checkpoints using stolen day commuter visas in the borderlands.

[352] Drug cartels have taken to kidnapping and terrorizing migrants in Mexico, sometimes to steal money from them or extort their relatives, other times to gain involuntary smugglers in the cartel's operations. So long as drug demand remained high in the remaining U.S. states, the same dynamics of murderous drug cartels and immigrant peril may take place, although one difference would be that Mexican migrants would no doubt employ more reliable means of transportation to jobs rather than using the highways and on-foot crossings through Northern Mexico that leave migrants in peril. As today, the migrant victims of drug cartel terror would tend to be vulnerable undocumented Central American migrants.

native inhabitants moved south and east.[353] Mexican sites farther south reveal the development of a farming culture by around 5000 B.C. that led indigenous tribes to adopt a sedentary village lifestyle.[354] Centuries before the arrival of European immigrants, indigenous societies like the Anasazi in today's states of New Mexico, Colorado, Utah, and Arizona lived in villages and farmed, while California was the most populated indigenous territory within Alto Mexico.[355] In the same way that Anglo immigrants devastated native populations in the Eastern United States and elsewhere with newly introduced diseases, Spanish settlers within Mexico and the Alto Mexico terrain decimated almost all the indigenous people, who lacked natural immunity to these imported pathogens, prompting deadly outbreaks of diphtheria, pneumonia, measles, small-pox, and venereal diseases. [356] The region's indigenous population declined radically as these epidemics swept native villages.[357] At the same time, offspring of Spanish settlers and indigenous peoples created the mestizo identity of mixed racial and cultural heritage that has since defined Mexico.

When Spanish settlers first arrived near today's Santa Fe, New Mexi-co, in 1598, later establishing it as the capital of a Spanish province, indigenous peoples had long populated the area. In contrast to the An-glo experience of settling the United States by driving out indigenous populations, Spanish and mestizo settlers within Alto Mexico aimed to convert native residents to "civilization" in the Spanish mission culture without ousting and relocating them, perhaps because land was plenti-ful in relation to the few Spanish settlers in the region. Missions were established throughout the Alto Mexico terrain, primarily in today's California (the site of twenty-one missions), New Mexico, and Texas (where twenty-nine missions were built). These Spanish missions had two ap-parent aims—to baptize indigenous residents into Christianity, as was done for nearly half a million natives in California,[358] and to exploit na-tive labor in the agricultural economy surrounding the missions. Despite the ostensible protection of Spanish law in 1512 governing Mexico and Alto Mexico that declared Indians as wards of the church and the crown, to be protected and Christianized,[359] natives were effectively treated as slave labor in a peonage system to support the Spanish mission econo-

---

[353] Martha Menchaca, *Recovering History, Constructing Race: The Indian, Black, and White Roots of Mexican Americans* (Austin: University of Texas, 2001), 26-27.
[354] Ibid., 27.
[355] Ibid., 31.
[356] Steven W. Hackel, *Children of Coyote, Missionaries of Saint Francis: Indian-Spanish Relations in Colonial California, 1769-1850* (Chapel Hill, NC: University of North Carolina Press, 2005), 113-115.
[357] Ibid., 58.
[358] Menchaca, *Recovering History*, 140.
[359] Ibid., 51.

my.[360] When Mexico won its independence from Spain, natives faired poorly despite legislation to dismantle slavery and to declare all groups—including natives, mestizos, and descendants (afromestizos) of relationships between African slaves and Spaniards—as equal Mexican citizens.[361] When the Mexican government secularized missions in Alto Mexico in 1833, and the economy shifted from a Spanish mission-based system to one supported by large rancho estates in private hands carved out of the mission lands, most natives lost their meager landholdings they had gained near the missions.[362] By the 1840s, many of California's 64,000 Christianized Indians[363] moved their labor to the Mexican rancho estates, controlled by a handful of Spanish/Mexican settlers and their descendants, supplying essentially free manual labor to sustain that rancho economy.[364]

By no means did the Spanish mission system Christianize all the Alto Mexico natives. Rather, indigenous nations such as the Apache, Navajo, Comanche, and Shoshone controlled extensive terrain within Alto Mexico and resisted Spanish, and then Mexican, efforts to conquer them. By the time of the U.S.-Mexican War, natives routinely raided Spanish/Mexican and Anglo ranchos and settlements within Alto Mexico, and in turn endured counter raids aiming to pacify the tribes, with all sides suffering significant casualties.[365] Despite the admonishment of Mexico's president in 1835 that Apache and Comanche tribes were in fact Mexican citizens yet to be tamed and "civilized,"[366] the reality was that these tribes within Alto Mexico never voluntarily recognized their governance by Spain, Mexico or, later, the United States in the wake of the U.S.-Mexican War. The violent conflict with tribes in Alto Mexico drew the attention of negotiators of the Treaty of Guadalupe Hidalgo, prompting an article obligating the United States to restrain ongoing tribal raids into Mexico's now dramatically smaller post-war territory, reading:

> Considering that a great part of the territories, which, by the present treaty, are to comprehended for the future within the limits of the United States, is now occupied by savage tribes, who will hereafter be under the exclusive control of the Gov-

---

[360] Liebman, *California Farmland*, 177.
[361] Menchaca, *Recovering History*, 159.
[362] Hackel, *Children of Coyote*, 374, 387.
[363] Menchaca, *Recovering History*, 209.
[364] Hackel, *Children of Coyote*, 389. Some Indians acculturated into the Spanish/Mexican culture succeeded in gaining their own rancho land grants from government officials. Ibid., 390.
[365] Bender, *Run for the Border*, 16; Brian DeLay, *War of a Thousand Deserts: Indian Raids and the U.S.-Mexican War* (New Haven, CT: Yale University Press, 2008), xv.
[366] Brian DeLay, "Independent Indians and the U.S.-Mexican War," *American Historical Review* 112 (February 2007): 35.

ernment of the United States, and whose incursions within the
territory of Mexico would be prejudicial in the extreme, it is
solemnly agreed that all such incursions shall be forcibly re-
strained by the Government of the United States whensoever
this may be necessary; and that when they cannot be prevented, they shall be punished by the said Government, and
satisfaction for the same shall be exacted—all in the same way,
and with equal diligence and energy, as if the same incursions
were mediated or committed within its own territory, against
its own citizens.[367]

Raids continued despite this treaty protection, and mounting Mexican
claims for restitution against the U.S. government prompted the United
States to buy its way out of the treaty's anti-raiding obligations as part of
the 1854 Gadsden Purchase. Today, some twenty-six U.S. federally recognized tribes occupy the U.S.-Mexico borderlands, in many instances
with their homelands severed by the current border, and 149 tribes
overall reside in the four U.S.-Mexico border states.[368]

Presumably, in the absence of the U.S.-Mexican War, these hostilities within Alto Mexico between indigenous tribes and Spanish/Mexican
settlers and their descendants would have continued with the outcome
dependent on how many military resources Mexico would have devoted
to suppress the raids in its northern territory. Potentially, these tribes
may have secured and maintained their independent territory within a
Mexico-governed Alto Mexico. Far more likely, as within Mexico today,
natives would have been conquered and subjected to a dichotomy of ostensible equal citizenship under Mexican law, while subordinated in
Mexico's economy and society in ways that still provoke outcry and rebellion, most notably in the ongoing struggle for recognition and rights
among indigenous residents of the southern Mexican state of Chiapas,
which has the highest concentration of indigenous residents in Mexico.[369] Today, Mexico's indigenous people suffer the highest illiteracy and
disease rates in the country,[370] and comprise a majority of the Mexican
population below the poverty line.[371] Among the foremost demands of
the Zapatista rebellion in Chiapas, drawing its name from Mexican
Revolution hero Emiliano Zapata and issuing its first public statement
on the day NAFTA took effect, is land rights, as evidenced by a negotia-

---

[367] Treaty of Guadalupe Hidalgo, art. XI.

[368] Bender, *Run for the Border*, 18.

[369] See generally George A. Collier and Elizabeth Lowery Quaratiello, *Basta!:
Land & The Zapatista Rebellion in Chiapas* (Oakland, CA: Food First Books, rev.
ed. 1999).

[370] Amy Chua, *World on Fire: How Exporting Free Market Democracy Breeds
Ethnic Hatred and Global Instability* (New York: Anchor Books, 2004), 59.

[371] Martínez, *Mexico's Uneven Development*, 57 (noting 79 percent of Mexico's
indigenous language-speakers were impoverished in 2010, albeit an improve-
ment over the 85 percent poverty rate in 2000).

tion agenda declaring: "Land is for the Indians and peasants who work for it, not for the large landlords. We demand that the copious lands in the hands of ranchers, foreign and national landlords, and other non-peasants be turned over to our communities, which totally lack land."[372] Dispossession of native lands in Mexico dates to the nineteenth century, where prerogatives of railroad development and wealthy foreigner interests trumped indigenous communal land holdings that the Mexican Revolution failed to restore.[373]

In contrast to the Spanish efforts to Christianize natives in Alto Mexico while sparring with tribes hostile to being conquered and assimilated into the Spanish mission and then the Mexican rancho economy and culture, the United States aimed to, and effectively did, exterminate, displace, isolate, and relocate tribes to less desirable agricultural terrain. Most infamously, the United States forced natives off their ancestral homelands onto distant reservations,[374] and through just one of those relocations caused one-fourth (an estimated 4,000 natives) of the Cherokee tribal nation to perish in their removal along the 1,000-mile Trail of Tears. When the United States seized ownership of Alto Mexico, an estimated 150,000 natives lived in California and, at the earlier time of its secession and independence, 80,000 in Texas. But by the end of the nineteenth century only about 25,000 survived in California, where the state government paid bounties on Indian heads, and only a couple thousand natives remained in Texas by 1875.[375]

Given these differences in conquering and subjugating natives in U.S. and Mexico-governed territory, it is difficult to predict how natives would have perished or prospered within a Mexico-governed Alto Mexico, particularly for those tribes unwilling to recognize Mexican control over their terrain. Clearly, Spanish/Mexican settlers and their descendants took the best land in Alto Mexico away from indigenous

---

[372] Collier and Quaratiello, *Basta!*, 64 (citing Zapatistas' 34-point agenda for negotiation in 1994).

[373] Shelley Brown Hatfield, *Chasing Shadows: Indians Along the United States-Mexico Border 1876-1911* (Albuquerque: University of New Mexico Press, 1998), 5, 142; Ethelia Ruiz Medrano, *Mexico's Indigenous Communities: Their Lands and Histories, 1500-2010* (Boulder, CO: University Press of Colorado, 2010) (describing how the policies of Mexican President Díaz in the late nineteenth century facilitated the divestment of vacant lands from Mexican Indians).

[374] See DeLay, *War of a Thousand Deserts*, 308 (describing how southern plains Indians left Texas in the 1860s for reservations in the Indian Territory of Oklahoma); Edward H. Spicer, *Cycles of Conquest: The Impact of Spain, Mexico, and the United States on the Indians of the Southwest, 1533-1960* (Tucson: University of Arizona Press, 1962), 345 (discussing how the Spanish and Mexican approach to incorporate natives into the nation as citizens was distinct from the Anglo approach to remove and isolate them using reservations).

[375] Felipe Fernández-Armesto, *Our America: A Hispanic History of the United States* (New York: W.W. Norton & Company, 2014), 177-179.

occupants,[376] as did Anglo settlers within the U.S.-governed South-west.[377] Nonetheless, natives who labored in the missions or ranchos sometimes secured modest land titles, and, in the Mexican state of Tejas, natives controlled about a third of the terrain.[378] In the aftermath of the U.S.-Mexican War, U.S. officials within Alto Mexico struggled to figure out how to treat rights and titles of the native population. Were they en-titled to the scant protections of other Mexicans secured under the Treaty of Guadalupe Hidalgo, or did they deserve less protection and even targeting for extermination?[379] Tribes not Christianized by the Spanish/Mexican government fared the least well, as the U.S. declared them enemies of the state and forcibly relocated them as desired to make way for Anglo settlements, with few natives surviving.[380] Even for so-called Christianized Indians, the United States failed to recognize them as equal citizens. For example, California's initial state constitu-tion denied Indians the right to vote.[381] In summary, whether in Mexico or the United States, indigenous residents remain marginalized and out-side the realm of a truly equal society and opportunity.

* * *

Chinese Americans comprise the largest Asian group in Alto Mexico's most populous state, California, with the 2010 Census counting 1.25 mil-lion Chinese residents. Most Chinese immigrants to the United States during the last two centuries settled on the West Coast, particularly in California with the lure of the Gold Rush, and within bustling San Fran-cisco, which serviced the Gold Rush industry.[382] U.S. laws, and those of

---

[376] Menchaca, *Recovering History*, 152 (describing the ways in which Spanish settlers took possession of tribal land).

[377] Cf. Gómez, *Manifest Destinies*, 56 (discussing how the Mexican government's declaration of equality of mestizos and Indians backfired for the Pueblo Indians of New Mexico, as mestizo settlers challenged the size of their land allowances and encroached on their territory).

[378] Fernández-Armesto, *Our America*, 177.ch

[379] Menchaca, *Recovering History*, 229-230 (stating that by the early 1860s, most nomadic Indian tribes in the Southwest were exterminated and those surviving, such as natives from the Comanches, were placed on reservations or, as in the case of the Apaches and Karankawas, pushed south into Mexico). On the uncer-tain land rights of Pueblo Indians in New Mexico, see *United States v. Joseph*, 94 U.S. 614 (1876); Christine A. Klein, "Treaties of Conquest: Property Rights, Indi-an Treaties, and the Treaty of Guadalupe Hidalgo," *New Mexico Law Review* 26 (1996): 201.

[380] Ibid., 223 (observing that the nomadic Indian population of California once under U.S. control decreased from 310,000 in 1850 to just 50,000 five years later).

[381] Ibid., 220.

[382] See Linda Heidenreich, *"This Land Was Mexican Once": Histories of Re-sistance from Northern California* (Austin: University of Texas Press, 2007), 152-166 (describing the impetus for Chinese migration and the violence and dis-crimination they faced in Northern California).

California, were particularly hostile toward Chinese immigrants, despite their vital labor contribution in the mines, in their building of the trans-continental railroad (resulting in the deaths of more than 1,200 Chinese), and elsewhere in the U.S. economy. The federal Chinese Exclusion Act of 1882 precluded Chinese immigration and their citizenship, while California's Alien Land Law barred Chinese (and other Asian immigrants) from purchasing or leasing land, with the intent of prohibiting Chinese and Japanese immigrants from controlling agricultural property in the state.[383] As described in Chapter 3, California's foreigner miner's tax enacted in 1850 favored Anglo settlers over Chinese and Mexican workers perceived as interlopers unentitled to share the state's mineral wealth of the Gold Rush era. Even local governments targeted Chinese residents with discriminatory laws, as San Francisco notoriously favored Anglo applicants for laundromat business permits, while denying applications from Chinese businessmen on unfounded safety concerns.[384]

With its encouragement of Chinese immigration at the same time the United States prohibited Chinese entry, Mexico seemingly was a more attractive destination for Chinese. In turn, the invitation of Chinese migration facially suggests that a Mexico-governed Alto Mexico might have received far more Chinese migrants than those Chinese who came to the United States in significant numbers. In reality, Mexico was no safe haven for Chinese migrants, who encountered restrictive laws and prejudices akin to those they faced in California and elsewhere in the United States. Presumably, then, Chinese would have migrated to a Mexico-governed Alto Mexico in similar numbers to those who came to the Western United States.

Once the United States barred Chinese entry, Chinese immigrants came in significant numbers to Mexico, settling especially in the northern Mexico regions near the U.S. border. By 1926, Chinese in Mexico, numbering more than 24,000 residents, constituted Mexico's second-largest immigrant group.[385] Mexico solicited them as agricultural laborers, but Chinese entrepreneurs soon found success in northern Mexico as merchants of groceries and dry goods, while other Chinese came to Mexico as a launching point for entering the United States surreptitiously as undocumented immigrants. Chinese immigrants were overwhelmingly male, and the same derogatory stereotypes that plagued Chinese immigrants in the United States affected their residency in Mexico. Particularly within the Mexican border state of Sonora, which includes 365 miles of U.S.-Mexico border frontage used to smuggle undocumented Chinese into the United States, and which hosts the twin

---

[383] Bender, *Tierra y Libertad*, 71.
[384] Ibid., 78 (also describing San Francisco's boarding house ordinance that facially protected against residential overcrowding but was a proxy for anti-Chinese sentiment).
[385] Robert Chao Romero, *The Chinese in Mexico 1882-1940* (Tucson: University of Arizona Press, 2010), 1.

city to Nogales, Arizona—Nogales, Sonora, virulent anti-Chinese sentiment surfaced during the Mexican Revolution. Fears of economic and
romantic competition from male Chinese storeowners perceived as dangerous foreign interlopers fueled the anti-Chinese campaign centered in
Sonora. Consequently, Chinese were driven from the region, and even
beaten and killed by the hundreds throughout Mexico.[386] At the same
time that U.S. Southwestern cities and states were forcibly repatriating
Mexicans to Mexico, the Mexican state of Sonora was ousting Chinese,
many of them leaving for the United States, while others returned to
China or hid within Mexico.[387] Augmenting the private campaign to ter-
rorize and oust Chinese, Sonora enacted discriminatory laws against
them, including a 1923 law prohibiting marriage between Chinese men
and Mexican women.[388]

The campaign to oust Chinese from Mexico was successful, as Mexico's Chinese population fell to fewer than 5,000 by 1940, and to just 92
residents in Sonora.[389] Although vibrant Chinese enclaves survived in
Mexico, such as in bordertown Mexicali, as one scholar put it, "To this
day, the Chinese immigrant community of Mexico has never recov-
ered."[390] Likely, then, the Chinese would have fared no better in a
Mexico-governed Alto Mexico than within the Southwest under U.S.
governance.

* * *

Since the Civil War, African Americans came west in search of economic
opportunity. For example, 25,000 blacks migrated to Portland, Oregon
during World War II to build ships for the military, although they were
urged to "go back home" after the war. Oregon, and the rest of the
Western United States, never welcomed black residents, with Oregon
law once forbidding blacks from settling in the region. Today, millions
of African Americans nonetheless live within Alto Mexico—2.3 million
in California and 3 million in Texas (about 500,000 in Houston alone,
the fourth largest black population in the United States), with much
smaller numbers in the other U.S. states that comprise Alto Mexico. As
detailed in Chapter 1, African Americans first came to Texas, when it was
the Mexican state of Coahuila y Tejas, as slaves of Anglo immigrants.

[386] Grace Peña Delgado, *Making the Chinese Mexican: Global Migration, Local-
ism, and the Exclusion in the U.S.-Mexico Borderlands* (Stanford, CA: Stanford
University Press, 2012), 105 (describing the murder of hundreds of Chinese
throughout Mexico as the "culmination of a nationalistic campaign that played
on the anxieties that Mexicans harbored about their own economic security,
their racial identity, and their role in the revolutionary project").
[387] Julia María Schiavone Camacho, *Chinese Mexicans: Transpacific Migration
and the Search for a Homeland, 1910-1960* (Chapel Hill, NC: University of North
Carolina Press, 2012), 68-69.
[388] Ibid., 49.
[389] Ibid., 70.
[390] Ibid. (quoting Robert Chao Romero).

The post-Civil War emancipation led many freed black slaves to migrate to Houston, joined throughout the next decades by rural blacks.[391] Whether a Mexico-governed Alto Mexico would include a similar black population turns on the same dominant factor for its Mexican and Anglo population—the extent of jobs over time that lured residents from other parts of the Americas. In contrast, given the relative absence of jobs in the Mexican interior as described in Chapter 5, most U.S. residents migrating to Mexico since the U.S.-Mexican War have done so either recently to retire or to enjoy Mexican resorts as part-time vacation residents, or to flee persecution and prosecution in the United States, as in the case of Mormons who fled the Alto Mexico terrain of Utah during the second half of the 19th century for northern Mexico, and Confederates from the U.S. South who fled to then French-controlled Mexico in 1865 at the conclusion of the Civil War, some to avoid imprisonment.[392] Similarly, black fugitive slaves before the Civil War fled Texas for Mexico, where the Mexican government offered sanctuary by refusing to extradite them back to their Anglo masters in the United States. But apart from the entry of these fugitive slaves, there have not been any significant migrations of U.S. blacks into Mexico, likely given the lesser financial opportunities there.

Stemming from the entry of some 200,000 African slaves when Spain controlled Mexico[393] rather than from the entry of U.S. blacks, a considerable number of Mexico residents today have direct African roots. The emphasis among U.S. anti-immigrant zealots on the Mexican national origin of most migrants to the United States in recent years obscures the reality that many of these migrants are black. A colorline dynamic in Mexico contributing to this northward migration is the longstanding discrimination there based on skin color. Whether in media, government, business leadership, or other professions of power and affluence, lighter-skinned Mexicans dominate, while darker-skinned Mexicans, whether of indigenous or African roots, are disproportionately poor.[394] Expectedly, then, a significant number of desperate Mexican migrants drawn north for low-wage employment in the United States have black and indigenous roots.

Discrimination on colorlines prevails in Mexico despite its longstanding abolition of de jure discrimination against blacks (and in-

---

[391] John D. Márquez, *Black-Brown Solidarity: Racial Politics in the New Gulf South* (Austin: University of Texas Press, 2013), 46-49 (describing how Latino/a residents surpassed blacks in number by 2000, after a century of a black population in Houston almost triple in size).

[392] Bender, *Run for the Border*, 13-14.

[393] Christina A. Sue, *Land of the Cosmic Race: Race Mixture, Racism, and Blackness in Mexico* (New York: Oxford University Press, 2013), 11 (noting that blacks outnumbered whites in Mexico for many years in its colonial history); see also Menchaca, *Recovering History*, 43 (noting that estimates of the number of black slaves brought to Mexico range from 150,000 to 200,000).

[394] Ibid., 6.

digenous communities), whether through its abolition of slavery decades before the United States, or through its early enactment after
independence from Spain of equality of citizenship through equal voting,
marriage, and land ownership rights.[395] Within the United States, black-
Mexican tensions have resulted in violence in immigrant communities
when Mexican immigrants bring their anti-black sentiments into the
United States, which fosters its own engrained culture of anti-black sub-
ordination.[396] The upshot is that whether in a Mexico- or U.S.-governed
Alto Mexico, black residents would face discrimination and violence, despite the longstanding declaration of equality for all groups in Mexico,
and the recent framing in the United States of a "postracial" society with
a supposed absence of de jure or de facto discrimination on color and
racial lines.[397] For black residents, then, a Mexico-governed Alto Mexico
would be no panacea for continuing and systemic racial inequalities in
education, housing, job opportunities, and beyond.

* * *

Yet another group likely to have fared equally poorly in a Mexico-
governed Alto Mexico is trans-migrants—those migrants to the United
States who enter the country through Mexico, and who are mostly un-
documented and primarily originating from the Central American
countries of El Salvador, Guatemala, Honduras and, to a lesser extent,
Nicaragua. These trans-migrants are often youth fleeing poverty and
violence, the latter sometimes sparked by the illicit drug trade serving
U.S. residents, or by gangs anchored by deportees from the United
States.[398] Lacking documentation both to enter the United States and
Mexico, these migrants often must brave traveling the entire length of
Mexico before reaching the United States, where they may need to repeat their undocumented crossing through yet another more fortified
border. Annually, estimates range from 100,000 to 400,000 Central
American trans-migrants crossing Mexico headed for U.S. employers,
primarily in the Los Angeles or San Francisco metropolitan areas.[399] In
2014, considerable numbers of youths fleeing violence in Central Ameri-

---

[395] Martha Menchaca, *Naturalizing Mexican Immigrants: A Texas History* (Austin: University of Texas Press, 2011), 19.
[396] See generally Tanya K. Hernandez, "Roots of Latino/Black Anger," *Los Angeles Times*, http://touch.latimes.com/#section/-1/article/p2p-27229891/ (posted
January 7, 2007; last visited June 1, 2014).
[397] See generally Bender, *Mea Culpa*, ch. 9.
[398] See Robert J. Lopez, Rich Connell, and Chris Kraul, "Gang Uses Deportation
to Its Advantage to Flourish in U.S.," http://touch.latimes.com/#section/-
1/article/p2p-21115923/ (posted October 30, 2005; last visited September 21, 2014)
(describing growth of Mala Salvatrucha gang network).
[399] See Raquel Aldana, Won Kidane, Beth Lyon, and Karla McKanders, *Global
Issues in Immigration Law* (St. Paul, MN: West Academic Publishing, 2013), 133
(100,000 estimate with 2005 as the peak year).

ca journeyed to the United States, creating a humanitarian crisis. Alto Mexico is the primary destination for most of these trans-migrants. Of the 1.8 million Salvadoran residents in the United States, half live in the two Alto Mexico states of California (36 percent) and Texas (13 percent).[400] Thirty-two percent of the estimated 1.2 million U.S. Guatemalan residents live in California.[401] Smaller numbers of Hondurans (702,000 as of 2011, 14 percent of them in Texas) and Nicaraguans (395,000, 31 percent in California alone) live in the United States. Presumably these census figures poorly count undocumented trans-migrants, most of whom reside in Alto Mexico.

If they reach the United States, these trans-migrants are subjected to the same deportation regime as other U.S. undocumented immigrants, seen notably in the workplace raid and mass deportation in 2008 of 398 mostly Mayan undocumented workers from Guatemala, employed at a kosher meatpacking plant in Postville, Iowa. Adding to the gauntlet they face, however, is the likelihood of their kidnapping, rape, or extortion along the migrant journey at the hands of Mexican drug cartels and others who take advantage of their vulnerable status traveling through Mexico, until recently accomplished by clinging to the roofs of train cars.[402] In one wrenching example from 2010, 72 Central and South American trans-migrants were killed for what is thought to be their refusal to assist a Mexican cartel in smuggling drugs to U.S. users. Augmenting this private terrorism against trans-migrants is the government immigration enforcement emphasis undertaken by Mexico in recent years to intercept and deport trans-migrants. Modeling its enforcement after the United States, Mexico established dozens of detention centers and a national immigration enforcement institute that

[400] Seth Motel and Eileen Patten, "Hispanics of Salvadoran Origin in the United States, 2010," Pew Research Center, http://www.pewhispanic.org/2012/06/27/hispanics-of-salvadoran-origin-in-the-united-states-2010/ (posted June 27, 2012; last visited June 10, 2014).
[401] Anna Brown and Eileen Patten, "Hispanics of Guatemalan Origin in the United States, 2011," http://www.pewhispanic.org/2013/06/19/hispanics-of-guatemalan-origin-in-the-united-states-2011/ (posted June 19, 2013; last visited June 10, 2014).
[402] For one young trans-migrant's harrowing journey through Mexico, and into the United States by fording the Rio Grande, see Sonia Nazario, *Enrique's Journey* (New York: Random House, 2006) (includes discussion of the unfriendliness trans-migrants face in the Mexican border state of Chiapas as compared to the more tolerant states of Oaxaca and Veracruz). For discussion of the variety of dangers trans-migrants face in Mexico, see Amnesty International, "Invisible Victims: Migrants on the Move in Mexico," http://www.amnesty.org/en/library/asset/AMR41/014/2010/en/8459f0ac-03ce-4302-8bd2-3305bdae9cde/amr410142010eng.pdf (comprehensive report published in 2010 before Mexico immigration reforms in 2011). Recently, crackdowns by the Mexican government along the train routes have forced migrants onto other equally perilous migration routes.

in its 2005 peak deported 235,297 undocumented foreigners from Mexico, most of them trans-migrants, 43 percent of them Guatemalans.[403] As with U.S. enforcement efforts directed at Mexican immigrants and Central American trans-migrants, the heightened Mexico-Guatemala border enforcement only increased the risk and cost of the trans-migrant's journey, prompting more reliance on oppressive human trafficking networks.

A glimmer of hope from Mexico was its adoption in 2011 of migratory law reform which supplies due process protections to undocumented migrants in their expulsion, and commits to their safety while in Mexico regardless of their immigration status.[404] A few years earlier, Mexico decriminalized migration without papers from a criminal violation to a civil one, landing intercepted migrants in a detention facility rather than a standard jail. Mexico's government, vocal in its condemnation of restrictive U.S. immigration enforcement policies, long faced criticism over its own poor treatment of trans-migrants despite its ratification of human rights treaties such as the International Convention on the Protection of the Rights of All Migrant Workers and Members of Their Families, which the United States has failed to join. Although it is too early to discern whether conditions in Mexico for trans-migrants will improve with these reforms, initial reports are disappointing. Mexico's Programa Frontera Sur (South Border Program), announced in 2014 and suspected of being prompted and funded by the United States, dramatically increased deportation raids on trans-migrants by Mexican police and immigration officials, reducing the number of trans-migrants making it to the U.S. border, but endangering the lives of migrants forced into more perilous routes through Mexico that place them at the mercy of cartels.[405] Aggravated by this program, Central American trans-migrants arguably face greater threats to their lives and safety while traveling in Mexico than once in the United States. Presumably the same threats would imperil those Central American migrants seeking passage through, or refuge and work in, a Mexico-governed Alto Mexico likely beset by similar drug cartel violence, as the next chapter suggests.[406]

---

[403] Rodolfo Casillas, "The Dark Side of Globalized Migration: The Rise and Peak of Criminal Networks—The Case of Central Americans in Mexico," *Globalizations* 8:3 (2011): 295, 298. See also González-Murphy, *Protecting Immigrant Rights*, 60-63 (describing militarization of Mexico's southern region against undocumented immigrants and the role of the United States in prompting such efforts).

[404] Aldana, Kidane, Lyon, and McKanders, *Global Issues in Immigration Law*, 137-145.

[405] Joseph Sorrentino, "How the U.S. 'Solved' the Central American Migrant Crisis," http://inthesetimes.com/article/17916/how-the-u.s.-solved-the-central-american-migrant-crisis (posted May 12, 2015; last visited August 18, 2015).

[406] If anything, that ill treatment might be more intense, as the better regard for trans-migrants by residents of Mexican states away from the Guatemala-Mexico

7. ON THE ALTO MEXICO BORDER

This isn't the real Mexico. You know that. All border towns bring out the worst in a country.

—Mexican Federal Narcotics Agent, Miguel "Mike" Vargas
(Charlton Heston), in Orson Welles's *Touch of Evil* (1958)

Borderlands terrain is ground zero for influencing and implementing U.S. immigration and drug enforcement policy, which in recent decades has emphasized fortifying the border. Accordingly, this chapter explores the Alto Mexico/United 44 States borderlands, in contrast to the current U.S.-Mexico border, the world's busiest border, to consider whether a relocated and reimagined border has fundamental consequences for U.S. immigration policy or drug enforcement, both of which dominate the current contentious debate on better securing the U.S.-Mexico border.

Following the U.S.-Mexican War and the subsequent Gadsden Purchase of parts of southern Arizona and southern New Mexico, the U.S. Mexico border has, for the most part, remained static aside from minor disputes over shifts in the Rio Grande channel.[407] Particularly since the end of the Spanish-American War at the close of the nineteenth century, the United States abandoned its expansionist model of seizing control of both desired mainland and outside territory such as Puerto Rico and Hawai'i. Stretching some 1,954 miles, the current U.S.-Mexico border spans the southern boundaries of California, Arizona, New Mexico, and Texas, with the Rio Grande accounting for about half its length. In contrast, the Alto Mexico/United 44 States border is significantly longer, following the boundaries of or cutting through the eight present-U.S. states of Oregon, Idaho, Wyoming, Colorado, Kansas, Oklahoma, Arkansas, and Louisiana, before reaching the Gulf of Mexico. For example,

---

borderlands may stem from the realization these migrants are aiming to reach the United States, rather than to stay and compete with Mexican nationals for jobs. Migrants from Central America coming to work in a Mexico-governed Alto Mexico would not enjoy the same tolerance.

[407] "Rio Grande Border Disputes," http://en.wikipedia.org/wiki/Rio_Grande_border_disputes (last visited June 21, 2014). In 1884, the United States and Mexico addressed shifts in the river's route by a new convention in which the national boundary would remain at the center of the river's "normal" channel. Although slow-arising changes in the channel through gradual erosion or deposits would, in effect, relocate the national border, shifts in the channel brought about suddenly by the force of current, such as during flood events, would not change the border. Paul Kramer, "A Border Crosses," http://www.newyorker.com/news/news-desk/moving-mexican-border (posted September 20, 2014; last visited September 25, 2014).

the Alto Mexico border follows the Sabine River that separates Texas from Louisiana, which is noted for its meandering path that near doubles an otherwise straightline border.

The terrain of the current U.S.-Mexico borderlands region is mostly scorching desert, yet subject to climate extremes with mountains that can imperil migrant crossers with winter snowstorms. Some of these borderlands are unpopulated or sparsely populated, particularly along much of the Texas and Arizona borders. A century ago, however, the border was even less settled and developed—long before the arrival of the maquiladora factories and the modern-day border security infrastructure. Due in part to the advent of maquiladoras and "sin" economies explained below, several border cities on the Mexico side ballooned in size during the 1900s. For example, before Prohibition, Tijuana was a tiny town of just 1,000 people. By the end of the Roaring Twenties, and the onset of Prohibition in the United States, Tijuana surged eightfold to 8,384 residents,[408] and today is the second-largest border city on the Mexico side, with 1.3 million residents.[409] Ciudad Juárez, with slightly more than 1.3 million, remains the most populous Mexican border city, with Mexicali third at 690,000 residents. An interesting border phenomenon is the presence of U.S. cities, effectively constituting sister cities, directly across the border from most every Mexican bordertown of consequence.[410] For example moving east, in California—San Diego-Chula Vista/Tijuana, Calexico/Mexicali; in Arizona—Nogales/Nogales; and in Texas, El Paso/Ciudad Juárez (among the largest world cities divided by an international border), Del Rio/Ciudad Acuña, Eagle Pass/Piedras Negras, Laredo/Nuevo Laredo, and Brownsville/Matamoros (450,000 residents) on the Gulf of Mexico.

In contrast, few large border cities lie along either side of the Alto Mexico/United 44 States border, which is desolate through much of its length, particularly when it follows current U.S. state borders such as between Oregon and California-Nevada. The explanation likely is that there is more impetus for economic growth and connectedness across national borders than across state lines, with exceptions elsewhere in the United States such as Washington state's city of Vancouver whose residents enjoy tax-free shopping in adjoining Portland, yet without Oregon's income tax. California's Crescent City and Oregon's Brookings are both a few miles from the Alto Mexico/United 44 States border that separates them, yet each is smaller than 10,000 residents. Jackpot, Nevada is a true Alto Mexico border town on the Mexican side directly abutting the border, but has only 1,200 residents and no true sister city. Across the state line from Jackpot, the closest town/city in Idaho, Twin

---

[408] Milo Kearney and Anthony Knopp, *Border Cuates: A History of the U.S.-Mexican Twin Cities* (Austin, TX: Eakin Press, 1995), 200.

[409] Population statistics come from the 2010 Mexico Census.

[410] In some instances, these sister cities resulted from the placement of the new national boundary line after events such as the U.S.-Mexican War.

Falls, is more than 40 miles away. Pueblo, Colorado, with 107,000 residents, is the most populous Alto Mexico/United 44 States border city, situated on both sides of the Arkansas River that once demarcated Mexican territory, and which presumably would constitute two cities if split by an international border. Garden City, Kansas, with 31,000 residents, lies on the northern side of the Arkansas River, on the once-U.S. side of the Alto Mexico border. In contrast, Dodge City, Kansas, 59 miles east and slightly smaller with a population of about 27,000 residents, would fall on the Mexico side of the Alto Mexico/United 44 States border. Texarkana, with 30,000 residents in the Arkansas city and 37,000 in the adjoining Texas city of the same name, is the closest model to the many sister cities along the current U.S.-Mexico border. Lying a few miles south of the once northern border of Mexico-governed Alto Mexico that followed the Red River, the twin cities of Texarkana tout their connectedness with the water tower, on the Texas (and thus once Mexican) side, proclaiming Texarkana "Is Twice As Nice." Near the Gulf of Mexico, Port Arthur (54,000 residents) on Sabine Lake, and Orange (19,000 residents) on the Sabine River, both in present-day Texas, would be significant Alto Mexico border cities on the Mexican side, although there is no companion city of consequence directly across the state/border-line in Louisiana—that state's seventh largest city of Lake Charles is about thirty-five miles east.

Today's U.S.-Mexico border is the world's most-crossed border, with hundreds of millions of crossings annually, the vast majority of them in accordance with the laws of both countries. Still, as a result of restrictive immigration laws that fail to keep pace with U.S. employer demand for low-wage workers, significant undocumented migration occurs along the border, no matter its militarization. As late as 1993, nine of ten undocumented Mexican migrants to the United States entered at or near Mexican border cities, such as Tijuana and Juárez,[411] particularly those connected to a U.S. city *en el otro lado* (the other side). Occasionally these migrants would rush the San Ysidro border station south of San Diego, at the beginning of Interstate 5 that traverses the Western U.S. coastal states of California, Oregon, and Washington, even running westward across those lanes of traffic once successfully past the border. During the Clinton presidency in the mid-1990s, however, the imperative of securing the U.S.-Mexico border against unchecked migration prompted by the fear of terrorist entries led to a border buildup that has continued for twenty years. Known variously as Operation Gatekeeper (at the San Diego/Tijuana border) and Operation Hold the Line (at the El Paso/Juárez border), beefed-up 1990s border enforcement targeted

---

[411] After the border fortification of recent decades, many unauthorized immigrants entered lawfully using temporary visas and simple overstayed the visa allowance. Bender, *Run for the Border*, 134 (citing a Pew Hispanic Center report in 2006 finding 45 percent of unauthorized migrants entered the United States in this manner).

borderlands urban areas in a show of strength using concrete and steel barriers. The Illegal Immigration Reform and Immigration Responsibility Act of 1996 added Border Patrol agents and financed construction of border walls and fencing. From 1994 to 1998 alone, the Border Patrol's annual budget more than doubled to $877 million,[412] still a mere shadow of the $3.5 billion budget in 2013.[413] Mexican (and Central American) migrants responded by shifting their undocumented crossing routes from populated regions now overrun with federal agents and obstacles, to isolated, perilous terrain, resulting in thousands of deaths while crossing. The resolve and desperation of migrants to keep coming despite the mounting death toll led U.S. lawmakers to react, not by decrying the deaths and rethinking the futility of urban border blockades, but by aiming to spread the clunky security infrastructure across the border's entire length to reach the new desolate crossing routes. Toward this end, Congress passed the Secure Fence Act in 2006, authorizing the construction of 700-miles of double-reinforced fencing along the U.S.-Mexico (but not the Canadian) border to augment the urban-focused border infrastructure. Although miles of new fencing resulted, only a few miles of the contemplated double fencing was actually built given the exorbitant cost of construction and the global economic crisis that soon followed, prompting calls for pledges by the 2012 U.S. presidential candidates to complete the double-reinforced border wall on the entirety of the border, echoed by Donald Trump in his 2016 campaign promise to successfully build a border "wall" that he suggested later would be a "great wall."[414] Today, much of the U.S.-Mexico border in isolated regions remains unmarked and unprotected from entry—only a third of its length is barricaded.[415] As suggested earlier, the cost of constructing a wall along the entirety of the Alto Mexico/United 44 States border would be even more expensive given the greater length of that border. Moreover, as considered in Chapter 3, the U.S. economic base shouldering that cost would be considerably smaller when missing the revenue contribution of Alto Mexico terrain and its residents who account for one-fourth of the current U.S. population, and its states of California and Texas that lead the United States in gross state product.

Predicting the economy and demographics of the Alto Mexico/United 44 States borderlands region requires examining the history of the present U.S.-Mexico border. Among other factors prompting their

---

[412] Ibid., 129 (from $354 million).

[413] http://www.cbp.gov/sites/default/files/documents/BP%20Budget%20 History%201990-2013.pdf (last visited July 31, 2014).

[414] Steven W. Bender, "Gringo Alley," *UC Davis Law Review* 45 (2012): 1925, 1931 n.19. An October 2011 survey found 46 percent of U.S. residents favored a fence along the entire U.S.-Mexico border, with 62 percent support from Republicans surveyed.

[415] Alana de Hinojosa, "Fortress America: How Walling Ourselves Off Can Kill," http://www.alternet.org/immigration/fortress-america-how-walling-ourselves-can-kill-0 (posted August 8, 2013; last visited November 22, 2013).

significant growth, the U.S.-Mexico border cities of Tijuana, Mexicali, and Juárez expanded in the 1900s when the sin trade brought visiting Anglos south of the border, and later when the entry of maquiladora factories pulled low-wage Mexican laborers north from Mexico's rural regions. Sin arrived first. As mentioned above, Tijuana was just a small town of 1,000 residents when Prohibition hit. Once the U.S. Congress enforced the Eighteenth Amendment through the Volstead Act to ban liquor sales, Tijuana lured U.S. residents with "scores of gambling devices, long drinking bars, dance halls, hop joints, cribs for prostitutes, cock fights, dog fights, [and] bull fights."[416] Its proximity to Hollywood and the advent of talking motion pictures, coinciding with Prohibition, attracted film stars to frolic in Tijuana resorts and bars. In Texas, which had outlawed alcohol in spring 1918 even before federal Prohibition, bordertown Ciudad Juárez (billed as the "Monte Carlo of America") drew hordes (418,735 border crossers from July 1919 to July 1920)[417] of Anglo visitors south through El Paso and Mexican workers north from Mexico's interior to service that sin industry. Bordering California's Calexico, Mexicali attracted Imperial Valley ranchers and smaller crowds of U.S. tourists, with its bars, prostitutes, and gambling casinos. Although the Great Depression and the end of federal Prohibition dampened sin traffic, the proximity of Tijuana and Juárez to U.S. military bases lifted these border towns during World War II as servicemen came to visit Mexican brothels and to drink alcohol. A few years after that War, in 1950, Tijuana had 65,346 residents on the cusp of the next and biggest boom when maquiladora factories arrived.

Presumably a Mexico-governed Alto Mexico would have supplied the same borderlands outlet for U.S. visitors thirsting for Prohibition-era booze and for prostitutes and gambling, among other vices. Although alcohol prohibitionist efforts spilled south of the border into Mexican state legislatures, revenues from Mexican taverns were too significant to seriously threaten the continuance of bordertown vice. Mexico, particularly the city of Juárez, even served as the launching point, as it does for today's illicit drug trafficking, of alcohol smuggling to supply thirsty inland U.S. residents during Prohibition. Within the United States, prohibitionists were particularly active on the East Coast, the South (including Texas), and the Midwest. Given that all U.S. states at the time, except Connecticut and Rhode Island, ratified the Eighteenth Amendment authorizing Prohibition, no doubt the same dynamics propelling federal Prohibition would have taken hold in the United 44 States to render it dry. Equally likely, Mexico would have served its same role selling booze to U.S. tourists while tolerating rum-runners across the Alto Mexico border destined for U.S. speakeasies and other flouting of Prohi-

---

[416] Oscar J. Martínez, "Prohibition and Depression in Ciudad Juárez-El Paso," in *U.S.-Mexico Borderlands: Historical and Contemporary Perspectives*, ed. Oscar J. Martínez (Wilmington, DE: SR Books, 1996), 151-152.

[417] Bender, *Run for the Border*, 58.

bition (although with the dominance of the Mormon religion and Mormon settlement in the Great Salt Lake area, it is unlikely that the Utah region of Alto Mexico would have contributed much to supplying vice). Despite the repeal of Prohibition, dry U.S. counties still exist by local vote, with most found in the East and South (including Texas).[418] In contrast, one would not expect to find dry zones in a Mexico-governed Alto Mexico, particularly in any tourist region, aside from the banning of alcohol sales, again outside of tourist areas, during Mexico elections. Presumably, then, sin traffic would have spurred considerable growth along a Mexico-governed Alto Mexico border.

As has been proven throughout the last 170 years of the U.S.-Mexico relationship, whatever is needed by one country, whether vice or labor, the other country (or its countrymen) supplies it. Even internal U.S. state bordertowns tend to take advantage of stiffer regulation in adjoining states to foster the local economy. As just one example, before the advent of a uniform drinking age, Washington State college students regularly drove eight miles to the University of Idaho college-town of Moscow to drink, where the drinking age was 19. Indeed, some fear Washington's legalization of recreational marijuana in 2012 will reverse that historic flow. Along the Alto Mexico/United 44 States border, several examples illustrate the ongoing cross-border sin traffic between U.S. states, much less countries. Texarkana, on the Texas side, was dry for years until voters in 2014 approved the sale of beer and wine. Of course, before then Texas residents could readily purchase their booze in adjoining Texarkana, Arkansas, where a trip to the liquor store was only as far from Texas as crossing the five-lane State Line Avenue to the drive-up liquor outlets fronting the boulevard that divides the two cities and states—a throwback to the days before border enforcement when the U.S.-Mexico border literally cut through saloons and other buildings.[419] Evanston, Wyoming, just across from the Utah border, serves the demand of Utahans for illegal fireworks, with a host of fireworks retailers along the highway. Utahans also cross the Wyoming border to purchase beer kegs for private parties, circumventing Utah liquor law that denies "kegger" parties and allows social hosts to serve only cans and bottles of beer. At least one unincorporated town, Jackpot, Nevada, appears to exist solely to serve cross-border vice. On the border between Idaho and Nevada, Jackpot was founded when Idaho banned casino gaming in 1954 and one of its casinos needed to relocate. Now home to casinos and ho-

---

[418] "Alcohol Control in the United States,"
http://en.wikipedia.org/wiki/File:Alcohol_control_in_the_United_States.svg
(last visited September 12, 2013).

[419] See McWilliams, *North From Mexico*, 65 (describing how before the U.S. government required sixty feet of free space and then armored the border, the mythical U.S.-Mexico border line sliced through buildings, including stores where the proprietor might evade the tax laws of the undesirable country by stepping to the other side of the counter).

tels that employ more Twin Falls residents than any one business in that Idaho city, Jackpot nonetheless does not appear to offer any brothels to Idaho travelers. They would need to drive another 67 miles south to Wells, Nevada, where two legal brothels operate—Bella's Hacienda Ranch and Donna's Ranch, the latter claiming to be the oldest of Nevada's active brothels, dating to the late 1800s. In the same vein as Jackpot, but on the other (U.S.) side of the Alto Mexico/United 44 States border, the Kiowa Casino in Oklahoma lies just across the border from the Texas city of Burkburnett, about 15 minutes north of Wichita Falls.

The U.S.-governed Alto Mexico in some respects beat Mexico at its own game. Gambling came under constant attack in Mexico, banned between 1911 and 1913, and then again by President Lázaro Cárdenas in 1935, forcing the closure of Tijuana's then famous Agua Caliente casino. But north of the U.S.-Mexico border, Nevada's legislature bucked the similar U.S. trend against gambling with its aptly-named "Wide Open Gambling Bill of 1931," prompting the opening of a casino that year in Las Vegas (meaning meadows in Spanish, as the valley was named by Mexican scouts), and launching today's Sin City that would replace the Mexican border as an international draw for vice tourism and excess. Query whether and where, if Mexico governed Alto Mexico today, the United 44 States equivalent of Las Vegas would exist—Atlantic City? New Orleans (which already suffers a murder rate more than five times higher than Mexico City)? Within Mexico (and presumably in a Mexico-governed Alto Mexico), the Mexican government finally lifted its federal ban on casinos in 2004, issuing limited permits that allowed Tijuana's historic Caliente casino to reopen its doors. Depending on competition from proximate U.S. tribal casinos, then, the Alto Mexico/United 44 States borderlands might offer gambling similar to "bordertown" Jackpot, Nevada. Yet few U.S. residents today cross the Mexico border with gambling in mind given the variety of more convenient U.S.-based alternatives.

Similar to the U.S. outcry in the early twentieth century against alcohol and gambling, morals attacks closed red-light districts in more than 2,000 towns across the United States from 1900 to 1917, prompting vice traffic from U.S. residents to Mexico's border brothels. Again, Nevada offers a vice alternative within the United States, with prostitution legal except in larger counties such as Clark (Las Vegas) and Washoe (Reno). Today, many cities in Mexico, particularly in the U.S.-Mexico borderlands, have red light districts with licensed (and unlicensed) prostitutes. As Mexican borderlands brothels served U.S. servicemen, youth coming of age, and other vice tourists for decades, presumably a Mexico-governed Alto Mexico borderlands region, and some Alto Mexico interior resort cities such as Los Angeles, would offer the same indulgences.

One difference in draw between the current U.S.-Mexico border and the Alto Mexico/United 44 States borderlands is the possibility of significant tourist traffic that is not sin-oriented. Tijuana in particular tried to reinvent itself in the 1970s as a family destination, particularly as the rise of U.S.-based topless bars and the U.S. pornography industry cut into the south-of-the-border sin business. But Mexico borderlands family tourism failed to take hold among U.S. Anglos. Today, the most popular Mexican beaches and family tourist attractions are far from the borderlands. In contrast, the Alto Mexico/United 44 States borderlands boasts several family-oriented attractions. They include rafting businesses lining the Arkansas River in Colorado, renowned ski resorts such as Colorado's Aspen and Telluride, Utah's Alta/Snowbird and Park City and, for summer excursions, the Great Salt Lake, as well as, at a greater distance from the borderlands, California's Lake Shasta and the Squaw Valley ski resort. Additional family-oriented opportunities exist in the Alto Mexico interior, as they do in Mexico away from the U.S.-Mexico border. Picaresque national parks within Alto Mexico include the Grand Canyon, Yosemite, Redwoods, Arches, and Carlsbad Caverns national parks. Southern California's beaches in Alto Mexico might be as popular for tourists from the United 44 States as today's Mexican beach resorts are for U.S. residents and spring breakers. Family theme parks such as Disneyland and Sea World lie within Alto Mexico, although their existence within a Mexico-governed Alto Mexico is speculative. Artist havens thrive within its borders—including California's Carmel, New Mexico's Santa Fe, Arizona's Sedona, and Marfa, Texas. Overall, rich opportunities for tourism beyond vice traffic exist in Alto Mexico both at and away from the borderlands.

Eventually manufacturing, not vice tourism, supplied the biggest boost to the current U.S.-Mexico borderlands economy and population. Reconstituting U.S.-Mexico border towns from purveyors of vice to manufacturing centers, the entry of maquiladora factories, especially in the 1970s, prompted huge labor migrations north from the Mexican interior. Tijuana, for example, grew from 65,346 residents in 1950 to more than 700,000 by 1980 once maquiladoras arrived.[420] Maquila factories were conceived when the U.S. Congress allowed the Bracero Program of guest labor to lapse in late 1964. Instead of sending Mexican laborers north as braceros, the 1965 Border Industrialization Program envisioned borderlands factories[421] serving U.S. consumer demand while freed from trade tariffs. For Mexico's part, it would receive raw materials from the United States duty-free and, once assembled by Mexican workers, the finished products would re-cross the border taxed only on the value added, essentially the cheap Mexican labor. Freed also from then-prevailing restrictions on majority foreign ownership of Mexican corporations, the maquiladora model soared in popularity in the late 1970s once economic distress in Mexico depressed Mexican currency and labor costs. Tijuana, Mexicali, and Juárez led the way as U.S. and other foreign investors, particularly from Asia, built borderlands factories to produce

---

[420] Bender, *Run for the Border*, 63.
[421] The free trade zone extended twenty-one kilometers into Mexico.

U.S.-bound clothing, electronics, and automobiles and to extract profits for foreign stockholders. By the early 1990s, more than 2,000 maquiladoras dotted the U.S.-Mexico border, employing about half a million Mexican workers.[422] Eventually, as many as half of all bordertown residents labored in the maquiladoras, effectively defining the U.S.-Mexico borderlands economies and contributing to a faster population growth rate in the second half of the 1900s in the northern Mexico border states than in the four U.S. border states.[423]

Whether the Alto Mexico/United 44 States border would replicate the maquiladora model depends, primarily, on the variable of wages. Maquilas import most of their parts, and must overcome transportation costs each way, leaving wages as the critical component to justify and render the model profitable. In practice, the great disparity of wages between the United States and Mexico ensured success, as Mexican workers tended to make just one-tenth of their counterparts in the United States. For example, in 1996, auto parts workers in maquiladoras made $2.75 an hour, high by Mexican standards, but well below the U.S. autoworker average then of $21.93 plus fringe benefits.[424] More in line with current wages, bordertown Mexican employees of clothier Levi Strauss made just 70 cents hourly in 1998, while U.S. Levi workers earned $10 to $15 hourly.[425] Bolstered by lesser standards for labor and environmental protection, or by their nonenforcement, bordertown maquiladoras eventually employed 1.35 million Mexican workers by 2000, and rose to a new peak of almost two million workers in 2007.[426] Yet, Mexico's low wages were soon undercut by other upstart countries, particularly China, India, and even other countries in Latin America and the Caribbean (such as those joining with the United States under the Dominican Republic-Central America-United States Free Trade Agreement). [427] Foreign competition especially threatened Mexican maquiladoras producing lighter and more cheaply transported items such as clothing. By 2013, however, the Mexican maquiladora model reignited as Chinese factory pay increased, yet still remained vulnerable to emerging lower-cost assembly locations, such as Haiti.[428] Even if maqui-

---

[422] Bender, *Run for the Border*, 43.

[423] Paul Ganster and David E. Lorey, *The U.S.-Mexican Border into the Twenty-First Century* (Lanham, MD: Rowman & Littlefield, 2d ed. 2008), 116.

[424] Bender, *Run for the Border*, 43.

[425] Ibid.

[426] Carolyn Tuttle, *Mexican Women in American Factories: Free Trade and Exploitation on the Border* (Austin, TX: University of Texas, 2012), 10.

[427] Known as CAFTA-DR (encompassing the United States, Costa Rica, the Dominican Republic, El Salvador, Guatemala, Honduras, and Nicaragua).

[428] "Mexico's Maquiladoras: Big Mac Attack," http://consciousnewsmedia.blogspot.com/2013/11/what-man-did-with-this-tree-trunk-will.html#.Uo5lQGAW9P4 (posted October 26, 2013; last visited November 21, 2013) (explaining how the maquiladora industry must constantly

ladoras took hold along the Alto Mexico/United 44 States border, then, the reality of today's manufacturers searching the globe for the cheapest and most exploitable labor force suggests their vulnerabilities along the Alto Mexico border.

Maquiladoras exact a heavy toll from their underpaid workers, many of them unable to afford adequate food or housing and forced to live in Mexican shantytown settlements. Many Mexican employers routinely flout overtime and maternity leave laws otherwise protecting their mostly female workforce. Workers must handle unsafe chemicals and endure dangerous workplaces, with many employees sickened or injured. Despite the crushing human toll of the sweatshop conditions found in many maquiladora workplaces, these consequences are invisible in the products sold within the United States. Equally out of view from much of the United States is the physical impact on the borderlands of thousands of maquiladora factories and the almost two million workers they drew to the region, who often live with their families near the factories. Given the twenty-one kilometer free trade zone and the need for proximity to markets to cut transportation costs, many of the factories are found on the southern outskirts of the major bordertowns, out of view from the U.S. side. Whether located along the current border, or the Alto Mexico/United 44 States border, the oppression of Mexican workers inherent in the maquiladora model would remain invisible to U.S. consumers.

U.S. environmentalists who have long fought industrial development in the West might imagine the impact along the Alto Mexico/United 44 States border of the perhaps thousands of maquiladora factories assembling (proportionately fewer) goods for export to the territorially and numerically smaller United States. More telling than their physical footprint would be the accompanying environmental degradation currently visited on Mexican soil. Despite ostensibly similar environmental laws to those in the United States, inadequate Mexican enforcement resources or bribes resulted in polluted air and watertables arguably responsible for increased cancers, birth defects, and disease along the border.[429] Despite being compelled by Border Environmental Agreements between the United States and Mexico (known as the La Paz Agreements) to return potentially hundreds of tons of hazardous wastes produced daily in U.S.-owned maquiladoras back to the country of origin, Mexico has served as a dumping ground for these wastes.[430] Most U.S. residents and consumers are immune from the impacts of this south-of-the-border environmental degradation. Rather than sprouting new towns in the desert, the maquiladora factories tended to be built in established bordertown cities, such as Mexicali and Juárez. Imagine, for example, if

---

reinvent the type of assembly work undertaken to stay competitive in global markets).
[429] Bender, *Run for the Border*, 46.
[430] Ibid.

hundreds of factories were built on the southern side of Pueblo, Colorado, drawing from the Arkansas River and, with the inadequate local sewer infrastructure to handle the huge influx of new resident workers, likely turning it into Mexicali's New River—once described as a "swirling, olive-green soup of chemicals and bacteria, reeking of dead animals, industrial waste and human excrement."[431] Or consider if maquiladoras arrived near the Colorado town of Kremmling, in the vicinity of the Alto Mexico/United 44 States border, and along the upper Colorado River, polluting that famous waterway through its course in Alto Mexico, as well as drawing huge amounts of water for industrial operations. Equally likely for development given proximity to water sources would be factories sited along the Red River separating Texas and Oklahoma, or the Sabine River, separating much of eastern Texas and Louisiana, both rivers once demarcating the U.S.-Mexico border. Maquiladoras have always been profit-driven, and the quality of life of the Mexican workers and Mexican neighbors matters little. As with Mexican workers inside Alto Mexico, or working in the United 44 States, the appeal of Mexican workers is their willingness to accept low wages, given their financial desperation. That desperation spurs much of the Mexican immigration to the United States, while enabling the other contentious border issue of drug trafficking, addressed next.

* * *

Arguably the commodity that has most influenced the U.S.-Mexico borderlands is illegal drugs. Dating back to opium smuggling from Mexico into the United States at least 100 years ago, and joined by trafficking in marijuana, cocaine, methamphetamine, and other narcotics desired by U.S. users, Mexican smugglers have long supplied the U.S. demand for drugs in the same way that Mexican migrants have served U.S. labor needs. Once offering opium dens along the border for nearby U.S. addicts, particularly in Mexicali's Chinatown, Mexicans now manage a lucrative, but bloody, delivery service to and within the United States that the border-arming policies of recent decades have failed to dent— as judged by the falling prices for cocaine in the United States. Tolerated for years by corrupt Mexican officials profiting from their illicit trade, traffickers confronted a new approach under Mexico's President Felipe Calderón (in office from 2006 to 2012). Calderón initiated a federal drug war in which tens of thousands of Mexicans perished, including many innocent bystanders, with bordertown Ciudad Juárez becoming, for a few years, the world's most murderous city. The materials below consid-

---

[431] Kori Westbrook, "The North American Free Trade Agreement's Effects on Mexico's Environment," *Currents: International Trade Law Journal* 10 (2001): 86, 89. See Waterman, *Journey From Source to Sea*, 272 (updating that with U.S. financing, Mexico agreed to treat its wastewater dumped into this river that flows toward California's Salton Sea).

er both the reality of the current bloody drug war within Mexico, and whether those dynamics would change if the U.S. Southwest were under Mexican control.

The roots of the current Mexican drug war extend to the 1800s when Mexico City banned the sale of marijuana in 1869.[432] Predating the "reefer madness" frenzy of regulation decades later in the United States, marijuana came to be seen in Mexico by the late nineteenth century as the "hardest" of narcotics, whose users were "furious madmen" and maniacs "akin to a wild beast."[433] Following its ban by Mexican states and additional cities in subsequent years, Mexico's federal government eventually outlawed marijuana cultivation and export in the 1920s.[434] Regulation in the United States began in the Southwest around this same time. As in Mexico, U.S. state and local governments reacted first to the supposed menace of marijuana, with legislators pointing condescendingly to the drug's origins in Mexico and the alleged criminal conduct resulting when Mexicans used this "killer weed."[435] Informed by such outrageous statements as one on the floor of the Texas Senate in the early 1900s that "[a]ll Mexicans are crazy, and this stuff is what makes them crazy,"[436] the U.S. Southwest led the charge for marijuana prohibition. California was the first Western state to regulate marijuana, with every state west of the Mississippi outlawing the drug by 1937. The city of El Paso did so much earlier—in 1914. Congress joined the prohibition bandwagon in 1937 with the federal Marihuana Tax Act banning nonmedical uses, followed by laws in the 1950s that established and then increased federal penalties for marijuana offenses, culminating in its listing by the federal Controlled Substances Act of 1970 as a Schedule 1 controlled substance, along with opiates and hallucinogens, as among the most dangerous of illicit drugs—what the U.S. Narcotics Bureau commissioner called an "assassin of youth."[437] Despite its prohibition in Mexico, marijuana trafficking began in earnest in the 1930s and 1940s from Mexican producers to U.S. users once the U.S. states banned marijuana. Opium too made its way from Mexican poppy farmers to U.S.

---

[432] Isaac Campos, *Home Grown: Marijuana and the Origins of Mexico's War on Drugs* (Chapel Hill, NC: University of North Carolina Press, 2012), 193-194.

[433] Ibid., 102.

[434] Ibid, 181 (reporting the federal ban on cultivation and sale as occurring in 1920); compare María Celia Toro, *Mexico's "War" on Drugs: Causes and Consequences* (Boulder, CO: Lynne Rienner Publishers, 1995), 8 (specifying 1927 as year of decree of Mexico's president banning exportation, and two years later a penal code revision imposing penalties on growers).

[435] Richard J. Bonnie & Charles H. Whitebread II, *The Marihuana Conviction: A History of Marihuana Prohibition in the United States* (Charlottesville, VA, University Press of Virginia, 1974), 39.

[436] Paul Butler, *Let's Get Free: A Hip-Hop Theory of Justice* (New York: New Press, 2009), 45.

[437] Doris Marie Provine, *Unequal Under Law: Race in the War on Drugs* (Chicago: University of Chicago Press, 2007), 96.

users, despite the Mexican government's 1920s prohibition on heroin exports and Mexican heroin smuggling's subordinate role, until recent decades, to opium supply chains arriving through the Middle East and Asia. The cocaine trade eventually swung through Mexico, using the same borderlands routes as other illicit drugs. Although still originating from South American producers in Colombia, Bolivia, and Peru, concentrated U.S. interdiction efforts in the "Miami Vice" region of Florida rerouted cocaine trafficking in recent decades through Mexico. Following U.S. efforts to regulate methamphetamine's core ingredient, pseudoephedrine, Mexican cartels took over the production and trade of much of the U.S. demand for meth. By 2010, a U.S. senator attributed 50 percent of the U.S. marijuana and methamphetamine supply to Mexico, and 90 percent of its cocaine.[438]

The upshot of this history of the Mexican supply chain is that Mexico will deliver, and produce where possible, whatever illicit drugs are desired by U.S. users, who voraciously consume more than half (60 percent) of the world's illegal narcotics.[439] Despite the bordertown visits by U.S. addicts to opium dens in the 1900s, most U.S. addictions cannot be served by south-of-the border travel, requiring the delivery of drugs across the border and into the United States. Notwithstanding the half-baked assertion in 2010 by Arizona Governor Jan Brewer that the majority of undocumented immigrants crossing from Mexico into Arizona were packing marijuana and other drugs, the reality is far different and illustrates the futility of border build-up designed to prevent drug trafficking as well as undocumented migrant entries. Rather than load migrants, many of whom are intercepted, with bulky packages of drugs, smugglers use a variety of techniques that utilize and exploit the entirety of the border. Traffickers often smuggle drugs within secret compartments of vehicles or inside truck cargo. Authorities have discovered drugs hidden inside everything from concrete furniture and oxygen tanks to big screen televisions and fake limes. Smugglers improve their odds against detection by bribing U.S. border officials, as well as Mexican officials on the smuggling route through Mexico to the border. When overland border crossings are too perilous, smugglers literally go underground, as authorities have discovered numerous sophisticated drug tunnels connecting U.S. borderlands homes and businesses to the Mexican side, some of the tunnels equipped with railroad tracks and carts to shuttle drugs.[440] Before the advent of enhanced radar detection, Mexican traffickers flew cocaine-laden planes into the United States, since replaced by motorized unmanned ultralights and even ocean transport to California ports, but mostly relying on smuggling at border entry stations. Given the concentrated dosage, only 13 truckloads of cocaine would supply U.S. demand for a year, with a street value in the

---

[438] Bender, *Run for the Border*, 98.
[439] Ibid., 103.
[440] Ibid., 107-108

billions of dollars. These economics ensure that illicit drugs continue to reach U.S. users through Mexican supply chains as they have for decades.

No doubt Mexico ownership of the U.S. Southwest would invite the same trafficking trajectories. Presumably the Alto Mexico borderlands would simply have become part of the northbound supply chain serving U.S. illicit drug demand—offering the advantage to cartels of an even longer physical border for trafficking breaches. Although the local drug of choice may differ based on such factors as socio-economics and de-mographics (as well as cultural changes over time), U.S. drug demand has no real dead zones or lulls in demand over time. Located within the United 44 States, Missouri is sometimes called the epicenter of meth-amphetamine abuse.[441] Washington D.C. has the highest cocaine use (indeed, on the day I wrote this section, a U.S. Congressman from Flori-da appeared in a D.C. court on a cocaine possession charge). Florida is seen as the leader of prescription drug abuse. Overall, Vermont is the U.S. state with the highest rate of illicit drug use.[442] Mexican cartels pre-sumably would continue to supply this constant demand throughout the United 44 States, particularly if differences in wages and opportunities for prosperity remain so stark between the two countries, ensuring re-placement Mexican smugglers no matter the peril of death or prison.

Border build-up has encouraged reliance where possible on produc-tion and supply chains within the United States, most notably in California's Humboldt County, famous for its illicit marijuana produc-tion and part of a three-county (with Mendocino and Trinity) coastal region (called the Emerald Triangle) that produces the most marijuana of any location within the United States. Ironically, those rich condi-tions for production of high-grade marijuana would fall within Mexican control in Alto Mexico. Post-NAFTA, Mexican farmers find it far more lucrative to grow marijuana and opium in Mexico than staple crops of corn and beans, suggesting a likely bonanza in this region even more than today where most every job in California's Emerald Triangle is seen as connected in some direct or indirect way to marijuana cultivation.

Although recreational legalization or decriminalization of marijuana and other narcotics might undermine the smuggling profits of Mexican cartels into the United 44 States, so far only Alaska, California, Maine, Massachusetts, Nevada, Oregon, Washington and Colorado (with most of its users residing in the more populous eastern side away from Alto Mexico) have authorized the production and sale of recreational mariju-ana. Twenty-nine states and the District of Columbia (which also legalized recreational use) permit use of marijuana for medical treat-ment, starting with California's voter-enacted Compassionate Use Act of 1996 and encompassing the current border states of Arizona and New

---

[441] http://www.voxmagazine.com/stories/2012/06/07/missouri-once-again-meth-capital-us/ (last visited November 20, 2013).
[442] http://www.businessinsider.com/15-maps-that-show-how-americans-use-drugs-2013-9 (posted September 26, 2013; last visited November 19, 2013).

Mexico, as well as the Alto Mexico border states of Oregon, Colorado, and Arkansas. Despite public opinion polling showing emerging support for broader legalization of marijuana across the United States, that outcome will likely arrive slowly, and not at all for other illegal drugs of choice for U.S. consumers. Predictably, Mexican cartels responded to lesser demand for marijuana given the emergence of legal markets for medical and recreational cannabis, shifting their emphasis to potent heroin and opiate products. U.S. users far from Mexico, such as in the Cape Cod region, happily obliged the uptick in supply, prompting a national heroin epidemic.[443]

Drug production and cartel trafficking in Mexico remain illegal despite Mexico's recent decriminalization of user quantities of drugs. Therefore, Mexican control of the Emerald Triangle of Northern California (and the rest of Alto Mexico), in theory, does not materially enhance the legality or opportunities for producing illicit drugs—moreover, cocaine is only grown in certain regions of South America. Nevertheless, until recently, drug trafficking in and through Mexico co-existed with its ostensible prohibition, utilizing bribes and law enforcement corruption networks so engrained that drug cartels operated more as legitimate businessmen than violent thugs. Of course, in the last decade, Mexico President Felipe Calderón upset that "gentlemen's agreement" and drew the Mexican army into a firefight with the drug cartels that claimed tens of thousands of Mexican lives. Presumably, the same dynamic might have emerged in a Mexico-governed Alto Mexico, with the United 44 States encouraging and even helping to fund that drug war on Mexico's own turf as the United States does now, no matter the innocent bloodshed that results outside the view of U.S. eyes.

Although Mexico's near tolerance of illicit trafficking was interrupted from time to time by enforcement offensives orchestrated by the United States, as with 1969's Operation Intercept allowing U.S. agents to surveil Mexican opium and marijuana cultivation and the 1970s Operation Condor dropping herbicides onto Mexican marijuana crops, the recent drug war is the bloodiest law enforcement campaign in Mexican history. President Vicente Fox, ironically now an ardent supporter of drug legalization and willing to produce a legal marijuana crop himself, first initiated what he called "The Mother of All Battles" against the Mexican cartels, but it was Calderón responsible for the most bloodshed.

---

[443] See Olga Khazan, "The New Heroin Epidemic," *Atlantic,* http://www.theatlantic.com/health/archive/2014/10/the-new-heroin-epidemic/382020/ (posted October 20, 2014; last visited February 10, 2016); *Heroin Cape Cod, USA* (HBO documentary, 2015) (attributing surge of heroin in U.S. user veins to Mexican drug cartels replacing lost marijuana revenue). See also Sam Quinones, *Dreamland: The True Tale of America's Opiate Epidemic* (New York: Bloomsbury, 2015) (describing a different distribution model of opiates than the violent Mexican cartel model, relying on small-time Mexican dealers from the same farming region who compete for U.S. customers with lowered prices rather than guns).

Calderón engaged the Mexican military and federal police to replace corrupt municipal police, prompting bloodshed from two directions as cartels fought turf battles with each other to fill the supply voids that emerged in the upheaval, and killed hundreds of federal officers and countless innocent bystanders in order to pressure the Mexican government to relent.

With its proximity to the United States and centrality within borderlands smuggling routes, Ciudad Juárez became the epicenter of drug war violence, with more than 10,000 killed on its streets since 2007. In January 2010, for example, cartel gunmen killed 16 people, most of them teenagers, celebrating a birthday at a Juárez residence. During just a 72-hour period in early 2011, 53 people died in Juárez drug violence, including four police officers. 2010 was the bloodiest year in Juárez, with 3,115 killed—by comparison, the more populous U.S. city of Chicago in 2012 experienced more than 500 homicides, a record that garnered national attention. As of early 2014, the violence in Juárez had cooled, in part as the battle for control between the rival Sinaloa and Juárez cartels quieted down (with the Sinaloa cartel victorious), and as Mexico's new president, Enrique Peña Nieto, infused the most violent cities with enhanced social resources and programs. But the violence simply migrated far inland to Mexican production zones and along supply routes. By late 2012, Juárez no longer served as the epicenter of drug war casualties, as, for example, the southern coastal Mexican state of Guerrero (home to the beach resort Acapulco) claimed that honor in September 2012 with 159 organized crime murders that month.

Within a Mexico-governed Alto Mexico, consider which city or region would replace Ciudad Juárez as the most violent city in the drug war debacle? Given the surprisingly low rate of violence in El Paso (in comparison to Juárez, which had 3,115 homicides in 2010, El Paso, albeit smaller in size, experienced only five murders that year)[444] and other U.S. bordertowns, that city or region would likely exist along the Mexico side of the Alto Mexico/United 44 States border. Candidates include Crescent City, near Humboldt County and the Northern California marijuana production zone, as well as Pueblo, Colorado (straddling both sides of the Arkansas River once dividing the United States from Mexico), which originated as a fort in the 1840s and later as the consolidation of four towns, and Texarkana, Texas, companion city to Texarkana, Arkansas. Likely the Alto Mexico/United 44 States border would have other substantial cities as the result of the sin and then the maquiladora economy that presumably would have enveloped those borderlands, with any of the Alto Mexico/United 44 States border cities a candidate for drug cartel violence, as would cities along the supply chain through

---

[444] Eichstaedt, *Dangerous Divide*, 64; Luis Alberto Urrea, "A Weird Calm at the Edge of the Abyss," *Playboy*, November 1, 2009, 40.

Alto Mexico, with possibilities such as Phoenix, Dallas, Houston, Los Angeles, and San Francisco.[445]

Perhaps the only hope for a different outcome in Mexico-governed Alto Mexico would be the potential of a stronger overall Mexican economy through its access to the resources and attractions in Alto Mexico. Given the reliance of cartels on the economic desperation of Mexican residents to recruit replacement couriers and killers as needed, a strong Mexican economy might be the only realistic variable in curbing drug trafficking though Mexico, as U.S. demand has never ceased and would likely find replacement supply chains.

Another approach to quell the drug violence, irrespective of which country owns the Southwest, would be for the United States to decriminalize small user quantities of drugs as Mexico has already done.[446] Of course, so long as the production and sale of drugs remain illegal, or in the United States the possession of drugs, the cartels will continue to flourish. Colorado's decriminalization of marijuana has raised the interesting specter of weed tourism to the state, expected to bring between $100 million and $500 million annually to the state's economy. Because the vast majority of lawful marijuana stores operate in Denver or elsewhere in the terrain of the state falling north or east of the reach of Alto Mexico, in a Colorado split between Mexico and U.S. ownership, reverse vice traffic might be possible with Mexican residents visiting nearby Denver for a Rocky Mountain "high"—Mexico law tolerates possession of only about four joints, whereas Coloradans can grow six marijuana plants or purchase an ounce of marijuana from licensed stores, with nonresidents able to purchase a quarter ounce. That proximity of disparate approaches to marijuana—with Mexico decriminalizing tiny user quantities but not their production and sale, and Denver outlets able to produce and sell marijuana in larger quantities, might bring the absurdity and futility of the ongoing War on Drugs into sharper focus.

In sum, the present U.S.-Mexico borderlands is ground zero for the two most contentious issues for U.S.-Mexico relations—undocumented migration and drug cartel smuggling. A relocated border between Alto Mexico and the United 44 States would do little to resolve those crossings, suggesting that instead of concentrating on the borderline itself in preventing undocumented migration and drug trafficking, we must look beyond the border and foster more compassionate, realistic solutions that account for our insatiable demand for cheap labor and illicit drugs.

* * *

---

[445] Of course, some cities in Alto Mexico, such as Phoenix, were established after the U.S. acquisition of the territory, and it is unclear whether these cities would have been established in a Mexico-governed Alto Mexico.

[446] See Andres Muñoz, "Blunt the Violence: How Legal Marijuana Regulation Can Help End the Cartel Violence in Mexico," *Seattle Journal for Social Justice* 13 (2014): 691.

Inexorably connected to the outcry over undocumented immigration, given the Mexican face of such immigrants in public perception, is the outcry over the supposed cultural war between Anglos and Mexicans in the United States. Chapter 8 describes this cultural battle in the United States between the Anglo culture and the perception that Mexican immigrants are unwilling to embrace it—resulting in laws evidencing our fear of Spanish, and anti-immigrant laws discussed in Chapter 4 that discourage Mexican entrants in the first instance. Most of that cultural tension within Alto Mexico is evident close to the current U.S.-Mexico border in places such as Southern California and Arizona. Less tension exists in the Alto Mexico/United 44 States borderlands, perhaps because these borderlands are sparsely populated, and the Mexican population is comparatively small in this region far from the Mexican population centers in Alto Mexico of Los Angeles and San Antonio, among others, and the Central California agricultural region dominated by Mexican labor—although Houston, with the third largest Mexican population in Alto Mexico, is not far from the Alto Mexico borderlands. The Alto Mexico borderlands are the terrain in Southern Oregon and Northern California of the proposed state of Jefferson,[447] reflecting the political conservatism of the region and its disdain for federal government control over natural resources such as water and grazing land, a sentiment that travels through the Oregon/Nevada borderlands as well. The Alto Mexico borderlands include northern Utah and northeastern Texas, with comparatively few Mexicans. The borderlands region with proportionately the most Mexican residents runs roughly from central Colorado into eastern Kansas. Here, in Colorado at least, are found the only towns and cities in the Alto Mexico borderlands with Spanish-derived names. In contrast, with a few scattered exceptions, Spanish-named towns and cities in California are located a few hundred miles from the Alto Mexico/United 44 States borderlands, with the cities of Santa Rosa and Sacramento ending the northern reach of California's Spanish-named settlements—generally Spanish/Mexican settlers lived away from the borderlands, with some areas devoid of settlers during Spanish/Mexican ownership, such as in Utah, Nevada, Wyoming and Kansas. The majority of Mexican residents in Alto Mexico at the time of its Mexican control lived in today's New Mexico state, its boundaries more than 50 miles from the Alto Mexico border traversing today's Colorado, Kansas, Oklahoma, and Texas. At the endpoints of that former border on the Mexican side are Crescent City, California (with a Mexican population of 25 percent in 2010) and Port Arthur, Texas, with a similar proportion (24 percent) of Mexican residents and a black plurality (41 percent), both boasting a higher proportion of Mexican residents than many cities and towns sited along or near the Alto Mexico/United 44 States borderlands. Still, Mexican and Latina/o culture increasingly is evident in many Alto

---

[447] See generally, Peter Laufer, *The Elusive State of Jefferson: A Journey through the 51st State* (Guilford, CT: TwoDot, 2013).

Mexico borderlands towns and cities, such as in Jackpot, Nevada, where the town grocery store stocks piñatas and Mexican treats for the Mexican casino workers, and Garden City, Kansas, home to a plurality of Latina/o residents, most of them Mexican (42 percent of the city's residents), where the meatpacking laborers can readily find Mexican goods in the local stores. Presumably in a Mexico-governed Alto Mexico, its borderlands would be home to considerably more Mexican residents, particularly if the maquiladora economy emerged as described above. In its entirely, if not its borderlands, the Alto Mexico terrain, home to millions of Mexican residents in numbers approaching the region's Anglo population, is a zone for the convergence of cultures and the potential emergence of the sentiment of shared destiny and challenge that will help unite its residents, and those of the United States and the Americas, as the remaining chapters explore.

8. ALTO MEXICO CULTURE SUPPRESSION AND SURVIVAL OF THE SPANISH LANGUAGE

[Mexico's government] hath sacrificed our welfare to the [Mexican] State of Coahuila, by which our interests have been continually depressed . . . in an unknown tongue.

—Texas Declaration of Independence (1836)[448]

Through sameness of language is produced sameness of sentiment, and thought; customs and habits are moulded and assimilated in the same way.

—U.S. Indian Peace Committee (1868)[449]

We have a country where to assimilate, you have to speak English. . . . This is a country where we speak English, not Spanish.

—Donald Trump (2015)

Anglo culture still defines the U.S. Southwest as it has for the last 170 years. Despite Latina/os, most of them of Mexican origin, in recent years surpassing the Anglo population in New Mexico, California and, soon, Texas, Anglos still outnumber Mexicans (and other Latina/os) in the entirety of the Alto Mexico terrain, as they do in much greater numbers in the United 44 States. Even with the fast rising population in Alto Mexico of residents of Mexican origin, the Southwest's cultural identity is still predominantly Anglo-centric.[450] Consider the cultural images and icons that represent the various states comprising the Alto Mexico terrain— for Utah it is likely Mormons (who settled as early as 1847 when Utah was still in Mexican ownership), for western Colorado, wealthy ski so-

---

[448] Declaration of Independence by the Republic of Texas, 1836, http://tarlton.law.utexas.edu/constitutions/doi1836 (last visited May 11, 2014).
[449] Allison M. Dussias, "Waging War with Words: Native Americans' Continuing Struggle Against the Suppression of Their Languages," *Ohio State Law Journal* 60 (1999): 901, 914 (quoting 1868 report of the Congressionally authorized Indian Peace Commission).
[450] Some border cities, notably Laredo, Texas, have always retained a Mexican majority—Laredo since its founding in 1775. Today one of Laredo's elementary schools is 99.9 percent Latina/o and overall the city is 96 percent Latina/o, most of them Mexicans attempting to navigate two cultures and languages. Damien Cave, "Deep Ties, Tested on Mexico's Border," *New York Times*, http://www.samachar.com/Deep-Ties-Tested-on-Mexicos-Border-ofsjM5idcjj.html (posted May 17, 2014; last visited June 3, 2014).

cialites. In Arizona, the dominant image is likely of white retirees or "snowbird" winter visitors, or staunch anti-immigrant enforcers such as former Governor Jan Brewer or the so-called former Toughest Sheriff in America Joe Arpaio, for Nevada, it is casino entertainers such as Mr. Las Vegas, Wayne Newton, for California as detailed below, lily-white Hollywood and the image of the sun-kissed beach blonde "California girl" and, for Texas as also examined below, the iconic image is probably still television's oil baron family, the Ewings from *Dallas*, or white cowboys such as actor John Travolta's *Urban Cowboy*, or the more diverse Dallas Cowboys football team—"America's Team," and its cheerleaders. Finally, New Mexico has perhaps the least dominant narrative in its cultural identity—its perception within the United States might be of the bohemian artists that populate Santa Fe, or the Native American tribal culture often appropriated by its tourist attractions and souvenirs.[451]

In the two most populous U.S. states, California and Texas, Anglo-dominated culture prevails despite the ascendancy of Latina/o population in recent decades. During the last fifty years, California's cultural image has evolved from one of the blonde-haired "Beach Boys" and surfer girls, with white suburban families driving their gas-guzzling automobiles on crowded Los Angeles freeways, to the 1980s Valley Girl stereotype, and finally to today's more complex blend of Silicon Valley entrepreneurs, wealthy Hollywood socialites, and beachgoing surfers and skaters. Yet, as within Hollywood's whitewashed film and television industry,[452] Anglos dominated every phase of this cultural evolution, at least as perceived by the rest of the United States. Still, Los Angeles emerged as home today to the largest U.S. city population of Mexicans, Koreans, Vietnamese, Salvadorans, and Thais—a veritable "cultural kaleidoscope of global proportions."[453] In the same way, Southern blacks moved in large numbers to Los Angeles, particularly in the 1950s, prompting local magazines to spotlight the "blackening" of post-World War II Los Angeles.[454] Rap music videos of the 1990s eventually stamped a black cultural identity within the U.S. imagination on suburbs south of Los Angeles such as Compton and Long Beach, sustained by the 2015 movie sensation *Straight Outta Compton*. Mexicans are surely an essential part of this complex cultural milieu in Los Angeles, in California, and elsewhere in the United States, but only in subordinate roles on the fringes of Anglo culture, if not entirely invisible. Well illustrating the dominant Anglo vision of California, and the concurrent societal marginalization of Mexicans, is the recent recurring *Saturday Night Live*

---

[451] See http://www.newmexico.org/native-american/ (last visited September 7, 2013).
[452] See generally Charles Phoenix, *Southern California in the '50s: Sun, Fun and Fantasy* (Santa Monica, CA: Angel City Press, 2001).
[453] Eric Avila, *Popular Culture in the Age of White Flight: Fear and Fantasy in Suburban Los Angeles* (Berkeley: University of California Press, 2004), 20.
[454] Ibid., 63.

comedy skit, "The Californians," a mock soap opera centered on a wealthy all-blonde Anglo family living in a Spanish-inspired mansion near a Southern California beach. Played by an Anglo woman, a Latina maid named Rosie completed the ensemble which delivered exaggerated Valley Girl and surfer dialogue and dialects. Although removed from the days when Anglos played themselves as Southern California maids, notably Alice from the 1970s Southern California television series *The Brady Bunch*, contemporary U.S. media still situates Latinas and Latinos (or Anglos portraying them) in subordinate roles despite their hard-fought ascendancy in recent years to all levels of economic and political power, as evidenced by Los Angeles' Mexican mayor from 2005 to 2013, Antonio Villaraigosa, the first Mexican mayor of the city in more than 100 years.

Familiar Texas cultural icons of Anglo cowboys and wealthy oil barons are best represented in popular culture by the 1980s television drama *Dallas* and the 1980 movie *Urban Cowboy*, both featuring prominent Anglo lead characters. *Dallas* did briefly include a Latina actress, Barbara Carrera, cast as a villainous CEO for one season, but otherwise tended to rely on Latina/o characters only when the cast crossed over to the wrong side of the tracks, as when J.R. Ewing's alcoholic wife, Sue Ellen, found herself recovering from a bender on the mean streets of Dallas, where she encountered Filipino actor Lou Diamond Phillips, a t-shirted street thug. Later, in the revived *Dallas* television series in 2012, at a time when about 40 percent of Dallas residents were Latina/o, most of them Mexican, the new series featured more Latina/o characters, albeit the most prominent one playing the Latina maid of the Southfork ranch. As one scholar put it, "The image of Texans has varied over the years, but whether the image was of a cowboy with a ten-gallon hat, or of a nouveau riche oil millionaire, Texans have traditionally been viewed as self-reliant, independent, English-speaking Anglo-Americans."[455]

This chapter details how Spanish and Mexican culture, once emblematic of the Southwest, as well as native tribal culture, gave way to an Anglo-dominant culture within the Southwest, as occurred for indigenous culture in the rest of the United States. The chapter also imagines the cultural composition of a Mexico-governed Alto Mexico, and ultimately concludes that the inevitable blending of cultures in the current U.S.-Mexico borderlands invites and suggests a cultural fusion throughout Alto Mexico that transcends national affiliation with the United States or Mexico. These materials emphasize language and, to a lesser extent, religion as two flashpoints of cultural convergence and disconnect, mindful that culture has other defining characteristics that include food, music, art, holidays, recreation, medicine, literature, values, and customs.

---

[455] José Roberto Juárez, Jr., "The American Tradition of Language Rights, ¡Que Viva Texas!: The Forgotten Right to Government in a "Known Tongue," *The Scholar: St. Mary's Law Review on Minority Issues* 1 (1999): 45, 53.

Spanish settlements within Alto Mexico, once clustered around missions seeking to "acculturate" local tribal populations with Catholicism and the Spanish language, evolved over time through enormous ranchland grants from the Spanish and then Mexican government. Enabled by these massive land grants, sprawling rancho estates eventually dotted the Southwest. Before the U.S.-Mexican War, Mexican residents of Alto Mexico's ranchos generally spoke Spanish in their households, and adhered to the Catholic faith, as they did in the former mission culture. In the Alto Mexico area of the most sustained pre-War push of Anglo migration, located within the Mexican state of Coahuila y Tejas, however, Anglos staked a different cultural legacy that was part of the catalyst for the upheaval that soon followed and delivered Alto Mexico to U.S. control.

Anglo immigrants arriving in Tejas were required to be or to become Catholics, although this dictate went unenforced.[456] The Mexican government also hoped the English-speaking immigrants in Tejas would learn the Spanish language, or at least that their children would become proficient. Toward this aim, Anglo Stephen F. Austin's empresario contract with Mexico required him to "promote the establishment of schools in the Spanish language."[457] Ignoring this directive, Anglo immigrants launched English language schools rather than teaching Spanish to their children, nor did they convert from Protestant faith to Catholicism. Although a Mexican official lamented that English was "almost the only language spoken in this section of the [Mexican] republic,"[458] Mexico did not force the issue. Still, educational instruction in the Catholic faith was mandated within Alto Mexico, evidenced by a Tejas statute that required that students learn reading, writing, math, arts and sciences, and dogma of the Catholic religion.[459] Increasing Anglo immigrant demands for government services in the English language led the Mexican Tejas state in 1835 to mandate publication of all laws in both Spanish and English.[460] Similarly, the Tejas legislature in 1833 agreed to provide interpreters in trials commenced or contested by the government involving persons who lacked Spanish language proficiency (in other words, Anglo immigrants). And a Tejas law in 1834 establishing the Department of Brazos (the regional political equivalent of today's county subdivision of state government, here named for the Brazos River region settled by Stephen F. Austin) decreed the equality of English

---

[456] Contract with the Government of the State for the Colonisation of Five Hundred Families, art. 4 (Apr. 27, 1825), reprinted in 1 Tex. Gen. Laws 48 (Gammel 1898), available at http://texashistory.unt.edu/ark:/67531/metapth5872/m1/55/ (last visited December 14, 2014) ("The families that are to compose this colony, besides being industrious as offered in the representation, must also be catholics, and of good moral habits ...").
[457] See Juárez, "American Tradition of Language Rights," 88.
[458] Ibid., 89.
[459] Ibid.
[460] Ibid., 96.

and Spanish through its dictate, as translated, providing "The Castilian and English [languages] shall be lawful languages in Texas; both may be used in the acts of the public administration as the case may require, except in communications with the supreme power, which shall be made expressly in Castilian."[461] But the Anglo immigrants weren't appeased by these concessions to the English-speakers of Tejas.

As Tejas/Texas transitioned from a Mexican state to an independent Republic, and then to a U.S. state, it became apparent that government willingness to embrace both the Anglo and Spanish/Mexican cultures by recognizing a bi/multilingual government had peaked in the era of Mexican control. As a U.S. state, Texas moved to suppress and subordinate the Spanish language, in the same way that the Southwest and the rest of the United States aimed to acculturate and Americanize both Mexican and native children.

Texas schools led the charge against Mexican culture. When Mexican immigrants came north to Texas in large numbers in the 1900s, adding to the U.S.-born Mexicans already there, some of them descendants of Mexican residents in the region before the U.S.-Mexican War, Texas schools enforced an imperative of educational instruction in English. Enacted in 1918, Texas law imposed criminal penalties for teaching children in languages other than English, except in a foreign language class, such as French, taught to older students.[462] In the same way that my 1960s Catholic school in the East Los Angeles barrio policed against the speaking of Spanish anywhere on the school grounds, in the 1900s Texas educational officials notoriously punished children for speaking Spanish while at school, even in school districts with students near exclusively of Mexican origin: "[A]s late as the 1950s [Texas] children who spoke Spanish in school were made to kneel on upturned bottle caps, forced to hold bricks in outstretched hands in the schoolyard, or told to put their nose in a chalk circle drawn on a blackboard."[463]

Although seemingly at odds with imperatives of Americanization through erasure of Mexican culture and immersion in Anglo norms, segregated schools throughout Texas and the rest of the U.S. Southwest kept Anglo and Mexican children apart until ruled unconstitutional in the seminal court decision involving black children, *Brown v. Board of Education*.[464] By means of the abusive Texas Rangers, lynchings,[465] and

---

[461] Ibid., 110.
[462] James Crawford, *Hold Your Tongue: Bilingualism and the Politics of "English Only"* (Reading, MA: Addison-Wesley Publishing, 1992), 72.
[463] Juan F. Perea, "English-Only Rules and the Right to Speak One's Primary Language in the Workplace," *University of Michigan Journal of Law Reform* 23 (1990): 265, 284.
[464] Previously, lawsuits successfully challenged segregated schools targeting Mexican children in Arizona, California, and Texas. E.g., *Westminster School Dist. of Orange County v. Mendez*, 161 F.2d 774 (9th Cir. 1947) (California's Orange County schools); *Romo v. Laird*, No. 21617, Maricopa County Superior Court (1925) (granting Mexican American parent's request to enroll children in

widespread segregated schools and whites-only restaurants, parks, movie theaters, and swimming pools, and even discriminatory cemeteries of the late 1800s into the early to mid-1900s excluding the Mexican dead, Texans reminded Mexican residents of their continued place as "not the white man's equal."[466] In one case that garnered national attention, a decorated World War II hero, Macario Garcia, was arrested for fighting after he was denied service at a Texas café bearing the sign, "No Dogs, No Mexicans."[467] Nor could Mexicans buy or rent homes in many areas, as their purchases and rentals were barred by restrictive covenants ensuring whites-only neighborhoods. As John Herrera, a renowned Texas civil rights lawyer in the mid-1900s, lamented about his personal experience with Texas discrimination:

> The signs in West Texas cafes: NO CHILI! "They mean us, son. Don't go in there," dad would admonish me. The rest of Texas was no better. Seguin [Texas]: a public park with the sign, Negros y Mexicanos Afuera! [out] In a Houston personnel office: "No Mexicans hired." On Washington Ave.: "No Mexicans Allowed in Dance Hall." In a refinery, all water fountains were painted white, black, or brown. You know where I had to drink.[468]

Although the segregated Texas courthouse bathrooms of the 1950s reading "Hombres Aqui" (essentially, "Mexican Men Here") are gone, the vestiges of racial segregation and the prevailing attitudes of a lesser humanity and hostility toward the Spanish language remain. A modern example of subordinating views toward Latina/o culture occurred when an Anglo Texas judge in 1995 told a Spanish-speaking mother that she was abusing her five-year-old child and relegating her to the status of a housemaid by speaking Spanish in the household, ordering the child will hear only English. Another occurred in 2013 when a principal near Houston announced over the school intercom that Spanish was not allowed in the school in order to "prevent disruptions."[469]

---

school with higher quality teachers that allowed only white students); Crawford, *Hold Your Tongue*, 73 (describing history of Texas anti-segregation litigation).
[465] Richard Delgado, "The Law of the Noose: A History of Latino Lynching," *Harvard Civil Rights-Civil Liberties Law Review* 44 (2009): 297.
[466] De León, *They Called Them Greasers*, 106.
[467] Suarez, *Latino Americans*, 102-104 (stating the criminal case was repeatedly postponed and ultimately dropped).
[468] John J. Herrera, "Letter to the Editor," *Houston Chronicle*, May 31, 1974, 27, quoted in Juan Francisco Perea, "*Mi Profundo Azul*: Why Latinos Have a Right to Sing the Blues," in *"Colored Men" and "Hombres Aquí"*: Hernandez v. Texas *and the Emergence of Mexican-American Lawyering*, ed. Michael A. Olivas (Houston: Arte Público Press, 2006), 91, 94.
[469] David Edwards, "Texas Principal Bans Hispanic Students from Speaking Spanish to 'Prevent Disruptions,'" http://www.rawstory.com/rs/2013/12/texas-

Multilingual recognition in state government flickered briefly in California, with its initial state constitution in 1849 providing that all laws would be published in English and Spanish.[470] By the time of the constitution's revision in 1879, no California convention delegates spoke Spanish and they eliminated the bilingual allowance, invoking the supposed justification that Mexican residents by then "had ample time to learn the [English] language,"[471] thus restricting official government proceedings to the English language. New Mexico, whose statehood awaited sufficient Anglo migration to the region as addressed in Chapter 2, better acknowledged and respected the culture of the Spanish language. Its initial state constitution provided for laws to be published in both English and Spanish, at least for twenty years, and guaranteed that no citizen's right to vote, hold office, or serve as a juror would be restricted by an inability to read or write English (or Spanish). Moreover, the New Mexico constitution provided for training in teacher proficiency in both Spanish and English.[472]

Apart from New Mexico, however, the ten U.S. states now comprising Alto Mexico generally failed to nurture the Spanish language. Eventually, by the late twentieth century, a new movement aimed at subordinating and shaming the Spanish language took hold in the Southwest and the United States generally, prompted by rising anti-Spanish language and anti-immigrant sentiment. In 1986, California voters passed an initiative declaring English the state's official language, to the symbolic degradation of Spanish, leading many private employers to embrace the law's anti-Spanish message and announce their own rules prohibiting Spanish in the workplace.[473] Colorado voters adopted a similar official English language initiative in 1988, prompting a school bus

---

principal-bans-hispanic-students-from-speaking-spanish-to-prevent-disruptions/ (posted December 4, 2013; last visited December 14, 2014). Related to cultural suppression, Texas officials even tried to deny U.S. born Mexican children their constitutionally mandated birthright citizenship, by withholding birth certificates to children of undocumented immigrants. *Serna v. Texas Department of State Health Services* (W.D. Tex. October 16, 2015) (denying temporary injunction and allowing continued denial of U.S. birth certificates to children whose parents cannot sufficiently prove their identity to Texas officials by a U.S. passport, U.S.-issued drivers license, or permanent resident card). Texas officials settled the lawsuit in 2016, agreeing to accept certain documents such as Mexican voter ID cards that undocumented immigrant parents might obtain from their U.S.-based consulates.

[470] "Spanish Language Rights in California: Constitutional Debates," in *Language Loyalties: A Source Book on the Official English Controversy*, ed. James Crawford (Chicago: University of Chicago Press, 1992), 51, 52.

[471] Steven W. Bender, *Comprende?: The Significance of Spanish in English-Only Times* (Mountain View, CA: Floricanto Press, 2008),

[472] http://sos.state.nm.us/pdf/2007nmconst.pdf (last visited February 22, 2014).

[473] See Steven W. Bender, "Direct Democracy and Distrust: The Relationship Between Language Law Rhetoric and the Language Vigilantism Experience," *Harvard Latino Law Review* 2 (1997): 145.

driver to interpret the symbolic language law as prohibiting the speaking of Spanish on his bus.[474] Arizona and Utah, relatedly, enacted more draconian English language laws by voter initiative. In addition to specifying English as the official state language, Arizona and Utah's language laws mandate official government action solely in the English language.[475] Demonstrating the punitive, broad reach of these laws, Utah officials had to redesign a website supplying government information in Spanish, deleting translated material on paying taxes and using state libraries, in order to fall within the law's narrow translation allowances for public safety (thereby permitting the website to address state health programs) and other limited purposes.[476] Initially, proponents of the Arizona English-Only law were reluctant to include a health and safety exception that encompassed 911-emergency operators, evidencing the imperative of cultural assimilation over human lives. In contrast to most every U.S. state comprising former Alto Mexico that adopted official English language laws (Arizona, California, Colorado, Kansas, Oklahoma, Utah, and Wyoming), typically in derogation of Spanish-speaking residents, Texas did not enact an official language law[477] nor did Nevada. Moreover, New Mexico's legislature by resolution embraced multilingualism in 1989 by rejecting official English language legislation and appreciating the need to preserve and value diverse cultures and languages, as well as to encourage proficiency in more than one language as an economic and cultural benefit to the state. Although some Southwest cities enacted localized official English language laws, such as Farmers Branch, Texas, the Texas bordertown of El Cenizo, Texas, with a population of about 3,000 predominantly Mexican residents, notoriously bucked the trend and adopted Spanish as its official language for government functions.

More than half of the U.S. states ultimately enacted official English laws. Once the momentum toward a federal official English law fizzled, opponents of the Spanish language broadened their local objectives and succeeded in obtaining laws invalidating bilingual education programs in California (1998, but effectively repealed by voters in 2016) and Arizo-

---

[474] Bender, *Comprende?*, 19.

[475] Although the Arizona Supreme Court struck down an earlier English-Only initiative as violating constitutional guarantees of free speech, *Ruiz v. Hall*, 957 P.2d 984 (Ariz. 1998), Arizona voters approved a slightly modified version of the prior law, exempting legislators and other government officials when communicating unofficially in the hopes of surviving constitutional challenge.

[476] Zach Patton, "In Utah, It's Gracias but no Gracias," http://www.governing.com/topics/education/In-Utah-It-Gracias-no-Gracias.html (posted July 2007; last visited February 22, 2014).

[477] See Juárez, "American Tradition of Language Rights," 55. At the same time, the Texas Court of Criminal Appeals failed to find any constitutional violation when a non-English speaking Latino was sentenced to jail rather than a probationary drunk driving diversion program available only to English-speakers. See *Flores v. State*, 904 S.W.2d 129 (Tex. Ct. Crim. App. 1995).

na (2000) schools (as well as in Massachusetts), effectively mandating an English-Only classroom that excludes Spanish language instruction. Gaining proficiency in Spanish is left to the Mexican child's own family. Additionally, that child must quickly acquire English proficiency, or be left behind in the study of math, history, and other subjects taught predominantly in English to Spanish-dominant children. Illustrating the prevailing hostility toward including Spanish in the U.S. classroom, conservative columnist Charles Krauthammer indicted bilingual education as a threat to the supposed imperative of Mexican assimilation, arguing "The real threat to the United States is not immigration per se, but bilingualism and, ultimately, biculturalism. . . . Our first task, therefore, should be abolishing bilingual education everywhere."[478]

Enacted in 2010, Arizona's anti-Ethnic Studies law further stripped the U.S. classroom of cultural and historical instruction on the Mexican American experience of lost territory and sustained discrimination.[479] Similarly, in 2014 the Texas State Board of Education rejected a proposal for a standardized Mexican American Studies class in Texas public high schools, fearing divisive indoctrination into racialized grievances, while allowing any interested school to teach the course. At stake, however, is a Mexican American student's right to learn about his or her history and culture in the classroom freed from localized opposition.[480] Shielded from that history of oppression, Mexican American children presumably will resist any tendency toward rebellion, cultural or physical, and accept the force-fed dictates of history. What will emerge, as hoped, is an English-speaking child conversant with only Anglo culture and history, or at least a sympathetic version of historical events that likely remembers the Alamo in ways that elide its history of preserving slavery and expressing disdain for rule by Mexicans seen as subordinate to Anglos. In Texas, in particular, what has emerged is a still subordinated Latina/o population that has the state's highest school drop-out rate, translating to weekly wages 46 percent lower on average than for Anglos and to a poverty rate of 25 percent unchanged for decades.[481]

Historically, the United States has suppressed non-Anglo cultures in its educational system, as it did when educating the children of Indian tribes. Of course, the Spanish mission system had similar aims to Chris-

---

[478] Lupe S. Salinas, "Linguaphobia, Language Rights, and the Right of Privacy," *Stanford Journal of Civil Rights & Civil Liberties* 3 (2007): 53, 55.

[479] A federal district court judge upheld most of the statute against various constitutional challenges, but in 2015 the Ninth Circuit federal appeals court required the trial judge to determine if the law was enacted with discriminatory intent. *Arce v. Douglas*, 793 F.3d 968 (9th Cir. 2015).

[480] Richard Delgado, "Precious Knowledge: State Bans on Ethnic Studies, Book Traffickers (Librotraficantes), and a New Type of Race Trial," *North Carolina Law Review* 91 (2013): 1513, 1518.

[481] Juan H. Flores and Rogelio Saenz, "Fading American Dream for Texas Hispanics," http://www.beyondchron.org/fading-american-dream-for-texas-hispanics/ (posted June 24, 2015; last visited September 11, 2015).

tianize natives and teach them Spanish to the exclusion of native languages.[482] But U.S.-governed education of natives had even broader aims than teaching children English and Christianizing them from their native religious practices seen as barbaric. U.S. schools sought further to reject tribal collectivism and replace community values with individualism and the virtue of accumulating personal wealth.[483] Americanization included giving indigenous children new Anglo names. Students were also trained in U.S. history and citizenship rather than tribal history and customs. Foremost in the curriculum was teaching the ability to read, write, and speak English, consistent with the imperative of the U.S. Indian Commissioner John Atkins who, calling native languages barbaric, wrote in 1887 that English "which is good enough for a white man or a black man ought to be good enough for a red man."[484] Toward this end, the Bureau of Indian Affairs issued an 1885 English-Only regulation applicable to all Indian schools, requiring that "[A]ll instruction must be in English, except in so far as the native language of the pupils shall be a necessary medium for conveying the knowledge of English, and the conversation of and communications between the pupils and with the teacher must be, as far as practicable, in English."[485] English-language imperatives were enforced strictly, even with the lash of a leather strap.[486] Probably the most horrific practice of these native Americanization schools was their frequent location far away from tribal reservations, with Indian children forcibly removed to these distant boarding schools, even for years at a time, in the singular interest of effectively assimilating them into the Anglo-Protestant culture.[487]

As was done to Native American children, early 1900s U.S. Americanization programs in the Southwest sought to assimilate Mexican children by teaching them English and ideals and expectations of Anglo culture. Explaining Americanization goals in 1923, the Los Angeles school superintendent suggested, "We have these [Mexican] immigrants

---

[482] Juárez, "American Tradition of Language Rights," 71-72.

[483] David Wallace Adams, *Education for Extinction: American Indians and the Boarding School Experience, 1875-1928* (Lawrence, KS: University Press of Kansas, 1995), 22.

[484] Charles L. Glen, *American Indian/First Nations Schooling: From the Colonial Period to the Present* (New York: Palgrave Macmillan, 2011), 132.

[485] See Dussias, "Waging War with Words," 912. Arizona's anti-bilingual education Proposition 203, modeled after California law and adopted in 2000, is very similar to the English imperatives of native instruction—the Arizona law mandates English in the classroom for all subjects except for "a minimal amount of the child's native language when necessary."

[486] Jon Reyhner, "Policies toward American Indian Languages: A Historical Sketch," in *Language Loyalties: A Source Book on the Official English Controversy*, ed. James Crawford (Chicago: University of Chicago Press, 1992), 41, 43.

[487] See generally Adams, *Education for Extinction*; David H. DeJong, *Promises of the Past: A History of Indian Education in the United States* (Golden, CO: North American Press, 1993).

to live with, and if we Americanize them, we can live with them."[488] California formalized its program by establishing the Division of Immigrant Education within its Department of Education. These Americanization programs in the Southwest for Mexicans emphasized English language instruction, with Arizona's superintendent of education once dictating that "every phase of school life [for Mexican children] should take part in promoting the meaningful use of English."[489] Going beyond replacing Spanish as the favored tongue, these programs relied on derogatory stereotypes to instruct Mexican children on how to avoid their supposed cultural propensities of laziness and uncleanliness, with many schools subjecting Mexican children to regular hygiene inspections in the same vein as U.S. immigration officials who doused incoming Mexican Bracero Program workers with pesticides. Although the phrasing of "Americanization" eventually lost favor as the popular term for assimilation imperatives, those efforts were ongoing and continue in today's schools within Alto Mexico that in some cases deny bilingual education. As one commentator explained the survival of anti-Mexican imperatives in U.S. education, "Language and culture continued to be major educational concerns, and the identification of the Spanish language and Mexican culture as contradictory to educational success lost no ground in conventional theory and practice."[490]

* * *

Concurrent with discrimination against Mexicans in the U.S. Southwest based on their perception as a subordinate people, anti-Catholic prejudice was rampant in the nineteenth and twentieth centuries, both within the Southwest and beyond. Despite the imperatives of religious freedom in the founding of the United States, religious discrimination is evident in the histories of a variety of U.S. venues ranging from the workplace to the voting booth to schools. Mexicans, most of them Catholics, are particularly affected by anti-Catholic discrimination. Under the Treaty of Guadalupe Hidalgo, Spanish-speaking Mexicans remaining in the United States were entitled to be "secured in the free expression of their religion without restriction."[491] Yet this treaty language did not protect against widespread attacks on the Catholic faith.

Anti-Catholic sentiment surfaced throughout the last two centuries. Notably, in the mid-nineteenth century, hatred of Irish and German Catholic immigrants prompted the establishment of a short-lived political party to suppress their influence—the Know-Nothing Party, also

---

[488] Gilbert G. Gonzalez, *Chicano Education in the Era of Segregation* (Philadelphia: Balch Institute Press, 1990), 36.
[489] Ibid., 43.
[490] Ibid., 45.
[491] Treaty of Guadalupe Hidalgo, art. IX.

called the American Party.[492] The despicable Ku Klux Klan organization led another mass movement against Catholics in the 1920s, viewing Catholics as the "unassimilated hordes of Europe" which threatened U.S. racial purity.[493] A Texas Court of Criminal Appeals decision in 1925 confronted an allegation by a Mexican charged with selling alcohol in dry times that Catholics were systematically excluded from the county grand jury, a precursor to a later challenge in Texas of the wholesale exclusion of Mexicans from all types of juries.[494]

Instructing children in the tenets of the Roman Catholic Church, private U.S. Catholic schools have long educated many Mexican and Anglo children outside the public school system. Evidencing anti-Catholic prejudice, state laws once targeted these schools, with Oregon's Klan-supported Compulsory Education Act requiring parents to send their children to public schools. Challenged by a Catholic school founded in 1880, the Oregon law (adopted by citizen initiative) failed constitutional scrutiny and was struck down by the Supreme Court in 1925 before it took effect.[495] As seen by the Court, the law unreasonably interfered with the constitutionally protected liberty of parents to direct their child's education, in the absence of any justifiable purpose for the state's parentalism. Rather than being "inherently harmful," the Court found Catholic school was "useful and meritorious." Ironic in this preservation of the cultural and educational mission of Catholicism is that Catholic schools were kindred instruments of Americanizing Mexican students, both in their longstanding aversion to the teaching and tolerance of Spanish—my childhood Catholic school prohibited speaking Spanish in the East Los Angeles barrio classroom and schoolyard, and in their failure to incorporate the Mexican cultural or historical experience in the classroom. Given that most of my teachers, and the priests connected to the barrio school, were Anglos, as were the school administrators, the institutional exclusion of the Mexican culture is not surprising. It seems ironic that on the same turf where Spanish missions once tried to Catholicize natives and teach them Spanish over their native language, that a U.S. Catholic school would aim to marginalize the Spanish language while teaching Mexican students, many with indigenous roots. But Alto Mexico is replete with ironies.

* * *

[492] Ray Allen Billington, *The Protestant Crusade 1800-1860: A Study of the Origins of American Nativism* (New York: Macmillan Company, 1938).
[493] Philip Jenkins, *The New Anti-Catholicism: The Last Acceptable Prejudice* (New York: Oxford University Press, 2003), 32.
[494] *Juarez v. State*, 277 S.W. 1091 (Tex. Crim. App. 1925) (concluding the court was obligated to hear evidence of prejudice against Catholics in constituting grand jury).
[495] *Pierce v. Society of the Sisters of the Holy Names of Jesus and Mary*, 268 U.S. 510 (1925).

Despite longstanding and ongoing efforts to stigmatize and suppress the Spanish language and the Mexican culture, it is evident, particularly within the Southwest, that the resiliency of language and culture is poised for a cultural renaissance connecting the United States and Mexico in ways that deemphasize national affiliation with a particular governing country, and which unite rather than divide. Within a U.S. Southwest rife with official English laws and past and present anti-bilingual education mandates, the Spanish language and culture nonetheless exude from near everyone's daily experience. Consider an average day in the life of a Californian, navigating traffic, eating, relaxing, and working. As just one 2012 sketch of *Saturday Night Live's* "The Californians" portrayed, directions for the coastal residents involved traveling on San Vicente Boulevard and the Santa Monica freeway, and included the destination of Marina del Rey (Spanish for king) reached by traveling through the city of El Segundo (apparently named for the second (segundo) Shell Oil refinery on the West Coast). The Californians entertained guests in their "Mexican country style chairs," enjoyed wine from Santa Barbara County, and nachos made with California avocadoes (derived from the Spanish word aguacate, from which guacamole results), while welcoming a fugitive who hitched a ride from prison on the back of a taco truck. The guitar melody of "Ventura [Spanish for fortune or luck] Highway" played between segments of the comedy sketch. Even the state name California came from Spanish explorers, and the region was known as Alta California during the period of Mexican control. Nevada (Spanish for snowy), Colorado (meaning reddish-colored), New Mexico, and Texas (Tejas) are similarly derived from Spanish language origins, as are iconic Southwest cities such as San Francisco, Los Angeles, Las Vegas, San Antonio, and Santa Fe. Geographies of the Southwest reveal Spanish/Mexican roots, with the Alto Mexican terrain of western and southern Colorado encompassing cities with names such as Pueblo, Durango, Salida, Alamosa, Trinidad, Cañon City, Cortez, and Buena Vista, and a number of Colorado counties carrying Spanish-derived names such as Baca, Conejos, Costilla, La Plata, Las Animas, Mesa, Montezuma, Rio Blanco, Rio Grande, San Juan, and San Miguel.[496]

California's iconic beach culture is steeped in Spanish origins, as evident in beach communities such as Laguna (Spanish for lagoon or pool of water), Redondo (round or perfect), and Hermosa (lovely) Beach. Other California waterfront communities include Santa Cruz (holy cross), Palos Verdes Estates (green sticks or trees), Corona Del Mar (crown of the sea), and Tiburon (shark) on the San Francisco Bay. Even

---

[496] Of course, Spanish names dot the U.S. landscape outside of Alto Mexico, evidencing the reach of Spain's ownership and exploration within the United States, including Florida (flowering land in Spanish) and such Florida cities as Boca Raton, and the Pacific Northwest (for example, the Strait of Juan de Fuca, named for the Spanish translation of a Greek explorer, separating Canada from Washington state).

the "Valley Girl" culture associated with shallow dialect and the excessive shopping propensities of well-to-do California teens, refers to residents of the Spanish-named San Fernando Valley region of Los Angeles.

The U.S. West's iconic cowboy culture—the stuff of Western movies and dime novels, television series, and country music, derives in both its origin and familiar terminology (such as rodeo, lasso, lariat, corral, stampede, chaps, poncho, chaparral, wrangler, and buckaroo) from Spanish influences. Spanish contributions to Western lore include the origin of the term cowboy (from the Spanish vaquero), at a time when Spanish vaqueros ran cattle and horses (including broncos and pintos and mestengos [mustangs]) in the rancho (source of the English term ranch) terrain of what eventually became the Anglo-dominated Southwest.[497]

Anyone turning the radio dial or television remote in the Southwest today can find a variety of Spanish-language television networks, such as Univision and Telemundo, offering news, telenovelas (short duration Spanish soap operas), and variety shows (such as Sábado Gigante which ran for 53 years until 2015), and radio stations playing an expansive variety of Mexican musical genres from Tejano to narcocorridos. Regional and local Spanish language newspapers augment television and radio coverage—Spanish language publications in the Southwest date to those originating in Mexico-owned Tejas in the 1820s, soon followed by those in California and New Mexico.[498] Driving through many Southwestern towns and cities, one can observe Mexican restaurants and markets ranging from national fast food chains to local eateries, butcher shops (carnicerías), bakeries (panaderías), and the increasingly iconic taco truck that revolutionized mobile food carts. Supermarkets in the Southwest often have Mexican or Hispanic food aisles, and now integrate Mexican foodstuffs with traditionally Anglo offerings, such as by including varieties of chiles and cilantro in the fresh vegetable section. Many Southwestern parks and athletic fields are filled with Mexican and Latina/o youth, and Anglo children too, playing soccer. Conjoining food and U.S. college football, the Tostitos Fiesta Bowl in Tempe, Arizona promoted Mexican food to the cultural mainstream (until its sponsorship ended in 2014), along with incessant Taco Bell commercials in U.S. media.[499]

A Mexico-governed Alto Mexico would amplify these cultural expressions. Presumably, Spanish would be the most spoken language and

---

[497] See generally Bender, *Comprende?*, 91-93; Robert N. Smead, *Vocabulario Vaquero/Cowboy Talk: A Dictionary of Spanish Terms from the American West* (Norman, OK: University of Oklahoma Press, 2004).

[498] Jean-Benoît Nadeau and Julie Barlow, *The Story of Spanish* (New York: St. Martin's Press, 2013), 236.

[499] See generally Gustavo Arellano, *Taco USA: How Mexican Food Conquered America* (New York: Scribner, 2012), 4.

the language of commerce, yet the likely presence of significant numbers of Anglo residents, as predicted in Chapter 5, might challenge that stature with official recognition of the English language within the region, as occurred in nineteenth century Tejas. Although some 95 percent of Mexico's population speaks Spanish, sometimes as a second language for an indigenous tongue, English is commonplace in Mexico's Anglo resort and retirement communities. Unclear too is the preeminence of the Catholic Church within a Mexico-governed Alto Mexico. Although Mexicans are leaving the Catholic Church in significant numbers, Mexicans remain overwhelmingly Catholic, with some 92.9 million of the 112 million Mexico residents still adherents of the Catholic faith, down from a whopping 98 percent Catholic in 1950.[500] Mexican Catholicism results in both legal and cultural differences from U.S. norms, including that most Mexican states prohibit or significantly regulate abortion,[501] and that Mexico has abolished the death penalty across its legal system,[502] both of these positions in contrast to the U.S. legal allowance of capital punishment (except as banned by some states) and its constitutionally sourced protection of a woman's right to reproductive choice.

With a relatively small Mexican population in relation to Alto Mexico, despite the inroads of Mexican migrants in recent decades, the United 44 States remains an even more apparent stronghold of Anglo culture. Still, its Anglo residents fear the cultural changes that arrive with new Mexican neighbors, despite their shared core values of love for family and the pursuit of economic security. Spanish language, in particular, is seen as the marker of hostility toward assimilating into the prevailing Anglo culture. Spanish language, however, has become dominant in the United States, as the most spoken non-English language in U.S. homes, even among non-Latina/o households.[503] Mexican residents, having reached every U.S. state, are infusing their new towns with cultural influences that Anglos can choose to embrace or repel. Situating Alto Mexico as the harbinger of future cultural convergence, the book's final chapter explores the potential for that multicultural renaissance uniting the Americas.

---

[500] Julian Rodriguez Marin, "More Than 1,000 Mexicans Leave Catholic Church Daily, Expert Says," *Latin American Herald Tribune*, http://www.laht.com/article.asp?ArticleId=390745&CategoryId=14091 (posted March 10, 2011; last visited June 11, 2014).

[501] Bender, *Run for the Border*, 180-181.

[502] Ibid., 21.

[503] Ana Gonzalez-Barrera and Mark Hugo Lopez, "Spanish is the Most-Spoken Non-English Language in U.S. Homes, Even Among Non-Hispanics," http://www.pewresearch.org/fact-tank/2013/08/13/spanish-is-the-most-spoken-non-english-language-in-u-s-homes-even-among-non-hispanics/ (posted August 12, 2013; last visited July 31, 2014).

9. FEARS OF LA RECONQUISTA SECESSION OR SYNERGY?

> In today's America, immigrants are welcomed by a society intoxicated with the idea of multiculturalism. Today's immigrants quickly become aware that there is no need to leave their old language or various attachments behind because the only cause they will be required to espouse is allegiance to the ideology of radical multiculturalism.
>
> —Tom Tancredo, *In Mortal Danger: The Battle for America's Border and Security* (2006), 22.

The legacy of U.S. conquest of Alto Mexico in the mid-1800s is fodder today for conspiracy theories of reconquest (derisively called la Reconquista) typically propagated to justify anti-immigrant legislation and policies. For example, the American Patrol organization accused the Mexican government and U.S. Mexican residents of a conspiracy to retake Alto Mexico in the name of the indigenous Mexican homeland of Aztlán.[504] These theories run the gamut from a bloodless demographic/cultural/political "invasion" to one employing military force, the latter suggestion farcically imagining that somehow Mexico might overcome a world superpower and physically retake the U.S. Southwest. During the U.S. Chicano Movement of the 1960s and 1970s, sporadic attempts to occupy Southwestern land were focused on smaller parcels and there was no comprehensive effort to regain the Southwest. In any event, these isolated events were quickly suppressed. In 1972, for example, a Chicana/o student group, the Brown Berets, briefly established a camp on a hillside of California's Santa Catalina Island and hoisted a Mexican flag, proclaiming the Channel Islands as Mexican lands. The activist group's creative theory, later dispelled by the Supreme Court, was that the Channel Islands, located off the California coast, were outside the scope of the Treaty of Guadalupe Hidalgo and remained in Mexican ownership. After a month of occupation, county sheriffs peaceably escorted the Brown Berets off the island.[505] Led by activist Reies Tijerina, a land grant movement in New Mexico in the 1960s deployed an equally inventive (and in this case legally defensible, if pursued by grant descendants) theory that the community allocation of ejido land grants from the Spanish/Mexican government was improperly dealt to the United States by the Supreme Court rather than to the collective control of the individual land claimants. Targeting the Carson National Forest, comprised

---

[504] Park and Pellow, *Slums of Aspen*, 10 (describing a radio production, "The Mexican Conquest of California," on the American Patrol website).
[505] Bender, *Tierra y Libertad*, 123.

of the former communal land of Spanish/Mexican villagers, Tijerina's organization, La Alianza Federal de Mercedes (the Federal Alliance of Land Grants), occupied a campground in the Carson National Forest, claiming all rights conferred by the King of Spain in the original 1808 land grant. In contrast to the Brown Beret occupation, the Alianza retaking turned violent when the group seized two federal park rangers and tried them for the criminal offenses of "trespassing and being a public nuisance," which prompted federal and state officials to clear out the campground and bring federal criminal charges against Tijerina and some of his followers.[506] Much earlier, in 1915, a revolutionary plot known as the Plan de San Diego, originating in the south Texas town of San Diego near Corpus Christi, called for an armed uprising by Mexicans against Anglo men with the goal of reclaiming Alto Mexico for Mexicans.[507] Quelled by the Texas Rangers after several violent skirmishes, speculation remains whether Mexico's President orchestrated the failed coup. In sum, these sporadic land occupations and uprisings during the last century failed to serve as any precursor to an actual forcible retaking of the entire Southwest, which remains the stuff of scare tactics of anti-immigrant zealots and not the reality of any realistically foreseeable conquest despite the irony of Mexico's bloody loss of Tejas/Texas following a surge of Anglo migration to the region. Therefore, despite the turns of history that brought rejection of slavery in the United States too late to preserve the Alto Mexico/United 44 States border, there is no chance (or desire) almost 200 years later of a forcible retaking to restore that historic border.

Glenn Spencer, founder of American Patrol and a strident backer of anti-immigrant policies, warns of a less bloody strategy of Reconquista involving the political takeover of the Southwest. Spencer fears that Mexican residents, once they become a majority of residents in Alto Mexico, "may vote to leave the union."[508] Most proponents of this political takeover theory point to the higher fertility rate of Mexicans, to unlawful immigration, and to the retention of Mexican citizenship by many immigrants as an expression of their allegiance to another country and to the inevitability of Mexican population growth in the United States. Of course, any suggestion of a political takeover is absurd, even at a time when these fearmongers can point to the 2014 Russian takeover of Ukraine's Crimea region, ostensibly through a democratic vote for joinder. Despite their raw numbers, Mexicans specifically, and Latina/os generally, are unable to realize political clout that corresponds to their significant population. Among the relevant factors explaining the still unrealized electoral potential of Latina/o residents are the noncitizen status of many Latina/os, as well as their relative youth, and more vexing concerns for Latina/o leaders such as their lower electoral

---

[506] Ibid., 123-124.
[507] Ganster and Lorey, *U.S.-Mexican*, 65.
[508] Eichstaedt, *Dangerous Divide*, 162.

participation and their failure, with some exceptions, to vote in bloc for Latina/o candidates, or even for uniquely Latina/o issues such as to oppose anti-immigrant laws.[509] Even if Mexican voters somehow managed to vote to secede from the union, in the manner of Texas that ostensibly left the United States to join the Confederate States of America, that vote would be illegal and contrary to the U.S. Constitution.[510] The U.S. Supreme Court said as much in an 1800s opinion concerning the Texas secession vote: "[A]s transactions under the [U.S.] Constitution, the ordinance of secession, adopted by the convention and ratified by a majority of the citizens of Texas, and all the acts of her legislature intended to give effect to that ordinance, were absolutely null." Rather, "[t]he obligations of the [Texas] State, as a member of the Union, and of every citizen of the State, as a citizen of the United States, remained perfect and unimpaired."[511] If Mexico seized on any such secession vote, however implausible, no doubt the United States would crush any attempted takeover with military force. As a military superpower, the United States is vastly distinct from Ukraine, itself a victim of superpower Russia claiming part of its territory with the ostensible approval of the Russian-leaning residents of the region. Alto Mexico is altogether distinct and any fears of some return to Mexican control by secession engineered through the ballot box are ludicrous.

The most feared blueprint for la Reconquista, rather than one of military conquest or political secession, is based on perceptions of runaway immigration of Mexican nationals and their alleged failure to assimilate to the predominant Anglo culture of the United States. The late Samuel Huntington, for example, wrote the anthem for doomsday xenophobes in calling Mexican immigration "a unique, disturbing, and looming challenge to our cultural integrity, our national identity, and potentially to

---

[509] See generally Steven W. Bender, "The Latina/o Influence on U.S. Politics: Reality and Potential," in *Twenty-First Century Dynamics of Multiculturalism: Beyond Post-Racial America*, ed. Martin Guevara Urbina (Springfield, IL: Charles C. Thomas, 2014), 81. See also Steven W. Bender, Keith Aoki, and Sylvia Lazos, "Race and the California Recall: A Top Ten List of Ironies," *Berkeley La Raza Law Journal* 16 (2005): 11 (discussing how a significant number of Latina/o voters favored the two Anglo Republican candidates over the Latino Cruz Bustamante in the 2003 California governor recall election); Rory Carroll, "Latinos Become California's Largest Demographic Though Political Clout Lags," http://www.theguardian.com/world/2014/mar/17/latinos-california-biggest-demographic-politics (posted March 17, 2014; last visited May 14, 2014).

[510] *Texas v. White*, 74 U.S. 700 (1869) (case involved the enforcement of bonds issued and payable to Texas by the United States in the 1850 Compromise of its border with New Mexico, and sold after secession by a military board to private buyers to aid in the rebellion against the United States).

[511] Ibid., 726.

our future as a county."[512] Fearing a bloodless "clash of civilizations," Huntington posited the "central elements of any culture or civilization" as language and religion. Huntington, a Harvard professor, accused Mexican immigrants of failing to assimilate as past European groups did, blaming their connectedness to neighboring Mexico, their concentration in the Southwest, their alleged resistance to assimilation, and their supposed desire to reclaim their former territory.[513] Huntington warned that "the results of American military expansion in the nineteenth century could be threatened and possibly reversed by Mexican demographic expansion in the twenty-first century,"[514] with the result that the United States "will become a cleft country with all the potentials for internal strife and disunion that entails."[515] As Huntington put it bluntly, "There is no Americano dream. There is only the American dream created by an Anglo-Protestant society. Mexican-Americans will share in that dream and in that society only if they dream in English."[516] Similarly, Pat Buchanan, in his apocalyptic book titled *The Death of the West: How Dying Populations and Immigrant Invasions Imperil Our Country and Civilization*, accuses Mexican immigrants of having no desire to learn English or to become citizens—instead, Buchanan warned, they create "Little Tijuanas" in the United States and foster a separatist culture "[w]ith their own radio and TV stations, newspapers, films, and magazines."[517] Cynthia Kendoll, president of Oregonians for Immigration Reform, calls undocumented immigration "an organized assault on our culture."[518] Former Arizona state school superintendent John Huppenthal complained too about balkanization of the United States, urging "no spanish radio stations, no spanish billboards, no spanish tv stations, [and] no spanish newspapers."[519] In the same vein, actor Ben Stein opined that Mexican immigrants "want to maintain their separate nationalist identi-

---

[512] Samuel P. Huntington, "Reconsidering Immigration: Is Mexico a Special Case?," http://www.cis.org/articles/2000/back1100.html (posted November 2000; last visited March 25, 2014).

[513] Samuel P. Huntington, *The Clash of Civilizations and the Remaking of World Order* (New York: Simon & Schuster, 1996), 206.

[514] Ibid.

[515] Ibid., 305.

[516] Samuel P. Huntington, *Who Are We?: The Challenges to America's National Identity* (New York: Simon & Schuster, 2004), 256.

[517] Patrick J. Buchanan, *The Death of the West: How Dying Populations and Immigrant Invasions Imperil Our Country and Civilization* (New York: St. Martin's Press, 2002), 125.

[518] Aaron Mesh, "Driving Her Loco," http://www.wweek.com/portland/article-23168-driving_her_loco.html (posted October 1, 2014; last visited October 16, 2014).

[519] Shadee Ashtari, "Arizona Official Pressured to Resign After Calling Welfare Recipients 'Lazy Pigs,'" http://www.huffingtonpost.com/2014/06/24/john-huppenthal-racist-comments_n_5527107.html?ncid=fcbklnkushpmg00000013 (posted June 24, 2014; last visited June 24, 2014).

ties, languages, and traditions—as it were, to assimilate the United States back into Mexico ('la Reconquista')."[520]

These wild-eyed claims of disloyalty and hostility to norms of assimilation, although sometimes cloaked in an appearance of scholarly argument, are readily debunked. Huntington, for example, cites opposition by Mexicans to California's anti-immigrant Proposition 187 as his sole evidence that Mexicans "tend to retain their Mexican identity"[521] rather than presumably embracing an Americanism that attacks vulnerable undocumented immigrants in their childhood education and receipt of vital health services. Typically, allegations of reluctance or inability of Mexican and other Latina/o immigrants to assimilate focus on their use and favoring of the Spanish language. Yet a study determined that more than 90 percent of Mexicans agreed, or strongly agreed, that "U.S. citizens and residents should learn English." Another survey of just Mexican immigrants similarly found 93 percent agreed U.S. residents should learn English.[522] Latina/o immigrants confirm these attitudes with the reality of their swift acquisition of English, learning English as fast or faster than past U.S. immigrant groups. Traditionally, English language acquisition and preference stretches three generations,[523] with most children of immigrants bilingual and most grandchildren of immigrants speaking English as the dominant language. A 2007 study confirmed that nearly all (88 percent) Latina/o adults born in the United States to immigrant parents spoke English very well.[524] Among Latina/os born in the United States, a significant majority gets its news in English, watches English language television, and listens to English language music.[525] My own family experience confirms these findings, with my two Mexican grandparents fluent in English yet much preferring Spanish at home, my mother fluent and speaking interchangeably in Spanish and English, and my dominant language of English. In contrast to the assimilatory desires and record of Mexican immigrants, recall that nineteenth century Anglo slaveholder immigrants to the Mexico-governed Tejas state continued to speak English and otherwise failed to assimilate into the Mexican culture of Catholicism, particularly if it meant giving up their black slaves. Apart from fears of a Mexican "Reconquista" in Alto Mexico, no doubt that earlier rejection of Mexican culture was the true "conquista" of the Southwest, accompanied by the suppression of indigenous culture.

---

[520] Stein and DeMuth, *How to Ruin the United States*, 125.
[521] Huntington, *Clash of Civilizations*, 206.
[522] Bender, *Comprende?*, 39.
[523] Jiménez, *Replenished Ethnicity*, 88.
[524] Bender, *Comprende?*, 40.
[525] Esther J. Cepeda, "Wrong in Any Language," *Washington Post*,
http://www.washingtonpost.com/opinions/esther-j-cepeda-diego-luna--wrong-in-any-language/2013/08/14/8c72de8e-052c-11e3-9259-e2aafe5a5f84_story.html
(last visited March 23, 2014).

Studies of Mexican immigrant language acquisition, although debunking any unwillingness to learn English, do confirm the maintenance of a strident bilingualism among the U.S. (and Southwest) Latina/o population that proves equally threatening as Spanish monolingualism to those U.S. residents (themselves monolingual English-speakers) who fear Spanish. As evident in the controversy over whether to offer bilingual education in U.S. schools and the outcry following the 2014 Super Bowl commercial for Coca-Cola with "America, The Beautiful" sung in different languages such as Spanish and Hindu, the United States is hardly at ease with multilingualism and multiculturalism. Yet there is room for optimism despite the controversy. Rather than any Reconquista in a tangible form, the increasing Mexican population in Alto Mexico holds a different and more optimistic future for those unafraid to dream of a hemispheric convergence of economy and culture. As I argued elsewhere,[526] the inroads of Spanish in current U.S. culture suggests a synergy of the two languages of Spanish and English, with an increasingly bilingual U.S. population able to navigate both languages and thus serving as a cultural bridge between the United States (and Canada), on the one hand, and the predominantly Spanish-speaking Mexico and Central and South American countries.[527] Indeed, the Alto Mexico terrain, rather than serving as some cultural battleground, can connect the U.S. culturally and hemispherically to its diverse and transformative future.

The United States and Mexico are already aligned economically, with NAFTA solidifying that relationship.[528] U.S. trade with Mexico exceeds one billion dollars each day, with more U.S. exports to Mexico than to China, India, Russia, and Brazil combined.[529] From Mexico's perspective, the United States is its most important trading partner, receiving about 80 percent of Mexican exports.[530] Mexico is the main or second destination of exports from twenty-one U.S. states, including Texas (35 percent), Arizona (33 percent), and California (16 percent).[531]

---

[526] Bender, *Comprende?*, 40.

[527] Of course, Latin America boasts a rich variety of languages, from colonizer languages such as Portuguese in Brazil, to the many indigenous languages still spoken in Mexico.

[528] Of course, NAFTA has created significant upheaval in the Mexican economy by, among other things, damaging Mexican farmers in staple crops such as corn, as these Mexican farmers do not enjoy the same government subsidies of U.S. agri-business. See Bill Ong Hing, *Ethical Borders: NAFTA, Globalization, and Mexican Migration* (Philadelphia: Temple University Press, 2010).

[529] Eichstaedt, *Dangerous Divide*, 72; see also "Top U.S. Trade Partners," http://www.trade.gov/mas/ian/build/groups/public/@tg_ian/documents/webc ontent/tg_ian_003364.pdf (last visited June 22, 2014) (2013 export data).

[530] Andrew Selee and Alberto Díaz-Cayeros, "The Dynamics of US-Mexican Relations," in *Mexico & the United States: The Politics of Partnership*, ed. Peter H. Smith and Andrew Selee (Boulder, CO: Lynne Rienner Publishers, 2013), 37, 41.

[531] Ibid., 42-43.

California and Mexico are particularly poised to build on their trading relationship, with Mexico reliant on California markets, capital, and technology.[532] In early 2014, newly elected Los Angeles mayor Eric Garcetti signed an economic alliance agreement with Mexico, the city's second-largest export market, aiming to broaden economic investment and trade and establish itself as the "go-to partner" for these opportunities.[533] Remittances in the many billions annually sent back to Mexico residents by Mexican immigrants working within the United States constitute a significant portion of the Mexican economy, reflecting the vital and ongoing labor contribution of Mexican immigrants in the United States.

Augmenting the economic interconnectedness of the United States and Mexico, cultural connections, predominantly through language, are equally evident, particularly in the borderlands but also throughout much of Alto Mexico. Rather than fearing Mexican immigration and the Spanish language, an embrace of the multilingualism and multiculturalism that accompany Mexican immigration will ensure the economic and cultural vibrancy of the U.S. Southwest (and the entire United States) in the global economy. As New Mexico's legislature recognized in adopting a multicultural resolution in 1989 urging its residents to develop proficiency in a second or multiple languages, "for survival in the twenty-first century our country needs both the preservation of culture and languages among us and the fostering in other languages on the part of its citizens." Resolving that multilingualism and multiculturalism do not threaten the dominance of the English language, the New Mexico legislature urged second language proficiency toward the economic and cultural betterment of the state and the nation. Fear of Spanish is antiquated in the globalized economy and in the United States, where Spanish is already the second most spoken language in all of the Alto Mexico states and in most of the United 44 States (with the exception of Alaska (the native Yupik language), Hawaii (Tagalog), Louisiana (French), Maine (French), New Hampshire (French), North Dakota (German), and Vermont (French)).[534] Rather than Spanish posing a

[532] Luis Rubio and Guillermo Trejo, "Reform, Globalization, and Structural Independence: New Economic Ties Between Mexico and California," in *The California-Mexico Connection*, ed. Abraham F. Lowenthal and Katrina Burgess (Stanford: Stanford University Press, 1993), 51, 59.
[533] "8 Reasons Los Angeles Depends on Mexico to Survive," http://www.huffingtonpost.com/2014/03/05/los-angeles-mexico-_n_4903438.html (posted March 5, 2014; last visited March 23, 2014).
[534] Alissa Walker, "The Most Common Languages Spoken in the U.S. After English and Spanish," http://gizmodo.com/the-most-common-languages-spoken-in-the-u-s-state-by-1575719698 (posted May 13, 2014; last visited June 11, 2014) (also mapping the most common language in the state after English and Spanish, and finding that Navajo was the most spoken in Arizona and New Mexico, Vietnamese in Texas and Oklahoma, German in Utah, Colorado, Kansas, and Wyoming, and Tagalog in California and Nevada).

threat to the Anglo culture, monolingualism poses the greater challenge to global viability and credibility today.

Despite the warnings of proponents of la Reconquista conspiracy theories,[535] there is simply no chance that Mexican residents in the Southwest will ever physically oust Anglo and other current residents, although some of those residents might choose to leave the Southwest because of their own prejudicial unwillingness to live with a Mexican neighbor. With Latina/os, most of them of Mexican heritage, becoming the largest racial/ethnic group (39 percent) in California in early 2014, and poised for the same status in Texas, joining the existing plurality of Latina/o residents in New Mexico, no doubt many Anglo residents already have Mexican neighbors they must either flee from or embrace. Absent an abusive repatriation campaign such as the 1950s Operation Wetback that implicated even U.S. citizens of Mexican origin, the demographic trend toward more Mexican residents in the Southwest will continue as the Anglo population ages and relies on Mexican immigrants (and those from other Latin feeder countries) to sustain the U.S. social security system and supply critical labor as they have been doing for the last several decades—Mexico's median age is only 27, in contrast to the U.S. median of 37. Rather than coming to seize governance of Alto Mexico from the United States, the extensive migration of Mexicans during the last 100 years came to take advantage of employment opportunities and better wages than available within Mexico—not the stuff of a Reconquista to hijack control of those industries from another government.

* * *

The arrival of significant numbers of Mexican immigrants, particularly during the past 50 years despite restrictive immigration laws, and the inevitable cultural fusion of Anglo and Mexicans (along with other groups such as natives, blacks, and Asians dominant in parts of the Southwest), raise an important question: Does it matter which country governs Alto Mexico? Which country really "won" the West? Is it possible that life would go on similarly no matter whether the United States or Mexico ostensibly controls and governs the terrain of Alto Mexico? No doubt there are some potentially significant differences in laws and values between the two countries. For example, Samuel Huntington once derisively called into question Mexico's ability to "adhere to North American concepts of liberty and the rule of law."[536] This view supposes

---

[535] "No One Has Asked: 'What Does Raza Studies Teach?' and Why We Want To Shut It Down," http://constitutionalvoices.org/bloggers/freedomblogger2/wp-content/uploads/2010/12/2.-What-does-RAZA-Studies-Teach3.pdf (last visited March 23, 2014) (warning of Mexican plan within the Southwest of an "'ethnic cleansing' on blacks, Asians, and Native Americans so that the land would be just for those of Mexican descent and no one else!").

[536] Huntington, *Clash of Civilizations*, 150.

that corruption in Mexico displaces law and order, and with longstanding corruption to the highest government levels there is surely support for this notion,[537] although the United States, with its green light for corporate purchase of elections and an active investigation of foreign meddling in the 2016 presidential election, is no haven against corruption.[538] Apart from certain constitutional rights lacking in Mexico, particularly in its corrupt criminal justice system that sometimes relies on torture in its War on Drugs, differences between the two countries in laws and culture include the engrained death penalty culture in most U.S. states, especially Texas, which prodigiously executes criminals (carrying out more than one-third of U.S. executions from 1977 to 2003),[539] in contrast to Mexico, which outlawed the death penalty in 2005 and has not executed anyone since 1961.[540] Despite these differences, would the daily lives of Alto Mexico residents be fundamentally different if under Mexican control?[541] Prior chapters have addressed and speculated on the economy and demographics of the Alto Mexico terrain, but here it is worth pondering just what practical impacts come with official governance. As North America unites economically in free trade, is populated in accordance with prevailing labor demand and desires for family reunification, and as cultural norms expand to encompass the legitimacy of the Spanish language in the cultural mainstream, it is a valid question

---

[537] See Anabel Hernández, *Narcoland: The Mexican Drug Lords and Their Godfathers* (New York: Verso, 2013) (English translation edition) (documenting how drug cartel corruption reaches the Mexican executive office).

[538] See *Citizens United v. Federal Election Commission*, 558 U.S. 310 (2010).

[539] Jon Sorensen and Rocky Leann Pilgrim, *Lethal Injection: Capital Punishment in Texas during the Modern Era* (Austin: University of Texas Press, 2006).

[540] When 51 Mexican nationals were awaiting execution in the United States in 2003, Mexico sought relief in the World Court in Hague, which responded by calling on the United States to review all pending death sentences to ensure prior compliance with the Vienna Convention, which requires informing foreign detainees of their right to contact the government's consulate for legal advice. If timely contacted, the Mexican government can supply legal assistance in criminal and capital punishment cases. One of the Mexican nationals, José Ernesto Medellín, while ostensibly protected by the ruling, was executed by the state of Texas, which ignored the World Court ruling by claiming the Court had no standing in Texas. See *Medellin v. Texas*, 129 S. Ct. 360 (2008) (refusing to bind Texas to the World Court ruling).

[541] One area of ostensible difference for residents is the reality of monopolies and oligopolies that dominate the Mexican marketplace, particularly in telecom and media, but also for bread, tortillas, cement, and sugar. Shannon K. O'Neil, *Two Nations Indivisible: Mexico, the United States, and the Road Ahead* (New York: Oxford University Press, 2013), 87. O'Neil also details the infrastructure deficits in Mexico, likely stemming from its low taxation rates for individuals and companies—among the lowest in the Western Hemisphere, resulting in a majority of its roads unpaved, and basic services such as treated water and sanitation services lacking for many rural residents. Ibid., 109.

whether it makes a significant difference if Alto Mexico is under Mexico or U.S. control.[542]

One possible difference of late is the narcoviolence that has swept Mexico in the last decade from the borderlands to the interior along drug supply chains, while leaving U.S. border cities relatively unscathed. Ironically, here, corruption within government once kept violence mostly at bay, as Mexican drug lords could operate more as businessmen than as domestic terrorists. But as addressed in Chapter 7, Mexico's recent campaign with U.S. backing to sweep corruption from drug enforcement and to confront drug cartels backfired and devolved into a bloody failure that killed tens of thousands of Mexicans. Presumably that same narcoviolence would demarcate the terrain of a Mexico-controlled Alto Mexico.

Probably the most fundamental impact on the lives (and deaths) of Mexicans migrating to or living in Alto Mexico is immigration policy. Here, governance of Alto Mexico would matter. As stated in Chapter 6, in Mexico-governed Alto Mexico, no Mexican migrant workers would need to die in their journey to jobs in the Southwest, nor would they be in constant risk of their families being ripped apart or their insecure status exploited by employers, landlords, and others. Still, the connectedness of the Americas means that Mexican immigrants would no doubt continue to serve the labor needs of the United 44 States, for which presumably the current restrictive U.S. federal and local immigration policies would govern. As Chapter 7 speculates, perhaps the current border chaos would merely shift to a militarized/securitized border to the north and east of the current configuration—thereby separating Alto Mexico from the United 44 States. This artificiality and fortuity of borders apparent in this book's historical examination of the U.S.-Mexico border, however, might spark a compassionate dialogue on the futility of excluding desperate migrants seeking a better life, which has caused many to perish on their dangerous journey. Particularly in the case of migrants from Mexico who have served the critical labor needs of U.S. agriculture and other industries for decades, it is time to reimagine borders and exclusions, and embrace a connectedness between the two countries in a spirit and ambition toward compassion and greatness.

---

[542] But see Acemoglu and Robinson, *Why Nations Fail* (positing that open and inclusive, pro-growth political systems are responsible for economic wealth of nations, in contrast to the political systems of poor nations, and discussing differences in wealth between United States and Mexico). On the political front, while difficult to predict how Mexico control of Alto Mexico would impact Mexico federal politics, with regard to the United 44 States the loss of electoral votes would have potentially minor impact. The six complete states within Alto Mexico awarded 66 electoral votes to the Democratic candidate in the 2016 presidential election and 55 to Republicans, evidencing the wide political spectrum of Alto Mexico voters.

CONCLUSION

> The river instead of separating them, rescued them from the
> desert and bound them together; . . . across its muddy channel
> the Mexicans intermarried, celebrated the same festivals, ob-
> served the same religious rites, rejoiced in the same feast days,
> and shared their sympathies, passions, and prejudices.
>
> —Walter Prescott Webb on El Paso/Ciudad Juárez[543]

As detailed above, in 2014, Latina/os, primarily of Mexican origin, overtook Anglos as California's largest racial/ethnic group with 39 percent of
the population, likely for the first time in history. Although Span-
iards/Mexicans once outnumbered Anglos in the region before the U.S.-
Mexican War and the Gold Rush, indigenous tribal residents of California at the time outnumbered them all. With the massive influx of
fortune seekers, California's Anglo population surged to almost 91 percent by 1900, and Latina/o residents, primarily Mexicans, decreased to
just four percent.[544] The state's Latina/o population stayed below ten
percent until 1970, when it reached 13.5 percent. Before that moment,
the die was cast for establishing California's cultural image as blondes
and "Beach Boys" during its Anglo super-majority era, but the resur-
gence of Latina/os since then led to the 2014 milestone of Latina/os
surpassing Anglos in number, with the next milestone likely by 2060—
Latina/os reaching half the state's population.[545]

Texas demographics followed a similar pattern, the difference being
the Anglo influx came without any gold fever, and arrived before the
U.S.-Mexican War at the invitation of the Mexican government to settle
the region with migrants it hoped to become loyal Mexican citizens.
Steady growth for decades of the border state's Latina/o population,
comprised mostly of residents of Mexican origin, means that Texas is
right behind California in the ascendancy of Latina/o residents over Anglos, with Latina/os expected to overtake Anglos in number by 2020.
The gap will only widen, based on the youth of the state's Latina/o population—Latina/o four-year-olds in Texas outnumber Anglos of the
same age 194,000 to 118,000.[546]

---

[543] McWilliams, *North From Mexico*, 65.

[544] Leslie Berestein-Rojas, "California's Latino Plurality Brings a Sense of Déjà
Vu," http://www.npr.org/blogs/codeswitch/2014/05/04/307954395/californias-
latino-plurality-brings-a-sense-of-d-j-vu (posted May 4, 2014; last visited June 10,
2014).

[545] Ibid.

[546] Gary Scharrer, "Look Into the Crystal Ball of Texas,"
http://www.texastotheworld.com/look-into-the-crystal-ball-of-texas/ (posted

Elsewhere in Alto Mexico, Latina/os eclipsed Anglo residents in New Mexico by the 2010 Census, with Anglos in 2012 constituting only 39.8 percent of the state's population and Latina/os (most of them of Mexican origin) 47 percent, another demographic trend expected to continue. Overall, despite the vast number of Anglo residents in Utah as compared to Latina/os, it seems inevitable someday that Latina/o residents, and eventually just those of Mexican origin, will surpass the number of Anglo residents in the whole of Alto Mexico.

Looking beyond Alto Mexico, as discussed in Chapter 4 the number of Mexican (and other Latina/o) residents is rising within the United 44 States through both immigrant arrivals and, since 2000, primarily from U.S. births.[547] Although it will take many decades for Latina/o residents to eclipse Anglos in the United 44 States, population trends suggest that day may eventually come.[548]

In the meantime, as detailed in Chapter 5, Mexico's Anglo population is rising, due primarily to south-of-the-border retirements of many Anglos for whom any difference in Mexico's law in relation to the United States has failed to discourage their migration. Although there is little likelihood in the foreseeable future that Anglos will surpass Mexican residents in number there, it is nonetheless the case that as the United 44 States is becoming more Mexican, Mexico is becoming more Anglo through the arrival of Anglo retirees and their culture, and by the Wal-Martization of Mexico through the inroads of U.S.-owned businesses. Where does this leave Alto Mexico, which is fast approaching an equal measure of Mexican and Anglo residents? I posit that Alto Mexico occupies a privileged status of opportunity—a convergence zone of culture and language that unifies Mexico with the rest of the United States, and the entirety of North America with the rest of the Western Hemisphere. Within the hybridity of Alto Mexico, residents increasingly will lead bilingual lives as U.S. residents able to navigate the Americas both linguistically and culturally.

Although it would not replace Mexico City, which has long been the hub and soul of Mexico and is the most populous city in North America, or the U.S. capital Washington D.C., with its rich political history, Los Angeles is well situated to serve as the de facto capital of this Alto Mexi-

---

April 1, 2014; last visited June 10, 2014) (lamenting the lack of educational spending in Texas on its majority-minority youth).

[547] Krogstad and Lopez, "Hispanic Nativity Shift," (noting that immigration outpaced native births from 1980 to 2000 in the United States, but since then the foreign-born percentage of the Latina/o population has been declining).

[548] Latina/o growth slowed in recent years, primarily due to a decline in Mexican immigration, with the annual growth rate in 2014 of just 2.1 percent after significantly larger growth in past recent decades. Jens Manuel Krogstad and Mark Hugo Lopez, "Hispanic Population Reaches Record 55 Million, But Growth Has Cooled," http://www.pewresearch.org/fact-tank/2015/06/25/u-s-hispanic-population-growth-surge-cools/ (posted June 25, 2015; last visited September 11, 2015).

co convergence zone. Transcending its significant metropolitan population of 12.8 million, the Los Angeles area is the United States,' and perhaps the hemispheric and even global, cultural trendsetter. As author Joel Garreau observed in mapping what he called the nine nations of North America, grouping Southern California with Mexico, as the image-creating "ground zero of the future," Los Angeles' "foremost importance may be its impact on the continental culture." From "this world television-and-film capital" comes the "majority of the images of who we are—and why."[549] Still, Los Angeles-based media has a long ways to go to adequately reflect the current diversity of the region and the demographic Latinization trend of the United States, as a 2014 report concluded that a "review of the top movies and television programs reveals that there is a narrower range of stories and roles, and fewer Latino lead actors in the entertainment industry today, than there were seventy years ago [when Latina/os comprised less than ten percent of California's population]."[550]

Today's Alto Mexico cultural convergence zone has emerged despite the ongoing fortification of the border between the United States and Mexico. Regardless of the legal and physical impediments to entry, undocumented immigrants from Mexico and the accompanying human spirit have found ways to enter the United States that no border feasibly will stop. Together with documented immigrants and U.S. born Mexicans, they have staked a legacy within Alto Mexico and the United 44 States that has altered and influenced the cultural composition of the country. Ultimately, the physical location of the U.S.-Mexico border, whether on the southern or northern/eastern boundary of Alto Mexico, is less important against the reality that the border, wherever located, fails to stop the entry of the two most contentious border issues—undocumented migrant laborers, and illicit drugs, bound respectively for U.S. employers and users. Although I have documented that failure elsewhere in discounting the utility of a fortified border, this book adds the conclusion that, particularly within the Alto Mexico convergence zone, governance of the zone is perhaps equally irrelevant. Differences in laws between the two jurisdictions are rarely a matter of life and death, other than the armored border imperiling migrant lives and the reliance in Texas on capital punishment. And the location of the border

---

[549] Joel Garreau, *The Nine Nations of North America* (Boston: Houghton Mifflin Company, 1981), 219. For an urban planning vision of a binational border city along the current U.S-Mexico border, see Tanvi Misra, "Instead of Trump's Wall, Why Not a Binational Border City?," http://citylab.com/
design/2016/09/instead-of-a-wall-build-a-binational-city-us-mexico-border-trump/499634 (posted September 19, 2016; last visited February 27, 2017).

[550] Frances Negrón-Muntaner, "The Latino Media Gap: A Report on the State of Latinos in U.S. Media,
http://www.columbia.edu/cu/cser/downloads/Latino_Media_Gap_Report.pdf (last visited June 22, 2014) (also concluding that when visible in media, Latina/os tend to be portrayed through decades-old derogatory stereotypes).

will supply no breakthrough for excluding the undocumented or illicit drugs from U.S. employers and users, aside from freeing up movement of labor, at least when those laborers are Mexicans, within the territory controlled by Mexicans. In the case of both labor and drugs, so long as there is significant disparity in economic opportunity between the two countries, Mexico and Mexicans will continue to supply needed labor and illicit drugs.

The futility of border armoring suggests that rather than spending wasteful resources trying to build a stronger border in the vision of Donald Trump's proposed multi-billion dollar wall (despite his ludicrous idea that Mexico and Mexicans would somehow finance it), we need to be open to other more humane solutions to the war on undocumented immigration, and the war on drugs. These solutions would honor the legacy of Mexican workers supplying vital labor to U.S. agriculture and industries, and return to the good neighbor policies of the pre-1965 immigration law that exempted Mexicans (and immigrants from other Western Hemisphere countries, particularly current trans-migrants from Central American countries, such as Guatemala, ravaged by drug cartel violence) from limits on U.S. immigration. Rather than the current restrictive limits and the hostile symbolism of the increasing fortification and militarization of the border, the United States and Mexico, along with the other Western Hemisphere countries, would function more like the European Union with residents enjoying freedom of movement toward jobs on par with the freedom accorded commercial interests under NAFTA for the movement of goods.[551]

On the drug front, as I have sketched in Chapter 7 and detailed more extensively elsewhere,[552] humane solutions would abandon or at least augment the costly war on drugs with selective decriminalization/legalization starting with marijuana, and aim to reduce drug demand through treatment programs rather than criminalization. Drugs will enter the United 44 States, as they will Alto Mexico, regardless of border impediments, or they will be produced domestically. Imagining the Southwest as Mexico-governed Alto Mexico helps crystalize the historical happenstance of borders which in turn reminds us that regardless of the border location, illicit drugs are here in our communities and we must protect against their abuse whether in the United States or Mexico, while focusing less on the supply chain that is ever-

[551] A 2005 survey found majority support in Canada and Mexico, and plurality support in the United States, for formation of a common market or economic union such as the European Union. At the time, a majority of respondents from all three countries believed it very or somewhat likely that such a union would be formed by 2015. See Pastor, *North American Idea*, 70. Another survey found significant support (42 percent) for abolishing the U.S.-Canada border but scant support (18 percent) among U.S. residents for abolishing the U.S.-Mexico border. Ibid., 72 (2000 survey). Yet a majority of Mexicans (51 percent, in 2005 data) favored removing the border.
[552] Bender, *Run for the Border*, ch. 12.

present and ever-malleable. Similarly, rather than the expensive and useless task of fortifying a national border against migrant entry, we must address the conditions that cause labor migrations out of economic desperation, and also the conditions and laws that allow or even encourage U.S. employers to seek out the most vulnerable workforce, which for several decades has been undocumented labor, rather than paying living wages and supplying a safe and tolerable workplace. In the same way, we must confront our drug demand as destabilizing the Western Hemisphere and prompting equally desperate survival migrants to journey north to escape cartel violence our demand has spawned.

Overall, these contentious problems traditionally seen as U.S.-Mexico border issues require the engagement of both countries toward compassionate and effective solutions that honor the humanity of residents of both countries, and aim to reduce the inequalities that foster migration and fuel the drug cartels. Compassion can begin in the borderlands, by drawing a line in the sand against future migrant deaths in transit, and then emanate to the U.S. interior far from the borderlands in the form of compassionate migration policies.[553] Surveying the Alto Mexico terrain in the materials above reveals the connectedness of the two countries, whose legacies and futures are bound together, as much as El Paso and Ciudad Juárez are connected by a muddy river,[554] and the two Texarkanas, separated only by asphalt, are joined by the synergy of together being "Twice as Nice."

---

[553] For a blueprint of these compassionate migration policies, see Steven W. Bender, "Compassionate Immigration Reform," 38 *Fordham Urban Law Journal* 107 (2010).

[554] An additional example of cross-border synergy is the annual border celebration Voices from Both Sides held in the Rio Grande-separated towns of Las Lajitas, Texas, and its Mexican neighbor Paso Lajitas. The festival unites the two communities through mutual river crossings in a return to the pre-border securitization times when border/river crossings and cross-cultural exchanges between the two communities were routine.

INDEX